INSPIRATIONAL
CLASSICS
FOR LATTER-DAY SAINTS

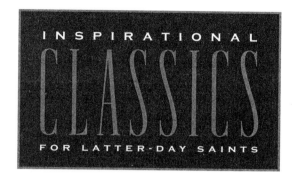

INSPIRATIONAL CLASSICS FOR LATTER-DAY SAINTS

COMPILED AND EDITED BY

JACK M. LYON

EAGLE GATE

SALT LAKE CITY, UTAH

Library of Congress Cataloging-in-Publication Data

Inspirational classics for Latter-day Saints / compiled by Jack M. Lyon.

   p. cm.

Includes bibliographical references and index.

ISBN 1-57345-778-7 (hardcover)

   1. Christian life. 2. Christian life—Mormon authors. 3. Spiritual life—Church of Jesus Christ of Latter-day Saints. I. Lyon, Jack M.

BX8656 .I58 2000

289.3'32—dc21
                                    00-027981

Printed in the United States of America   72082-6667

10   9   8   7   6   5   4   3   2   1

"Except a living man there is nothing more wonderful than a book, a message to us from the dead, . . . from human souls we never saw, who lived perhaps thousands of miles away. And yet these, in those little sheets of paper, speak to us, terrify us, teach us, comfort us, open their hearts to us as brothers."

—CHARLES KINGSLEY

CONTENTS

PREFACE

Over the years, certain inspirational books have become classics, motivating young and old to improve their lives, reach their goals, and grow closer to the Lord. Often these books are based on the scriptures, and they have occasionally been quoted by General Authorities of The Church of Jesus Christ of Latter-day Saints to illustrate a point, touch hearts, and change lives. In so doing, the Brethren have often provided helpful commentary on the works themselves, opening them more fully to our understanding and helping us to apply them, along with the scriptures, to our daily walk and talk.

President Gordon B. Hinckley said, "I love books. There is something wonderful about a good book. . . . You can pick it up. You can heft it. You can read it. You can set it down. You can think of what you have read. It does something for you. You can share great minds and great actions and great undertaking in the pages of a book." (*The Teachings of Gordon B. Hinckley* [Salt Lake City: Deseret Book Co., 1997], 315–16.)

President Thomas S. Monson commented, "Reading is one of the true pleasures of life. In our age of mass culture, when so much that we encounter is abridged, adapted, adulterated, shredded, and boiled down, and commercialism's loudspeakers are incessantly braying, it is mind-easing and mind-inspiring to sit down privately with a good book. (*Pathways to Perfection* [Salt Lake City: Deseret Book Co., 1984], 109.)

And President James E. Faust wrote, "Members of the Church are encouraged to seek learning from all good books and from any source.

For 'if there is anything virtuous, lovely, or of good report or praise-worthy, we seek after these things.' (Article of Faith 13.)" (*To Reach Even unto You* [Salt Lake City: Deseret Book Co., 1980], 37.)

President Heber J. Grant also appreciated good books and often gave them as gifts to family and friends, as explained by his daughter Lucy: "[Father] remarked that he had never kept any record of the number of books he had given away but that roughly estimating he could count up to one hundred thousand." (*Improvement Era*, November 1936, 674.) On many of these books, President Grant wrote these lines by Horace G. Whitney:

> *What though the price be paltry and small,*
> *What though the cover be old and thin,*
> *What though there be no cover at all,*
> *If worth and merit are written within.*

In that spirit, several inspirational classics are presented together in this volume. Though these works were not written by Latter-day Saints and do not always agree precisely with Latter-day Saint belief, they contain valuable insights and admonitions. Even passages that at first may seem questionable offer wisdom to those who read carefully and with the intent to understand rather than condemn.

Although the language of these classics may sometimes sound old-fashioned to our modern ears, their messages are often timeless, as applicable today as when they were first written. They are reprinted here with brief commentaries that, it is hoped, will make them live again in the hearts and lives of Latter-day Saints.

AS A MAN THINKETH

James Allen

James Allen was born in Leicester, England, on November 28, 1864. In 1879 his father traveled to America, where he hoped to improve his family's financial situation after a business loss. Before he could send for his family, he was robbed and murdered. Fifteen-year-old James had to leave school to work and eventually served as a private secretary for various manufacturing firms. Having a philosophical turn of mind and a natural power of expression, he decided in 1902 to write full time. After finishing his first book, *From Poverty to Power,* he moved to the small resort town of Ilfracombe, on the southwest coast of England. There he studied, kept his garden, strolled the hills overlooking the sea, and produced his second book, *As a Man Thinketh.* Dissatisfied with the work, Allen published it in 1904 only upon the insistence of his wife, Lily. During his remaining years, he wrote eighteen other books. He died in 1912.

Despite Allen's dissatisfaction with *As a Man Thinketh,* it has probably been read by more people and quoted by more speakers and writers than any other inspirational classic. The point of the book is that the circumstances of our lives are largely influenced by our own thoughts and attitudes.

Elder Milton R. Hunter, a member of the First Council of the Seventy from 1945 until his death in 1975, explained the book's message in this way:

"Keep your mind and heart clean and pure at all times. The scriptures truthfully declared: 'For as . . . [a man] thinketh in his heart, so is he.' (Prov. 23:7.) Our thoughts are like seeds planted in a fertile garden. They take root, grow, and eventually mature in full bloom. Thus the very center of our character-growth is our inner thoughts. Our thoughts precede our actions. They are the underlying forces that shape our destiny. . . .

"It is definitely true that each person is the product of his own individual thinking. Mr. James Allen aptly declared: 'Whatever your present environment may be, you will fall, remain, or rise with your thoughts, your Vision, or your Ideals. You will become as small as your controlling desire, as great as your dominating aspiration.' . . .

"Thus let me advise: . . . guard your mind and your thinking continuously. Do not listen to impure or indecent stories. . . . Remember never to let anything come from your lips that is indecent, suggestive, degrading, or of an immoral nature in any respect. The Savior declared: 'Blessed are the pure in heart: for they shall see God.' (Matt. 5:8.)" (Conference Report, April 1963, 15.)

AS A MAN THINKETH

Foreword

This little volume (the result of meditation and experience) is not intended as an exhaustive treatise on the much-written-upon subject of the power of thought. It is suggestive rather than explanatory, its object being to stimulate men and women to the discovery and perception of the truth that—

"They themselves are makers of themselves"
by virtue of the thoughts which they choose and encourage; that mind is the master-weaver, both of the inner garment of character and the outer garment of circumstance, and that, as they may have hitherto woven in ignorance and pain they may now weave in enlightenment and happiness.

Thought and Character

The aphorism, "As a man thinketh in his heart so is he," not only embraces the whole of a man's being, but is so comprehensive as to reach out to every condition and circumstance of his life. A man is literally *what he thinks,* his character being the complete sum of all his thoughts.

As the plant springs from, and could not be without, the seed, so every act of a man springs from the hidden seeds of thought, and could not have appeared without them. This applies equally to those acts called "spontaneous" and "unpremeditated" as to those which are deliberately executed.

Act is the blossom of thought, and joy and suffering are its fruits; thus does a man garner in the sweet and bitter fruitage of his own husbandry.

> *Thought in the mind hath made us. What we are*
> *By thought we wrought and built. If a man's mind*
> *Hath evil thoughts, pain comes on him as comes*
> *The wheel the ox behind. . . . If one endure*
> *In purity of thought, joy follows him*
> *As his own shadow—sure.*

Man is a growth by law, and not a creation by artifice, and cause and effect is as absolute and undeviating in the hidden realm of thought as in the world of visible and material things. A noble and Godlike character is not a thing of favor or chance, but is the natural result of continued effort in right thinking, the effect of long-cherished association with Godlike thoughts. An ignoble and bestial character, by the same process, is the result of the continued harboring of grovelling thoughts.

Man is made or unmade by himself; in the armoury of thought he forges the weapons by which he destroys himself. He also fashions the tools with which he builds for himself heavenly mansions of joy and strength and peace. By the right choice and true application of thought, man ascends to the Divine Perfection; by the abuse and wrong application of thought, he descends below the level of the beast. Between these two extremes are all the grades of character, and man is their maker and master.

Of all the beautiful truths pertaining to the soul which have been restored and brought to light in this age, none is more gladdening or fruitful of divine promise and confidence than this—that man is the master of thought, the moulder of character, and maker and shaper of condition, environment, and destiny.

As a being of Power, Intelligence, and Love, and the lord of his own thoughts, man holds the key to every situation, and contains within himself that transforming and regenerative agency by which he may make himself what he wills.

Man is always the master, even in his weakest and most abandoned state; but in his weakness and degradation he is the foolish master who misgoverns his "household." When he begins to reflect upon his condition, and to search diligently for the Law upon which his being is established, he then becomes the wise master, directing his energies with intelligence, and fashioning his thoughts to fruitful issues. Such is the *conscious* master, and man can only thus become by discovering *within himself* the laws of thought; which discovery is totally a matter of application, self-analysis, and experience.

Only by much searching and mining are gold and diamonds obtained, and man can find every truth connected with his being if he will dig deep into the mine of his soul; and that he is the maker of his character, the moulder of his life, and the builder of his destiny, he may unerringly prove, if he will watch, control, and alter his thoughts, tracing their effects upon himself, upon others, and upon his life and circumstances, linking cause and effect by patient practice and investigation, utilizing his every experience, even to the most trivial, everyday occurrence, as a means of obtaining that knowledge of himself which is Understanding, Wisdom, Power. In this direction, as in no other, is the law absolute that "He that seeketh findeth; and to him that knocketh it shall be opened"; for only by patience, practice, and ceaseless importunity can a man enter the Door of the Temple of Knowledge.

Effect of Thought on Circumstances

A man's mind may be likened to a garden, which may be intelligently cultivated or allowed to run wild; but whether cultivated or neglected, it must, and will, *bring forth*. If no useful seeds are *put* into it, then an abundance of useless weed-seeds will *fall* therein, and will continue to produce their kind.

Just as a gardener cultivates his plot, keeping it free from weeds, and growing the flowers and fruits which he requires, so may a man tend the garden of his mind, weeding out all the wrong, useless, and impure thoughts, and cultivating toward perfection the flowers and fruits of right, useful, and pure thoughts. By pursuing this process, a man sooner or later discovers that he is the master gardener of his soul, the director of his life. He also reveals, within himself, the laws of thought, and understands with ever-increasing accuracy, how the thought-forces and mind-elements operate in the shaping of his character, circumstances, and destiny.

Thought and character are one, and as character can only manifest and discover itself through environment and circumstance, the outer conditions of a person's life will always be found to be harmoniously related to his inner state. This does not mean that a man's circumstances at any given time are an indication of his *entire* character, but that those circumstances are so intimately connected with some vital thought-element within himself that, for the time being, they are indispensable to his development.

Every man is where he is by the law of his being; the thoughts which he has built into his character have brought him there, and in the arrangement of his life there is no element of chance, but all is the result of a law which cannot err. This is just as true of those who feel "out of harmony" with their surroundings as of those who are contented with them.

As the progressive and evolving being, man is where he is that he may learn that he may grow; and as he learns the spiritual lesson which any circumstance contains for him, it passes away and gives place to other circumstances.

Man is buffeted by circumstances so long as he believes himself to be the creature of outside conditions, but when he realizes that he may command the hidden soil and seeds of his being out of which circumstances grow, he then becomes the rightful master of himself.

That circumstances *grow* out of thought every man knows who has for any length of time practiced self-control and self-purification, for he will have noticed that the alteration in his circumstances has been in exact ratio with his altered mental condition. So true is this that when a man earnestly applies himself to remedy the defects in his character, and makes swift and marked progress, he passes rapidly through a succession of vicissitudes.

The soul attracts that which it secretly harbors; that which it loves, and also that which it fears; it reaches the height of its cherished aspirations; it falls to the level of its unchastened desires, and circumstances are the means by which the soul receives its own.

Every thought-seed sown or allowed to fall into the mind, and to take root there, produces its own, blossoming sooner or later into act, and bearing its own fruitage of opportunity and circumstance. Good thoughts bear good fruit, bad thoughts bad fruit.

The outer world of circumstance shapes itself to the inner world of thought, and both pleasant and unpleasant external conditions are factors which make for the ultimate good of the individual. As the reaper of his own harvest, man learns both by suffering and bliss.

Following the inmost desires, aspirations, thoughts, by which he allows himself to be dominated (pursuing the will-o'-the-wisps of impure imaginings or steadfastly walking the highway of strong and high endeavour), a man at last arrives at their fruition and fulfilment in the outer conditions of his life. The laws of growth and adjustment everywhere obtain.

A man does not come to the almshouse or the jail by the tyranny of fate or circumstance, but by the pathway of grovelling thoughts and base desires. Nor does a pure-minded man fall suddenly into crime by stress of any mere external force; the criminal thought had long been secretly fostered in the heart, and the hour of opportunity revealed its gathered power. Circumstance does not make the man; it reveals him to himself. No such conditions can exist as descending into vice and its attendant sufferings apart from vicious inclinations, or ascending into virtue and its pure happiness without the continued cultivation of virtuous aspirations; and man, therefore, as the lord and master of thought, is the maker of himself, the shaper and author of environment. Even at birth the soul comes to its own, and through every step of its earthly pilgrimage it attracts those combinations of conditions which reveal itself, which are the reflections of its own purity and impurity, its strength and weakness.

Men do not attract that which they *want,* but that which they *are.* Their whims, fancies, and ambitions are thwarted at every step, but their inmost thoughts and desires are fed with their own food, be it foul or clean. The "divinity that shapes our ends" is in ourselves; it is our very self. Man is manacled only by himself: thought and action are the jailers of Fate—they imprison, being base; they are also the angels of Freedom—they liberate, being noble. Not what he wishes and prays for does a man get, but what he justly earns. His wishes and prayers are only gratified and answered when they harmonize with his thoughts and actions.

In the light of this truth, what, then, is the meaning of "fighting against circumstances"? It means that a man is continually revolting against an *effect* without, while all the time he is nourishing and preserving its *cause* in his heart. That cause may take the form of a conscious vice or an unconscious weakness; but whatever it is, it stubbornly retards the efforts of its possessor, and thus calls aloud for remedy.

Men are anxious to improve their circumstances, but are unwilling to improve themselves. They therefore remain bound. The man who does not shrink from self-crucifixion can never fail to accomplish the object upon which his heart is set. This is as true of earthly as of heavenly things. Even the man whose sole object is to acquire wealth must be prepared to make great personal sacrifices before he can accomplish his object; and how much more so he who would realize a strong and well-poised life?

Here is a man who is wretchedly poor. He is extremely anxious that his surroundings and home comforts should be improved, yet all the time he shirks his work, and considers he is justified in trying to deceive his employer on the ground of the insufficiency of his wages. Such a man does not understand the simplest rudiments of those principles which are the basis of true prosperity. He is not only totally unfitted to rise out of his wretchedness, but is actually attracting to himself a still deeper wretchedness by dwelling in, and acting out, indolent, deceptive, and unmanly thoughts.

Here is a rich man who is the victim of a painful and persistent disease as the result of gluttony. He is willing to give large sums of money to get rid of it, but he will not sacrifice his gluttonous desires. He wants to gratify his taste for rich and unnatural viands and have his health as well. Such a man is totally unfit to have health, because he has not yet learned the first principles of a healthy life.

Here is an employer of labour who adopts crooked measures to avoid paying the regulation wage, and, in the hope of making larger profits, reduces the wages of his work-people. Such a man is altogether unfitted for prosperity. And when he finds himself bankrupt, both as regards reputation and riches, he blames circumstances, not knowing that he is the sole author of his condition.

I have introduced these three cases merely as illustrative of the truth that man is the causer (though nearly always unconsciously) of his circumstances, and that, while aiming at the good end, he is continually frustrating its accomplishment by encouraging thoughts and desires which cannot possibly harmonize with that end. Such cases could be multiplied and varied almost indefinitely, but this is not necessary, as the reader can, if he so resolves, trace the action of the laws of thought in his own mind and life, and until this is done, mere external facts cannot serve as a ground of reasoning.

Circumstances, however, are so complicated, thought is so deeply rooted, and the conditions of happiness vary so vastly with individuals, that a man's *entire* soul-condition (although it may be known to himself) cannot be judged by another from the external aspect of his life alone.

A man may be honest in certain directions, yet suffer privations; a man may be dishonest in certain directions, yet acquire wealth; but the conclusion usually formed that the one man fails *because of his particular honesty,* and that the other prospers *because of his particular dishonesty,* is the result of a superficial judgment, which assumes that the dishonest man is almost totally corrupt, and the honest man almost entirely virtuous. In the light of a deeper knowledge and wider experience, such judgment is found to be erroneous. The dishonest man may have some admirable virtues which the other does not possess; and the honest man obnoxious vices which are absent in the other. The honest man reaps the good results of his honest thoughts and acts; he also brings upon himself the sufferings which his vices produce. The dishonest man likewise garners his own suffering and happiness.

It is pleasing to human vanity to believe that one suffers because of one's virtue; but not until a man has extirpated every sickly, bitter, and impure thought from his mind, and washed every sinful stain from his soul, can he be in a position to know and declare that his sufferings are the result of his good, and not of his bad qualities; and on the way to that supreme perfection, he will have found working in his mind and life, the Great Law which is absolutely just, and which cannot, therefore, give good for evil, evil for good. Possessed of such knowledge, he will then know, looking back upon his past ignorance and blindness, that his life is, and always was, justly ordered, and that all his past experiences, good and bad, were the equitable outworking of his evolving, yet unevolved self.

Good thoughts and actions can never produce bad results; bad thoughts and actions can never produce good results. This is but saying that nothing can come from corn but corn, nothing from nettles but nettles. Men understand this law in the natural world, and work with it. But few understand it in the mental and moral world (though its operation there is just as simple and undeviating), and they, therefore, do not cooperate with it.

Suffering is *always* the effect of wrong thought in some direction. It is an indication that the individual is out of harmony with himself, with the Law of his being. The sole and supreme use of suffering is to purify, to burn out all that is useless and impure. Suffering ceases for him who is pure. There could be no object in burning gold after the dross had been removed, and a perfectly pure and enlightened being could not suffer.

The circumstances which a man encounters with suffering are the result of his own mental in harmony. The circumstances which a man encounters with blessedness are the result of his own mental harmony. Blessedness, not material possessions, is the measure of right thought; wretchedness, not lack of material possessions, is the measure of wrong thought. A man may be cursed and rich; he may be blessed and poor. Blessedness and riches are only joined together when the riches are rightly and wisely used; and the poor man only descends into wretchedness when he regards his lot as a burden unjustly imposed.

Indigence and indulgence are the two extremes of wretchedness. They are both equally unnatural and the result of mental disorder. A man is not rightly conditioned until he is a happy, healthy, and prosperous being; and happiness, health, and prosperity are the result of a harmonious adjustment of the inner with the outer, of the man with his surroundings.

A man only begins to be a man when he ceases to whine and revile, and commences to search for the hidden justice which regulates his life. And as he adapts his mind to that regulating factor, he ceases to accuse others as the cause of his condition, and builds himself up in strong and noble thoughts; he ceases to kick against circumstances, but begins to *use* them as aids to his more rapid progress, and as a means of discovering the hidden powers and possibilities within himself.

Law, not confusion, is the dominating principle in the universe; justice, not injustice, is the soul and substance of life; and righteousness, not corruption, is the moulding and moving force in the spiritual government of the world. This being so, man has but to right himself to find that the universe is right; and during the process of putting himself right, he will find that as he alters his thoughts towards things and other people, things and other people will alter towards him.

The proof of this truth is in every person, and it therefore admits of easy investigation by systematic introspection and self-analysis. Let a man radically alter his thoughts, and he will be astonished at the rapid transformation it will effect in the material conditions of his life. Men imagine that thought can be kept secret, but it cannot; it rapidly crystallizes into habit, and habit solidifies into circumstance. Bestial thoughts crystallize into habits of drunkenness and sensuality, which solidify into circumstances of destitution and disease: impure thoughts of every kind crystallize into enervating and confusing habits, which solidify into distracting and adverse circumstances: thoughts of fear, doubt, and indecision crystallize into weak, unmanly, and irresolute habits, which solidify into circumstances of failure, indigence, and slavish dependence: lazy thoughts crystallize into habits of uncleanliness and dishonesty, which solidify into circumstances of foulness and beggary: hateful and condemnatory thoughts crystallize into habits of accusation and violence, which solidify into circumstances of injury and persecution: selfish thoughts of all kinds crystallize into habits of self-seeking, which solidify into circumstances more or less distressing. On the other hand, beautiful thoughts of all kinds crystallize into habits of grace and kindliness, which solidify into genial and sunny circumstances: pure thoughts crystallize into habits of temperance and self-control, which solidify into circumstances of repose and peace: thoughts of courage, self-reliance, and decision crystallize into manly habits, which solidify into circumstances of success, plenty, and freedom: energetic thoughts crystallize into habits of cleanliness and industry, which solidify into circumstances of pleasantness: gentle and forgiving thoughts crystallize into habits of gentleness, which solidify into protective and preservative circumstances: loving and unselfish thoughts crystallize into habits of self-forgetfulness for others, which solidify into circumstances of sure and abiding prosperity and true riches.

A particular train of thought persisted in, be it good or bad, cannot fail to produce its results on the character and circumstances. A man cannot *directly* choose his circumstances, but he can choose his thoughts, and so indirectly, yet surely, shape his circumstances.

Nature helps every man to the gratification of the thoughts which he most encourages, and opportunities are presented which will most speedily bring to the surface both the good and evil thoughts.

Let a man cease from his sinful thoughts, and all the world will soften towards him, and be ready to help him; let him put away his weakly and sickly thoughts, and lo! opportunities will spring up on every hand to aid his strong resolves; let him encourage good thoughts, and no hard fate shall bind him down to wretchedness and shame. The world is your kaleidoscope, and the varying combinations of colours which at every succeeding moment it presents to you are the exquisitely adjusted pictures of your ever-moving thoughts.

> *You will be what you will to be;*
>   *Let failure find its false content*
> *In that poor word, "environment,"*
>   *But spirit scorns it, and is free.*
>
> *It masters time, it conquers space;*
>   *It cows that boastful trickster, Chance,*
> *And bids the tyrant Circumstance*
>   *Uncrown, and fill a servant's place.*
>
> *The human Will, that force unseen,*
>   *The offspring of a deathless Soul,*
> *Can hew a way to any goal,*
>   *Though walls of granite intervene.*
>
> *Be not impatient in delay,*
>   *But wait as one who understands;*
> *When spirit rises and commands,*
>   *The gods are ready to obey.*

Effect of Thought on Health and the Body

The body is the servant of the mind. It obeys the operations of the mind, whether they be deliberately chosen or automatically expressed. At the bidding of unlawful thoughts the body sinks rapidly into disease and decay; at the command of glad and beautiful thoughts it becomes clothed with youthfulness and beauty.

Disease and health, like circumstances, are rooted in thought. Sickly thoughts will express themselves through a sickly body. Thoughts of fear have been known to kill a man as speedily as a bullet, and they are continually killing thousands of people just as surely though less rapidly. The people who live in fear of disease are the people who get it. Anxiety quickly demoralizes the whole body, and lays it open to the entrance of disease; while impure thoughts, even if not physically indulged, will soon shatter the nervous system.

Strong, pure, and happy thoughts build up the body in vigour and grace. The body is a delicate and plastic instrument, which responds readily to the thoughts by which it is impressed, and habits of thought will produce their own effects, good or bad, upon it.

Men will continue to have impure and poisoned blood so long as they propagate unclean thoughts. Out of a clean heart comes a clean life and a clean body. Out of a defiled mind proceeds a defiled life and corrupt body. Thought is the fount of action, life, and manifestation; make the fountain pure, and all will be pure.

Change of diet will not help a man who will not change his thoughts. When a man makes his thoughts pure, he no longer desires impure food.

Clean thoughts make clean habits. The so-called saint who does not wash his body is not a saint. He who has strengthened and purified his thoughts does not need to consider the malevolent microbe.

If you would perfect your body, guard your mind. If you would renew your body, beautify your mind. Thoughts of malice, envy, disappointment, despondency, rob the body of its health and grace. A sour face does not come by chance; it is made by sour thoughts. Wrinkles that mar are drawn by folly, passion, pride.

I know a woman of ninety-six who has the bright, innocent face of a girl. I know a man well under middle age whose face is drawn into inharmonious contours. The one is the result of a sweet and sunny disposition; the other is the outcome of passion and discontent.

As you cannot have a sweet and wholesome abode unless you admit the air and sunshine freely into your rooms, so a strong body and a bright, happy, or serene countenance can only result from the free admittance into the mind of thoughts of joy and goodwill and serenity.

On the faces of the aged there are wrinkles made by sympathy; others by strong and pure thought, others are carved by passion: who cannot distinguish them? With those who have lived righteously, age is calm, peaceful, and softly mellowed, like the setting sun. I have recently seen a philosopher on his death-bed. He was not old except in years. He died as sweetly and peacefully as he had lived.

There is no physician like cheerful thought for dissipating the ills of the body; there is no comforter to compare with goodwill for dispersing the shadows of grief and sorrow. To live continually in thoughts of ill-will, cynicism, suspicion, and envy, is to be confined in a self-made prison hole. But to think well of all, to be cheerful with all, to patiently learn to find the good in all—such unselfish thoughts are the very portals of heaven; and to dwell day to day in thoughts of peace toward every creature will bring abounding peace to their possessor.

Thought and Purpose

Until thought is linked with purpose there is no intelligent accomplishment. With the majority the barque of thought is allowed to "drift" upon the ocean of life. Aimlessness is a vice, and such drifting must not continue for him who would steer clear of catastrophe and destruction.

They who have no central purpose in their life fall an easy prey to petty worries, fears, troubles, and self-pityings, all of which are indications of weakness, which lead, just as surely as deliberately planned sins (though by a different route), to failure, unhappiness, and loss, for weakness cannot persist in a power-evolving universe.

A man should conceive of a legitimate purpose in his heart, and set out to accomplish it. He should make this purpose the centralizing point of his thoughts. It may take the form of a spiritual ideal, or it may be a worldly object, according to his nature at the time being; but whichever it is, he should steadily focus his thought-forces upon the object which he has set before him. He should make this purpose his supreme duty, and should devote himself to its attainment, not allowing his thoughts to wander away into ephemeral fancies, longings, and imaginings. This is the royal road to self-control and true concentration of thought. Even if he fails again and again to accomplish his purpose (as he necessarily must until weakness is overcome), the *strength of character gained* will be the measure of his *true* success, and this will form a new starting point for future power and triumph.

Those who are not prepared for the apprehension of a *great* purpose, should fix the thoughts upon the faultless performance of their duty, no matter how insignificant their task may appear. Only in this way can the thoughts be gathered and focused, and resolution and energy be developed, which being done, there is nothing which may not be accomplished.

The weakest soul, knowing its own weakness, and believing this truth—*that strength can only be developed by effort and practice,* will at once begin to exert itself, and, thus believing, adding effort to effort, patience to patience, and strength to strength, will never cease to develop, and will at last grow divinely strong.

As the physically weak man can make himself strong by careful and patient training, so the man of weak thoughts can make them strong by exercising himself in right thinking.

To put away aimlessness and weakness, and to begin to think with purpose, is to enter the ranks of those strong ones who only recognize failure as one of the pathways to attainment; who make all conditions serve them, and who think strongly, attempt fearlessly, and accomplish masterfully.

Having conceived of his purpose, a man should mentally mark out a *straight* pathway to its achievement, looking neither to the right nor to the left. Doubts and fears should be rigorously excluded; they are disintegrating elements which break up the straight line of effort, rendering it crooked, ineffectual, useless. Thoughts of doubt and fear never accomplish anything, and never can. They always lead to failure.

Purpose, energy, power to do, and all strong thoughts cease when doubt and fear creep in.

The will to do springs from the knowledge that we *can* do. Doubt and fear are the great enemies of knowledge, and he who encourages them, who does not slay them, thwarts himself at every step.

He who has conquered doubt and fear has conquered failure. His every thought is allied with power, and all difficulties are bravely met and wisely overcome. His purposes are seasonably planted, and they bloom and bring forth fruit which does not fall prematurely to the ground.

Thought allied fearlessly to purpose becomes creative force: he who *knows* this is ready to become something higher and stronger than a mere bundle of wavering thoughts and fluctuating sensations: he who *does* this has become the conscious and intelligent wielder of his mental powers.

The Thought-Factor in Achievement

All that a man achieves and all that he fails to achieve is the direct result of his own thoughts. In a justly ordered universe, where loss of equipoise would mean total destruction, individual responsibility must be absolute. A man's weakness and strength, purity and impurity, are his own, and not another man's: they are brought about by himself, and not by another; and they can only be altered by himself, never by another. His condition is also his own, and not another man's. His suffering and his happiness are evolved from within. As he thinks, so he is; as he continues to think, so he remains.

A strong man cannot help a weaker unless the weaker is *willing* to be helped, and even then the weak man must become strong of himself; he must, by his own efforts, develop the strength which he admires in another. None but himself can alter his condition.

It has been usual for men to think and to say, "Many men are slaves because one is an oppressor; let us hate the oppressor." Now, however, there is amongst an increasing few a tendency to reverse this judgment, and to say, "One man is an oppressor because many are slaves; let us despise the slaves." The truth is that oppressor and slave are co-operators in ignorance, and, while seeming to afflict each other, are in reality afflicting themselves. A perfect Knowledge perceives the action of law in the weakness of the oppressed and the misapplied power of the oppressor; a perfect Love, seeing the suffering which both states entail, condemns neither; a perfect Compassion embraces both oppressor and oppressed.

He who has conquered weakness, and has put away all selfish thoughts, belongs neither to oppressor nor oppressed. He is free.

A man can only rise, conquer, and achieve by lifting up his thoughts. He can only remain weak, and abject, and miserable by refusing to lift up his thoughts.

Before a man can achieve anything, even in worldly things, he must lift his thoughts above slavish animal indulgence. He may not, in order to succeed, give up *all* animality and selfishness, by any means; but a portion of it must, at least, be sacrificed. A man whose first thought is bestial indulgence could neither think clearly nor plan methodically; he could not find and develop his latent resources, and would fail in any undertaking. Not having commenced manfully to control his thoughts, he is not in a position to control affairs and to adopt serious responsibilities. He is not fit to act independently and stand alone, but he is limited only by the thoughts which he chooses.

There can be no progress, no achievement without sacrifice. A man's worldly success will be in the measure that he sacrifices his confused animal thoughts, and fixes his mind on the development of his plans, and the strengthening of his resolution and self-reliance. And the higher he lifts his thoughts, the more manly, upright, and righteous he becomes, the greater will be his success, the more blessed and enduring will be his achievements.

The universe does not favor the greedy, the dishonest, the vicious, although on the mere surface it may sometimes appear to do so; it helps the honest, the magnanimous, the virtuous. All the great Teachers of the ages have declared this in varying forms, and to prove and know it a man has but to persist in making himself more and more virtuous by lifting up his thoughts.

Intellectual achievements are the result of thought consecrated to the search for knowledge, or for the beautiful and true in life and nature. Such achievements may be sometimes connected with vanity and ambition but they are not the outcome of those characteristics; they are the natural outgrowth of long and arduous effort, and of pure and unselfish thoughts.

Spiritual achievements are the consummation of holy aspirations. He who lives constantly in the conception of noble and lofty thoughts, who dwells upon all that is pure and unselfish, will, as surely as the sun reaches its zenith and the moon its full, become wise and noble in character, and rise into a position of influence and blessedness.

Achievement, of whatever kind, is the crown of effort, the diadem of thought. By the aid of self-control, resolution, purity, righteousness, and well-directed thought a man ascends; by the aid of animality, indolence, impurity, corruption, and confusion of thought a man descends.

A man may rise to high success in the world, and even to lofty altitudes in the spiritual realm, and again descend into weakness and wretchedness by allowing arrogant, selfish, and corrupt thoughts to take possession of him.

Victories attained by right thought can only be maintained by watchfulness. Many give way when success is assured, and rapidly fall back into failure.

All achievements, whether in the business, intellectual, or spiritual world, are the result of definitely directed thought, are governed by the same law and are of the same method; the only difference lies in *the object of attainment.*

He who would accomplish little must sacrifice little; he who would achieve much must sacrifice much; he who would attain highly must sacrifice greatly.

Visions and Ideals

The dreamers are the saviours of the world. As the visible world is sustained by the invisible, so men, through all their trials and sins and sordid vocations, are nourished by the beautiful visions of their solitary dreamers. Humanity cannot forget its dreamers; it cannot let their ideals fade and die; it lives in them; it knows them in the *realities* which it shall one day see and know.

Composer, sculptor, painter, poet, prophet, sage, these are the makers of the afterworld, the architects of heaven. The world is beautiful because they have lived; without them, laboring humanity would perish.

He who cherishes a beautiful vision, a lofty ideal in his heart, will one day realize it. Columbus cherished a vision of another world, and he discovered it; Copernicus fostered the vision of a multiplicity of worlds and a wider universe, and he revealed it; Buddha beheld the vision of a spiritual world of stainless beauty and perfect peace, and he entered into it.

Cherish your visions; cherish your ideals; cherish the music that stirs in your heart, the beauty that forms in your mind, the loveliness that drapes your purest thoughts, for out of them will grow all delightful conditions, all heavenly environment; of these, if you but remain true to them, your world will at last be built.

To desire is to obtain; to aspire is to achieve. Shall man's basest desires receive the fullest measure of gratification, and his purest aspirations starve for lack of sustenance? Such is not the Law: such a condition of things can never obtain: "Ask and receive."

Dream lofty dreams, and as you dream, so shall you become. Your Vision is the promise of what you shall one day be; your Ideal is the prophecy of what you shall at last unveil.

The greatest achievement was at first and for a time a dream. The oak sleeps in the acorn; the bird waits in the egg; and in the highest vision of the soul a waking angel stirs. Dreams are the seedlings of realities.

Your circumstances may be uncongenial, but they shall not long remain so if you but perceive an Ideal and strive to reach it. You cannot travel *within* and stand still *without*. Here is a youth hard pressed by poverty and labor; confined long hours in an unhealthy workshop; unschooled, and lacking all the arts of refinement. But he dreams of better things; he thinks of intelligence, of refinement, of grace and beauty. He conceives of, mentally builds up, an ideal condition of life; the vision of the wider liberty and a larger scope takes possession of him; unrest urges him to action, and he utilizes all his spare time and means, small though they are, to the development of his latent powers and resources. Very soon so altered has his mind become that the workshop can no longer hold him. It has become so out of harmony with his mentality that it falls out of his life as a garment is cast aside, and with the growth of opportunities which fit the scope of his expanding powers, he passes out of it forever. Years later we see this youth as a full-grown man. We find him a master of certain forces of the mind which he wields with world-wide influence and almost unequaled power. In his hands he holds the cords of gigantic responsibilities; he speaks, and lo! lives are changed; men and women hang upon his words and remould their characters, and, sunlike, he becomes the fixed and luminous centre round which innumerable destinies revolve. He has realized the Vision of his youth. He has become one with his Ideal.

And you, too, youthful reader, will realize the Vision (not the idle wish) of your heart, be it base or beautiful, or a mixture of both, for you will always gravitate toward that which you, secretly, most love. Into your hands will be placed the exact results of your own thoughts; you will receive that which you earn; no more, no less. Whatever your present environment may be, you will fall, remain, or rise with your thoughts, your Vision, your Ideal. You will become as small as your controlling desire; as great as your dominant aspiration; in the beautiful words of Stanton Kirkham Davis, "You may be keeping accounts, and presently you shall walk out of the door that for so long has seemed to you the barrier of your ideals, and shall find yourself before an audience—the pen still behind your ear, the ink stains on your fingers—and then and there shall pour out the torrent of your inspiration. You may be driving sheep, and you shall wander to the city—bucolic and open-mouthed; shall wander under the intrepid guidance of the spirit into the studio of the master, and after a time he shall say, 'I have nothing more to teach you.' And now you have become the master, who did so recently dream of great things while driving sheep. You shall lay down the saw and the plane to take upon yourself the regeneration of the world."

The thoughtless, the ignorant, and the indolent, seeing only the apparent effects of things and not the things themselves, talk of luck, of fortune, and chance. Seeing a man grow rich, they say, "How lucky he is!" Observing another become intellectual, they exclaim, "How highly favored he is!" And noting the saintly character and wide influence of another, they remark, "How chance aids him at every turn!" They do not see the trials and failures and struggles which these men have voluntarily encountered in order to gain their experience; have no knowledge of the sacrifices they have made, of the undaunted efforts they have put forth, of the faith they have exercised, that they might overcome the apparently insurmountable, and realize the Vision of their heart. They do not know the darkness and the heartaches; they only see the light and joy, and call it "luck"; do not see the long and arduous journey, but only behold the pleasant goal, and call it "good fortune"; do not understand the process, but only perceive the result, and call it "chance."

In all human affairs there are *efforts,* and there are *results,* and the strength of the effort is the measure of the result. Chance is not. "Gifts," powers, material, intellectual, and spiritual possessions are the fruits of effort; they are thoughts completed, objects accomplished, visions realized.

The Vision that you glorify in your mind, the Ideal that you enthrone in your heart—this you will build your life by, this you will become.

Serenity

Calmness of mind is one of the beautiful jewels of wisdom. It is the result of long and patient effort in self-control. Its presence is an indication of ripened experience, and of a more than ordinary knowledge of the laws and operations of thought.

A man becomes calm in the measure that he understands himself as a thought-evolved being, for such knowledge necessitates the understanding of others as the result of thought, and as he develops a right understanding, and sees more and more clearly the internal relations of things by the action of cause and effect, he ceases to fuss and fume and worry and grieve, and remains poised, steadfast, serene.

The calm man, having learned how to govern himself, knows how to adapt himself to others; and they, in turn, reverence his spiritual strength, and feel that they can learn of him and rely upon him. The more tranquil a man becomes, the greater is his success, his influence, his power for good. Even the ordinary trader will find his business prosperity increase as he develops a greater self-control and equanimity, for people will always prefer to deal with a man whose demeanor is strongly equable.

The strong, calm man is always loved and revered. He is like a shade-giving tree in a thirsty land, or a sheltering rock in a storm. Who does not love a tranquil heart, a sweet-tempered, balanced life? It does not matter whether it rains or shines, or what changes come to those possessing these blessings, for they are always sweet, serene, and calm. That exquisite poise of character which we call serenity is the last lesson of culture; it is the flowering of life, the fruitage of the soul. It is precious as wisdom, more to be desired than gold—yea, than even fine gold. How insignificant mere money-seeking looks in comparison with a serene life—a life that dwells in the ocean of Truth, beneath the waves, beyond the reach of tempests, in the Eternal Calm!

"How many people we know who sour their lives, who ruin all that is sweet and beautiful by explosive tempers, who destroy their poise of character, and make bad blood! It is a question whether the great majority of people do not ruin their lives and mar their happiness by lack of self-control. How few people we meet in life who are well-balanced, who have that exquisite poise which is characteristic of the finished character!"

Yes, humanity surges with uncontrolled passion, is tumultuous with ungoverned grief, is blown about by anxiety and doubt. Only the wise man, only he whose thoughts are controlled and purified, makes the winds and the storms of the soul obey him.

Tempest-tossed souls, wherever ye may be, under whatsoever conditions ye may live, know this—in the ocean of life the isles of Blessedness are smiling, and the sunny shore of your ideal awaits your coming. Keep your hand firmly upon the helm of thought. In the barque of your soul reclines the commanding Master; He does but sleep; wake Him. Self-control is strength; Right Thought is mastery; Calmness is power.

Say unto your heart, "Peace, be still!"

THE GREAT STONE FACE

Nathaniel Hawthorne

Nathaniel Hawthorne, born in Salem, Massachusetts, in 1804 (just a year before the birth of Joseph Smith), is famous as a master of American fiction. Best known for his novel *The Scarlet Letter,* published in 1850, he also wrote several collections of highly symbolic short stories, many on moral and spiritual themes. One of these was *The Great Stone Face* (published in 1851), whose message is similar to that of *As a Man Thinketh:* That which we think about, we become.

The Great Stone Face—the rock formation about which the story is told—recalls the words of Helaman to his sons: "Remember that it is upon the rock of our Redeemer, who is Christ, the Son of God, that ye must build your foundation; that when the devil shall send forth his mighty winds, yea, his shafts in the whirlwind, yea, when all his hail and his mighty storm shall beat upon you, it shall have no power over you to drag you down to the gulf of misery and endless wo, because of the rock upon which ye are built, which is a sure foundation, a foundation whereon if men build they cannot fall." (Helaman 5:12.)

It also recalls the words of John the Beloved: "Now are we the sons of God, and it doth not yet appear what we shall be: but we know that, when he shall appear, we shall be like him; for we shall see him as he is. And every man that hath this hope in him purifieth himself, even as he is pure." (1 John 3:2–3.)

THE GREAT STONE FACE

One afternoon, when the sun was going down, a mother and her little boy sat at the door of their cottage, talking about the Great Stone Face. They had but to lift their eyes, and there it was plainly to be seen, though miles away, with the sunshine brightening all its features.

And what was the Great Stone Face?

Embosomed amongst a family of lofty mountains, there was a valley so spacious that it contained many thousand inhabitants. Some of these good people dwelt in log huts, with the black forest all around them, on the steep and difficult hill-sides. Others had their homes in comfortable farm-houses, and cultivated the rich soil on the gentle slopes or level surfaces of the valley. Others, again, were congregated into populous villages, where some wild, highland rivulet, tumbling down from its birthplace in the upper mountain region, had been caught and tamed by human cunning, and compelled to turn the machinery of cotton factories. The inhabitants of this valley, in short, were numerous, and of many modes of life. But all of them, grown people and children, had a kind of familiarity with the Great Stone Face, although some possessed the gift of distinguishing this grand natural phenomenon more perfectly than many of their neighbors.

The Great Stone Face, then, was a work of Nature in her mood of majestic playfulness, formed on the perpendicular side of a mountain by some immense rocks, which had been thrown together in such a position as, when viewed at a proper distance, precisely to resemble the features of the human countenance. It seemed as if an enormous giant, or a Titan, had sculptured his own likeness on the precipice. There was the broad arch of the forehead, a hundred feet in height; the nose, with its long bridge; and the vast lips, which, if they could have spoken, would have rolled their thunder accents from one end of the valley to the other. True it is, that if the spectator approached too near, he lost the outline of the gigantic visage, and could discern only a heap of ponderous and gigantic rocks, piled in chaotic ruin one upon another. Retracing his steps, however, the wondrous features would again be seen; and the further he withdrew from them, the more like a human face, with all its original divinity intact, did they appear; until, as it grew dim in the distance, with the clouds and glorified vapor of the mountains clustering about it, the Great Stone Face seemed positively to be alive.

It was a happy lot for children to grow up to manhood or womanhood with the Great Stone Face before their eyes, for all the features were noble, and the expression was at once grand and sweet, as if it were the glow of a vast, warm heart, that embraced all mankind in its affections, and had room for more. It was an education only to look at it. According to the belief of many people, the valley owed much of its fertility to this benign aspect that was continually beaming over it, illuminating the clouds, and infusing its tenderness into the sunshine.

As we began with saying, a mother and her little boy sat at their cottage door, gazing at the Great Stone Face, and talking about it. The child's name was Ernest.

"Mother," said he, while the Titanic visage smiled on him, "I wish that it could speak, for it looks so very kindly that its voice must needs be pleasant. If I were to see a man with such a face, I should love him dearly."

"If an old prophecy should come to pass," answered his mother, "we may see a man, some time or other, with exactly such a face as that."

"What prophecy do you mean, dear mother?" eagerly inquired Ernest. "Pray tell me all about it!"

So his mother told him a story that her own mother had told to her, when she herself was younger than little Ernest; a story, not of things that were past, but of what was yet to come; a story, nevertheless, so very old, that even the Indians, who formerly inhabited this valley, had heard it from their forefathers, to whom, as they affirmed, it had been murmured by the mountain streams, and whispered by the wind among the tree-tops. The purport was, that, at some future day, a child should be born hereabouts, who was destined to become the greatest and noblest personage of his time, and whose countenance, in manhood, should bear an exact resemblance to the Great Stone Face. Not a few old-fashioned people, and young ones likewise, in the ardor of their hopes, still cherished an enduring faith in this old prophecy. But others, who had seen more of the world, had watched and waited till they were weary, and had beheld no man with such a face, nor any man that proved to be much greater or nobler than his neighbors, concluded it to be nothing but an idle tale. At all events, the great man of the prophecy had not yet appeared.

"O, mother, dear mother!" cried Ernest, clapping his hands above his head, "I do hope that I shall live to see him!"

His mother was an affectionate and thoughtful woman, and felt that it was wisest not to discourage the generous hopes of her little boy. So she only said to him, "Perhaps you may."

And Ernest never forgot the story that his mother told him. It was always in his mind, whenever he looked upon the Great Stone Face. He spent his childhood in the log-cottage where he was born, and was dutiful to his mother, and helpful to her in many things, assisting her much with his little hands, and more with his loving heart. In this manner, from a happy yet often pensive child, he grew up to be a mild, quiet, unobtrusive boy, and sun-browned with labor in the fields, but with more intelligence brightening his aspect than is seen in many lads who have been taught at famous schools. Yet Ernest had had no teacher, save only that the Great Stone Face became one to him. When the toil of the day was over, he would gaze at it for hours, until he began to imagine that those vast features recognized him, and gave him a smile of kindness and encouragement, responsive to his own look of veneration. We must not take upon us to affirm that this was a mistake, although the Face may have looked no more kindly at Ernest than at all the world besides. But the secret was, that the boy's tender and confiding simplicity discerned what other people could not see; and thus the love, which was meant for all, became his peculiar portion.

About this time, there went a rumor throughout the valley, that the great man, foretold from ages long ago, who was to bear a resemblance to the Great Stone Face, had appeared at last. It seems that, many years before, a young man had migrated from the valley and settled at a distant seaport, where, after getting together a little money, he had set up as a shopkeeper. His name—but I could never learn whether it was his real one, or a nickname that had grown out of his habits and success in life—was Gathergold. Being shrewd and active, and endowed by Providence with that inscrutable faculty which develops itself in what the world calls luck, he became an exceedingly rich merchant, and owner of a whole fleet of bulky-bottomed ships. All the countries of the globe appeared to join hands for the mere purpose of adding heap after heap to the mountainous accumulation of this one man's wealth. The cold regions of the north, almost within the gloom and shadow of the Arctic Circle, sent him their tribute in the shape of furs; hot Africa sifted for him the golden sands of her rivers, and gathered up the ivory tusks of her great elephants out of the forests; the East came bringing him the rich shawls, and spices, and teas, and the effulgence of diamonds, and the gleaming purity of large pearls. The ocean, not to be behindhand with the earth, yielded up her mighty whales, that Mr. Gathergold might sell their oil, and make a profit on it. Be the original commodity what it might, it was gold within his grasp. It might be said of him, as of Midas in the fable, that whatever he touched with his finger immediately glistened, and grew yellow, and was changed at once into sterling metal, or, which suited him still better, into piles of coin. And, when Mr. Gathergold had become so very rich that it would have taken him a hundred years only to count his wealth, he bethought himself of his native valley, and resolved to go back thither, and end his days where he was born. With this purpose in view, he sent a skilful architect to build him such a palace as should be fit for a man of his vast wealth to live in.

As I have said above, it had already been rumored in the valley that Mr. Gathergold had turned out to be the prophetic personage so long and vainly looked for, and that his visage was the perfect and undeniable similitude of the Great Stone Face. People were the more ready to believe that this must needs be the fact, when they beheld the splendid edifice that rose, as if by enchantment, on the site of his father's old weather-beaten farm-house. The exterior was of marble, so dazzlingly white that it seemed as though the whole structure might melt away in the sunshine, like those humbler ones which Mr. Gathergold, in his young play-days, before his fingers were gifted with the touch of transmutation, had been accustomed to build of snow. It had a richly ornamented portico, supported by tall pillars, beneath which was a lofty door, studded with silver knobs, and made of a kind of variegated wood that had been brought from beyond the sea. The windows, from the floor to the ceiling of each stately apartment, were composed, respectively, of but one enormous pane of glass, so transparently pure that it was said to be a finer medium than even the vacant atmosphere. Hardly anybody had been permitted to see the interior of this palace; but it was reported, and with good semblance of truth, to be far more gorgeous than the outside, insomuch that whatever was iron or brass in other houses, was silver or gold in this; and Mr. Gathergold's bed-chamber, especially, made such a glittering appearance that no ordinary man would have been able to close his eyes there. But, on the other hand, Mr. Gathergold was now so inured to wealth, that perhaps he could not have closed his eyes unless where the gleam of it was certain to find its way beneath his eyelids.

In due time, the mansion was finished; next came the upholsterers, with magnificent furniture; then, a whole troop of black and white servants, the harbingers of Mr. Gathergold, who, in his own majestic person was expected to arrive at sunset. Our friend Ernest, meanwhile, had been deeply stirred by the idea that the great man, the noble man, the man of prophecy, after so many ages of delay, was at length to be made manifest to his native valley. He knew, boy as he was, that there were a thousand ways in which Mr. Gathergold, with his vast wealth, might transform himself into an angel of beneficence, and assume a control over human affairs as wide and benignant as the smile of the Great Stone Face. Full of faith and hope, Ernest doubted not that what the people said was true, and that now he was to behold the living likeness of those wondrous features on the mountain-side. While the boy was still gazing up the valley, and fancying, as he always did, that the Great Stone Face returned his gaze and looked kindly at him, the rumbling of wheels was heard, approaching swiftly along the winding road.

"Here he comes!" cried a group of people who were assembled to witness the arrival. "Here comes the great Mr. Gathergold!"

A carriage, drawn by four horses, dashed round the turn of the road. Within it, thrust partly out of the window, appeared the physiognomy of a little old man, with a skin as yellow as if his own Midas-hand had transmuted it. He had a low forehead, small, sharp eyes, puckered about with innumerable wrinkles, and very thin lips, which he made still thinner by pressing them forcibly together.

"The very image of the Great Stone Face!" shouted the people. "Sure enough, the old prophecy is true; and here we have the great man come, at last!"

And, what greatly perplexed Ernest, they seemed actually to believe that here was the likeness which they spoke of. By the roadside there chanced to be an old beggar-woman and two little beggar-children, stragglers from some far-off region, who, as the carriage rolled onward, held out their hands and lifted up their doleful voices, most piteously beseeching charity. A yellow claw—the very same that had clawed together so much wealth—poked itself out of the coach-window, and dropt some copper coins upon the ground; so that, though the great man's name seems to have been Gathergold, he might just as suitably have been nicknamed Scattercopper. Still, nevertheless, with an earnest shout, and evidently with as much good faith as ever, the people bellowed,

"He is the very image of the Great Stone Face!"

But Ernest turned sadly from the wrinkled shrewdness of that sordid visage, and gazed up the valley, where, amid a gathering mist, gilded by the last sunbeams, he could still distinguish those glorious features which had impressed themselves into his soul. Their aspect cheered him. What did the benign lips seem to say?

"He will come! Fear not, Ernest; the man will come!"

The years went on, and Ernest ceased to be a boy. He had grown to be a young man now. He attracted little notice from the other inhabitants of the valley; for they saw nothing remarkable in his way of life, save that, when the labor of the day was over, he still loved to go apart and gaze and meditate upon the Great Stone Face. According to their idea of the matter, it was a folly, indeed, but pardonable, inasmuch as Ernest was industrious, kind, and neighborly, and neglected no duty for the sake of indulging this idle habit. They knew not that the Great Stone Face had become a teacher to him, and that the sentiment which was expressed in it would enlarge the young man's heart, and fill it with wider and deeper sympathies than other hearts. They knew not that thence would come a better wisdom than could be learned from books, and a better life than could be moulded on the defaced example of other human lives. Neither did Ernest know that the thoughts and affections which came to him so naturally, in the fields and at the fireside, and wherever he communed with himself, were of a higher tone than those which all men shared with him. A simple soul—simple as when his mother first taught him the old prophecy—he beheld the marvellous features beaming adown the valley, and still wondered that their human counterpart was so long in making his appearance.

By this time poor Mr. Gathergold was dead and buried; and the oddest part of the matter was, that his wealth, which was the body and spirit of his existence, had disappeared before his death, leaving nothing of him but a living skeleton, covered over with a wrinkled, yellow skin. Since the melting away of his gold, it had been very generally conceded that there was no such striking resemblance, after all, betwixt the ignoble features of the ruined merchant and that majestic face upon the mountain side. So the people ceased to honor him during his lifetime, and quietly consigned him to forgetfulness after his decease. Once in a while, it is true, his memory was brought up in connection with the magnificent palace which he had built, and which had long ago been turned into a hotel for the accommodation of strangers, multitudes of whom came, every summer, to visit that famous natural curiosity, the Great Stone Face. Thus, Mr. Gathergold being discredited and thrown into the shade, the man of prophecy was yet to come.

It so happened that a native-born son of the valley, many years before, had enlisted as a soldier, and, after a great deal of hard fighting, had now become an illustrious commander. Whatever he may be called in history, he was known in camps and on the battle-field under the nick-name of Old Blood-and-Thunder. This war-worn veteran, being now infirm with age and wounds, and weary of the turmoil of a military life, and of the roll of the drum and the clangor of the trumpet, that had so long been ringing in his ears, had lately signified a purpose of returning to his native valley, hoping to find repose where he remembered to have left it. The inhabitants, his old neighbors and their grown-up children, were resolved to welcome the renowned warrior with a salute of cannon and a public dinner; and all the more enthusiastically, it being affirmed that now, at last, the likeness of the Great Stone Face had actually appeared. An aid-de-camp of Old Blood-and-Thunder, travelling through the valley, was said to have been struck with the resemblance. Moreover, the schoolmates and early acquaintances of the general were ready to testify, on oath, that, to the best of their recollection, the aforesaid general had been exceedingly like the majestic image, even when a boy, only that the idea had never occurred to them at that period. Great, therefore, was the excitement throughout the valley; and many people, who had never once thought of glancing at the Great Stone Face for years before, now spent their time in gazing at it, for the sake of knowing exactly how General Blood-and-Thunder looked.

On the day of the great festival, Ernest, with all the other people of the valley, left their work, and proceeded to the spot where the sylvan banquet was prepared. As he approached, the loud voice of the Reverend Doctor Battleblast was heard, beseeching a blessing on the good things set before them, and on the distinguished friend of peace in whose honor they were assembled. The tables were arranged in a cleared space of the woods, shut in by the surrounding trees, except where a vista opened eastward, and afforded a distant view of the Great Stone Face. Over the general's chair, which was a relic from the home of Washington, there was an arch of verdant boughs, with the laurel profusely intermixed, and surmounted by his country's banner, beneath which he had won his victories. Our friend Ernest raised himself on his tip-toes, in hopes to get a glimpse of the celebrated guest; but there was a mighty crowd about the tables anxious to hear the toasts and speeches, and to catch any word that might fall from the general in reply; and a volunteer company, doing duty as a guard, pricked ruthlessly with their bayonets at any particularly quiet person among the throng. So Ernest, being of an unobtrusive character, was thrust quite into the background, where he could see no more of Old Blood-and-Thunder's physiognomy than if it had been still blazing on the battle-field. To console himself, he turned towards the Great Stone Face, which, like a faithful and long-remembered friend, looked back and smiled upon him through the vista of the forest. Meantime, however, he could overhear the remarks of various individuals, who were comparing the features of the hero with the face on the distant mountain side.

"'Tis the same face, to a hair!" cried one man, cutting a caper for joy.

"Wonderfully like, that's a fact!" responded another.

"Like! why, I call it Old Blood-and-Thunder himself, in a monstrous looking-glass!" cried a third. "And why not! He's the greatest man of this or any other age, beyond a doubt."

And then all three of the speakers gave a great shout, which communicated electricity to the crowd, and called forth a roar from a thousand voices, that went reverberating for miles among the mountains, until you might have supposed that the Great Stone Face had poured its thunder-breath into the cry. All these comments, and this vast enthusiasm, served the more to interest our friend; nor did he think of questioning that now, at length, the mountain-visage had found its human counterpart. It is true, Ernest had imagined that this long-looked-for personage would appear in the character of a man of peace, uttering wisdom, and doing good, and making people happy. But, taking an habitual breadth of view, with all his simplicity, he contended that Providence should choose its own method of blessing mankind, and could conceive that this great end might be effected even by a warrior and a bloody sword, should inscrutable wisdom see fit to order matters so. "The general! the general!" was now the cry. "Hush! silence! Old Blood-and-Thunder's going to make a speech."

Even so; for, the cloth being removed, the general's health had been drunk amid shouts of applause, and he now stood upon his feet to thank the company. Ernest saw him. There he was, over the shoulders of the crowd, from the two glittering epaulets and embroidered collar upward, beneath the arch of green boughs with inter-twined laurell and the banner drooping as if to shade his brow! And there, too, visible in the same glance, through the vista of the forest, appeared the Great Stone Face! And was there, indeed, such a resemblance as the crowd had testified? Alas, Ernest could not recognize it! He beheld a war-worn and weather-beaten countenance, full of energy, and expressive of an iron will; but the gentle wisdom, the deep, broad, tender sympathies, were altogether wanting in Old Blood-and-Thunder's visage; and even if the Great Stone Face had assumed his look of stern command, the milder traits would still have tempered it.

"This is not the man of prophecy," sighed Ernest to himself, as he made his way out of the throng. "And must the world wait longer yet?" The mists had congregated about the distant mountain-side, and there were seen the grand and awful features of the Great Stone Face, awful but benignant, as if a mighty angel were sitting among the hills, and enrobing himself in a cloud-vesture of gold and purple. As he looked, Ernest could hardly believe but that a smile beamed over the whole visage, with a radiance still brightening, although without motion of the lips. It was probably the effect of the western sunshine, melting through the thinly diffused vapors that had swept between him and the object that he gazed at. But—as it always did—the aspect of his marvellous friend made Ernest as hopeful as if he had never hoped in vain.

"Fear not, Ernest," said his heart, even as if the Great Face were whispering to him, "fear not, Ernest; he will come."

More years sped swiftly and tranquilly away. Ernest still dwelt in his native valley, and was now a man of middle age. By imperceptible degrees, he had become known among the people. Now, as heretofore, he labored for his bread, and was the same simple-hearted man that he had always been. But he had thought and felt so much, he had given so many of the best hours of his life to unworldly hopes for some great good to mankind, that it seemed as though he had been talking with the angels, and had imbibed a portion of their wisdom unawares. It was visible in the calm and well-considered beneficence of his daily life, the quiet stream of which had made a wide green margin all along its course. Not a day passed by, that the world was not the better because this man, humble as he was, had lived. He never stepped aside from his own path, yet would always reach a blessing to his neighbor. Almost involuntarily, too, he had become a preacher. The pure and high simplicity of his thought, which, as one of its manifestations, took shape in the good deeds that dropped silently from his hand, flowed also forth in speech. He uttered truths that wrought upon and moulded the lives of those who heard him. His auditors, it may be, never suspected that Ernest, their own neighbor and familiar friend, was more than an ordinary man; least of all did Ernest himself suspect it; but, inevitably as the murmur of a rivulet, came thoughts out of his mouth that no other human lips had spoken.

When the people's minds had had a little time to cool, they were ready enough to acknowledge their mistake in imagining a similarity between General Blood-and-Thunder's truculent physiognomy and the benign visage on the mountain side. But now, again, there were reports and many paragraphs in the newspapers, affirming that the likeness of the Great Stone Face had appeared upon the broad shoulders of a certain eminent statesman. He, like Mr. Gathergold and Old Blood-and-Thunder, was a native of the valley, but had left it in his early days, and taken up the trades of law and politics. Instead of the rich man's wealth and the warrior's sword, he had but a tongue, and it was mightier than both together. So wonderfully eloquent was he, that whatever he might choose to say, his auditors had no choice but to believe him; wrong looked like right, and right like wrong; for when it pleased him, he could make a kind of illuminated fog with his mere breath, and obscure the natural daylight with it. His tongue, indeed, was a magic instrument: sometimes it rumbled like the thunder; sometimes it warbled like the sweetest music. It was the blast of war—the song of peace; and it seemed to have a heart in it, when there was no such matter. In good truth, he was a wondrous man; and when his tongue had acquired him all other imaginable success—when it had been heard in halls of state, and in the courts of princes and potentates—after it had made him known all over the world, even as a voice crying from shore to shore— it finally persuaded his countrymen to select him for the presidency. Before this time—indeed, as soon as he began to grow celebrated—his admirers had found out the resemblance between him and the Great Stone Face; and so much were they struck by it, that throughout the country this distinguished gentleman was known by the name of Old Stony Phiz. The phrase was considered as giving a highly favorable aspect to his political prospects; for, as is likewise the case with the

Popedom, nobody ever becomes president without taking a name other than his own.

While his friends were doing their best to make him president, Old Stony Phiz, as he was called, set out on a visit to the valley where he was born. Of course, he had no other object than to shake hands with his fellow-citizens, and neither thought nor cared about any effect which his progress through the country might have upon the election. Magnificent preparations were made to receive the illustrious statesman; a cavalcade of horsemen set forth to meet him at the boundary line of the state, and all the people left their business and gathered along the wayside to see him pass. Among these was Ernest. Though more than once disappointed, as we have seen, he had such a hopeful and confiding nature, that he was always ready to believe in whatever seemed beautiful and good. He kept his heart continually open, and thus was sure to catch the blessing from on high, when it should come. So now again, as buoyantly as ever, he went forth to behold the likeness of the Great Stone Face.

The cavalcade came prancing along the road, with a great clattering of hoofs and a mighty cloud of dust, which rose up so dense and high that the visage of the mountain side was completely hidden from Ernest's eyes. All the great men of the neighborhood were there on horseback: militia officers, in uniform; the member of Congress; the sheriff of the county; the editors of newspapers; and many a farmer, too, had mounted his patient steed, with his Sunday coat upon his back. It really was a very brilliant spectacle, especially as there were numerous banners flaunting over the cavalcade, on some of which were gorgeous portraits of the illustrious statesman and the Great Stone Face, smiling familiarly at one another, like two brothers. If the pictures were to be trusted, the mutual resemblance, it must be confessed, was marvellous. We must not forget to mention that there was a band of music, which made the echoes of the mountains ring and reverberate with the loud triumph of its strains; so that airy and soul-thrilling melodies broke out among all the heights and hollows as if every nook of his native valley had found a voice to welcome the distinguished guest. But the grandest effect was when the far-off mountain precipice flung back the music; for then the Great Stone Face itself seemed to be swelling the triumphant chorus, in acknowledgment that, at length, the man of prophecy was come.

All this while the people were throwing up their hats and shouting, with enthusiasm so contagious that the heart of Ernest kindled up, and he likewise threw up his hat, and shouted, as loudly as the loudest, "Huzza for the great man! Huzza for Old Stony Phiz!" But as yet he had not seen him.

"Here he is, now!" cried those who stood near Ernest. "There! There! Look at Old Stony Phiz and then at the Old Man of the Mountain, and see if they are not as like as two twin-brothers!"

In the midst of all this gallant array, came an open barouche, drawn by four white horses; and in the barouche, with his massive head uncovered, sat the illustrious statesman, Old Stony Phiz himself.

"Confess it," said one of Ernest's neighbors to him, "the Great Stone Face has met its match at last!"

Now, it must be owned that, at his first glimpse of the countenance which was bowing and smiling from the barouche, Ernest did fancy that there was a resemblance between it and the old familiar face upon the mountain side. The brow, with its massive depth and loftiness, and all the other features, indeed, were boldly and strongly hewn, as if in emulation of a more than heroic, of a Titanic model. But the sublimity and stateliness, the grand expression of a divine sympathy, that illuminated the mountain visage, and etherealized its ponderous granite substance into spirit, might here be sought in vain. Something had been originally left out, or had departed. And therefore the marvellously gifted statesman had always a weary gloom in the deep caverns of his eyes, as of a child that has outgrown its playthings, or a man of mighty faculties and little aims, whose life, with all its high performances, was vague and empty, because no high purpose had endowed it with reality.

Still, Ernest's neighbor was thrusting his elbow into his side, and pressing him for an answer.

"Confess! confess! Is not he the very picture of your Old Man of the Mountain?"

"No!" said Ernest, bluntly, "I see little or no likeness."

"Then so much the worse for the Great Stone Face!" answered his neighbor; and again he set up a shout for Old Stony Phiz.

But Ernest turned away, melancholy, and almost despondent; for this was the saddest of his disappointments, to behold a man who might have fulfilled the prophecy, and had not willed to do so. Meantime, the cavalcade, the banners, the music, and the barouches, swept past him, with the vociferous crowd in the rear, leaving the dust to settle down, and the Great Stone Face to be revealed again, with the grandeur that it had worn for untold centuries.

"Lo, here I am, Ernest!" the benign lips seemed to say. "I have waited longer than thou, and am not yet weary. Fear not; the man will come."

The years hurried onward, treading in their haste on one another's heels. And now they began to bring white hairs, and scatter them over the head of Ernest; they made reverend wrinkles across his forehead, and furrows in his cheeks. He was an aged man. But not in vain had he grown old: more than the white hairs on his head were the sage thoughts in his mind; his wrinkles and furrows were inscriptions that Time had graved, and in which he had written legends of wisdom that had been tested by the tenor of a life. And Ernest had ceased to be obscure. Unsought for, undesired, had come the fame which so many seek, and made him known in the great world, beyond the limits of the valley in which he had dwelt so quietly. College professors, and even the active men of cities, came from far to see and converse with Ernest; for the report had gone abroad that this simple husbandman had ideas unlike those of other men, not gained from books, but of a higher tone—a tranquil and familiar majesty, as if he had been talking with the angels as his daily friends. Whether it were sage, statesman, or philanthropist, Ernest received these visitors with the gentle sincerity that had characterized him from boyhood, and spoke freely with them of whatever came uppermost, or lay deepest in his heart or their own. While they talked together, his face would kindle, unawares, and shine upon them, as with a mild evening light. Pensive with the fulness of such discourse, his guests took leave and went their way; and, passing up the valley, paused to look at the Great Stone Face, imagining that they had seen its likeness in a human countenance, but could not remember where.

While Ernest had been growing up and growing old, a bountiful Providence had granted a new poet to this earth. He, likewise, was a native of the valley but had spent the greater part of his life at a distance from that romantic region, pouring out his sweet music amid the bustle and din of cities. Often, however, did the mountains which had been familiar to him in his childhood lift their snowy peaks into the clear atmosphere of his poetry. Neither was the Great Stone Face forgotten, for the poet had celebrated it in an ode, which was grand enough to have been uttered by its own majestic lips. This man of genius, we may say, had come down from heaven with wonderful endowments. If he sang of a mountain, the eyes of all mankind beheld a mightier grandeur reposing on its breast, or soaring to its summit, than had before been seen there. If his theme were a lovely lake, a celestial smile had now been thrown over it, to gleam forever on its surface. If it were the vast old sea, even the deep immensity of its dread bosom seemed to swell the higher, as if moved by the emotions of the song. Thus the world assumed another and a better aspect from the hour that the poet blessed it with his happy eyes. The Creator had bestowed him, as the last, best touch to his own handiwork. Creation was not finished till the poet came to interpret, and so complete it.

The effect was no less high and beautiful, when his human brethren were the subject of his verse. The man or woman, sordid with the common dust of life, who crossed his daily path, and the little child who played in it, were glorified if he beheld them in his mood of poetic faith. He showed the golden links of the great chain that intertwined them with an angelic kindred; he brought out the hidden traits of a celestial birth that made them worthy of such kin. Some, indeed, there were, who thought to show the soundness of their judgment by affirming that all the beauty and dignity of the natural world existed only in the poet's fancy. Let such men speak for themselves, who undoubtedly appear to have been spawned forth by Nature with a contemptuous bitterness; she having plastered them up out of her refuse stuff, after all the swine were made. As respects all things else, the poet's ideal was the truest truth.

The songs of this poet found their way to Ernest. He read them, after his customary toil, seated on the bench before his cottage door, where, for such a length of time, he had filled his repose with thought by gazing at the Great Stone Face. And now, as he read stanzas that caused the soul to thrill within him, he lifted his eyes to the vast countenance beaming on him so benignantly.

"O, majestic friend," he murmured, addressing the Great Stone Face, "is not this man worthy to resemble thee?"

The Face seemed to smile, but answered not a word.

Now it happened that the poet, though he dwelt so far away, had not only heard of Ernest, but had meditated much upon his character, until he deemed nothing so desirable as to meet this man, whose untaught wisdom walked hand in hand with the noble simplicity of his life. One summer morning, therefore, he took passage by the railroad, and, in the decline of the afternoon, alighted from the cars at no great distance from Ernest's cottage. The great hotel, which had formerly been the palace of Mr. Gathergold, was close at hand, but the poet with his carpet-bag on his arm, inquired at once where Ernest dwelt, and was resolved to be accepted as his guest.

Approaching the door, he there found the good old man, holding a volume in his hand, which alternately he read, and then, with a finger between the leaves, looked lovingly at the Great Stone Face.

"Good evening," said the poet. "Can you give a traveller a night's lodging?"

"Willingly," answered Ernest; and then he added, smiling, "Methinks I never saw the Great Stone Face look so hospitably at a stranger."

The poet sat down on the bench beside him, and he and Ernest talked together. Often had the poet held intercourse with the wittiest and the wisest, but never before with a man like Ernest, whose thoughts and feelings gushed up with such a natural freedom, and who made great truths so familiar by his simple utterance of them. Angels, as had been so often said, seemed to have wrought with him at his labor in the fields; angels seemed to have sat with him by the fireside; and, dwelling with angels as friend with friends, he had imbibed the sublimity of their ideas, and imbued it with the sweet and lowly charm of household words. So thought the poet. And Ernest, on the other hand, was moved and agitated by the living images which the poet flung out of his mind, and which peopled all the air about the cottage door with shapes of beauty, both gay and pensive. The sympathies of these two men instructed them with a profounder sense than either could have attained alone. Their minds accorded into one strain, and made delightful music which neither of them could have claimed as all his own, nor distinguished his own share from the other's. They led one another, as it were, into a high pavilion of their thoughts, so remote, and hitherto so dim, that they had never entered it before, and so beautiful that they desired to be there always.

As Ernest listened to the poet, he imagined that the Great Stone Face was bending forward to listen too. He gazed earnestly into the poet's glowing eyes.

"Who are you, my strangely gifted guest?" he said.

The poet laid his finger on the volume that Ernest had been reading.

"You have read these poems," said he. "You know me, then—for I wrote them."

Again, and still more earnestly than before, Ernest examined the poet's features; then turned towards the Great Stone Face; then back, with an uncertain aspect, to his guest. But his countenance fell; he shook his head, and sighed.

"Wherefore are you sad?" inquired the poet.

"Because," replied Ernest, "all through life I have awaited the fulfilment of a prophecy; and, when I read these poems, I hoped that it might be fulfilled in you."

"You hoped," answered the poet, faintly smiling, "to find in me the likeness of the Great Stone Face. And you are disappointed, as formerly with Mr. Gathergold, and Old Blood-and-Thunder, and Old Stony Phiz. Yes, Ernest, it is my doom. You must add my name to the illustrious three, and record another failure of your hopes. For—in shame and sadness do I speak it, Ernest—I am not worthy to be typified by yonder benign and majestic image."

"And why?" asked Ernest. He pointed to the volume—"Are not those thoughts divine?"

"They have a strain of the Divinity," replied the poet. "You can hear in them the far-off echo of a heavenly song. But my life, dear Ernest, has not corresponded with my thought. I have had grand dreams, but they have been only dreams, because I have lived—and that, too, by own choice—among poor and mean realities. Sometimes even—shall I dare to say it?—I lack faith in the grandeur, the beauty, and the goodness, which my own works are said to have made more evident in nature and in human life. Why, then, pure seeker of the good and true, shouldst thou hope to find me, in yonder image of the divine!"

The poet spoke sadly, and his eyes were dim with tears. So, likewise, were those of Ernest.

At the hour of sunset, as had long been his frequent custom, Ernest was to discourse to an assemblage of the neighboring inhabitants, in the open air. He and the poet, arm in arm, still talking together as they went along, proceeded to the spot. It was a small nook among the hills, with a gray precipice behind, the stern front of which was relieved by the pleasant foliage of many creeping plants, that made a tapestry for the naked rock, by hanging their festoons from all its rugged angles. At a small elevation above the ground, set in a rich frame-work of verdure, there appeared a niche, spacious enough to admit a human figure, with freedom for such gestures as spontaneously accompany earnest thought and genuine emotion. Into this natural pulpit Ernest ascended, and threw a look of familiar kindness around upon his audience. They stood, or sat, or reclined upon the grass, as seemed good to each, with the departing sunshine falling obliquely over them, and mingling its subdued cheerfulness with the solemnity of a grove of ancient trees, beneath and amid the boughs of which the golden rays were constrained to pass. In another direction was seen the Great Stone Face, with the same cheer, combined with the same solemnity, in its benignant aspect.

Ernest began to speak, giving to the people of what was in his heart and mind. His words had power, because they accorded with his thoughts; and his thoughts had reality and depth, because they harmonized with the life which he had always lived. It was not mere breath that this preacher uttered; they were the words of life, because a life of good deeds and holy love was melted into them. Pearls, pure and rich, had been dissolved into this precious draught. The poet, as he listened, felt that the being and character of Ernest were a nobler strain of poetry than he had ever written. His eyes glistening with tears, he gazed reverentially at the venerable man, and said within himself that never was there an aspect so worthy of a prophet and a sage as that mild, sweet, thoughtful countenance, with the glory of white hair diffused about it. At a distance, but distinctly to be seen, high up in the golden light of the setting sun, appeared the Great Stone Face, with hoary mists around it, like the white hairs around the brow of Ernest. Its look of grand beneficence seemed to embrace the world.

At that moment, in sympathy with a thought which he was about to utter, the face of Ernest assumed a grandeur of expression, so imbued with benevolence, that the poet, by an irresistible impulse, threw his arms aloft, and shouted,

"Behold! Behold! Ernest is himself the likeness of the Great Stone Face!"

Then all the people looked, and saw that what the deep-sighted poet said was true. The prophecy was fulfilled. But Ernest, having finished what he had to say, took the poet's arm, and walked slowly homeward, still hoping that some wiser and better man than himself would by and by appear, bearing a resemblance to the GREAT STONE FACE.

THE MANSION

Henry Van Dyke

Best known as the author of a Christmas tale, "The Story of the Other Wise Man," Henry Van Dyke was born in 1852 in Germantown, Pennsylvania. He graduated from Princeton's theological seminary in 1877 and became a minister in the Presbyterian Church. He first read "The Story of the Other Wise Man" to his congregation in 1896 and "The First Christmas Tree" in 1897. Soon he was publishing his stories in such volumes as *The Ruling Passion* (1901) and *The Blue Flower* (1902).

Van Dyke's story "The Mansion" is an impressive tale of someone who learns that service to others should be given anonymously, without expectation of reward or thought of self-aggrandizement. President Thomas S. Monson used this classic story as an illustration in general conference of April 1983, noting the selfishness of the protagonist, John Weightman, who says, "You have to be careful how you give, in order to secure the best results—no indiscriminate giving—no pennies in beggars' hats! . . . Try to put your gifts where they can be identified and do good all around." But the Savior said, "Take heed that ye do not your alms before men, to be seen of them: otherwise ye have no reward of your Father which is in heaven. Therefore when thou doest thine alms, do not sound a trumpet before thee, as the hypocrites do in the synagogues and in the streets, that they may have glory of men. *Verily I say unto you, They have their reward.* But when thou doest alms, let not thy left hand know what thy right hand doeth: that thine alms may be in secret: and thy Father which seeth in secret himself shall reward thee openly." (Matthew 6:1–4; italics added.)

THE MANSION

There was an air of calm and reserved opulence about the Weightman mansion that spoke not of money squandered, but of wealth prudently applied. Standing on a corner of the Avenue no longer fashionable for residence, it looked upon the swelling tide of business with an expression of complacency and half-disdain.

The house was not beautiful. There was nothing in its straight front of chocolate-colored stone, its heavy cornices, its broad, staring windows of plate glass, its carved and bronze-bedecked mahogany doors at the top of the wide stoop, to charm the eye or fascinate the imagination. But it was eminently respectable, and in its way imposing. It seemed to say that the glittering shops of the jewelers, the milliners, the confectioners, the florists, the picture-dealers, the furriers, the makers of rare and costly antiquities, retail traders in luxuries of life, were beneath the notice of a house that had its foundations in the high finance, and was built literally and figuratively in the shadow of St. Petronius' Church.

At the same time there was something self-pleased and congratulatory in the way in which the mansion held its own amid the changing neighborhood. It almost seemed to be lifted up a little, among the tall buildings near at hand, as if it felt the rising value of the land on which it stood.

John Weightman was like the house into which he had built himself thirty years ago, and in which his ideals and ambitions were incrusted. He was a self-made man. But in making himself he had chosen a highly esteemed pattern and worked according to the approved rules. There was nothing irregular, questionable, flamboyant about him. He was solid, correct, and justly successful.

His minor tastes, of course, had been carefully kept up to date. At the proper time, pictures of the Barbizon masters, old English plate and portraits, bronzes by Barye and marbles by Rodin, Persian carpets and Chinese porcelains, had been introduced to the mansion. It contained a Louis Quinze reception-room, an Empire drawing-room, a Jacobean dining-room, and various apartments dimly reminiscent of the styles of furniture affected by deceased monarchs. That the hallways were too short for the historic perspective did not make much difference. American decorative art is *capable de tout,* it absorbs all periods. Of each period Mr. Weightman wished to have something of the best. He understood its value, present as a certificate, and prospective as an investment.

It was only in the architecture of his town house that he remained conservative, immovable, one might almost say Early-Victorian-Christian. His country house at Dulwich-on-the-Sound was a palace of the Italian Renaissance. But in town he adhered to an architecture which had moral associations, the Nineteenth-Century-Brownstone epoch. It was a symbol of his social position, his religious doctrine, and even, in a way, of his business creed.

"A man of fixed principles," he would say, "should express them in the looks of his house. New York changes its domestic architecture too rapidly. It is like divorce. It is not dignified. I don't like it. Extravagance and fickleness are advertised in most of these new houses. I wish to be known for different qualities. Dignity and prudence are the things that people trust. Every one knows that I can afford to live in the house that suits me. It is a guarantee to the public. It inspires confidence. It helps my influence. There is a text in the Bible about 'a house that hath foundations.' That is the proper kind of a mansion for a solid man."

Harold Weightman had often listened to his father discoursing in this fashion on the fundamental principles of life, and always with a divided mind. He admired immensely his father's talents and the single-minded energy with which he improved them. But in the paternal philosophy there was something that disquieted and oppressed the young man, and made him gasp inwardly for fresh air and free action.

At times, during his college course and his years at the law school, he had yielded to this impulse and broken away—now toward extravagance and dissipation, and then, when the reaction came, toward a romantic devotion to work among the poor. He had felt his father's disapproval for both of these forms of imprudence; but it was never expressed in a harsh or violent way, always with a certain tolerant patience, such as one might show for the mistakes and vagaries of the very young. John Weightman was not hasty, impulsive, inconsiderate, even toward his own children. With them, as with the rest of the world, he felt that he had a reputation to maintain, a theory to vindicate. He could afford to give them time to see that he was absolutely right.

One of his favorite Scripture quotations was, "Wait on the Lord." He had applied it to real estate and to people, with profitable results.

But to human persons the sensation of being waited for is not always agreeable. Sometimes, especially with the young, it produces a vague restlessness, a dumb resentment, which is increased by the fact that one can hardly explain or justify it. Of this John Weightman was not conscious. It lay beyond his horizon. He did not take it into account in the plan of life which he made for himself and for his family as the sharers and inheritors of his success.

"Father plays us," said Harold, in a moment of irritation, to his mother, "like pieces in a game of chess."

"My dear," said that lady, whose faith in her husband was religious, "you ought not to speak so impatiently. At least he wins the game. He is one of the most respected men in New York. And he is very generous, too."

"I wish he would be more generous in letting us be ourselves," said the young man. "He always has something in view for us and expects to move us up to it."

"But isn't it always for our benefit?" replied his mother. "Look what a position we have. No one can say there is any taint on our money. There are no rumors about your father. He has kept the laws of God and of man. He has never made any mistakes."

Harold got up from his chair and poked the fire. Then he came back to the ample, well-gowned, firm-looking lady, and sat beside her on the sofa. He took her hand gently and looked at the two rings—a thin band of yellow gold, and a small solitaire diamond—which kept their place on her third finger in modest dignity, as if not shamed, but rather justified, by the splendor of the emerald which glittered beside them.

"Mother," he said, "you have a wonderful hand. And father made no mistake when he won you. But are you sure he has always been so inerrant?"

"Harold," she exclaimed, a little stiffly, "what do you mean? His life is an open book."

"Oh," he answered, "I don't mean anything bad, mother dear. I know the governor's life is an open book—a ledger, if you like, kept in the best bookkeeping hand, and always ready for inspection—every page correct, and showing a handsome balance. But isn't it a mistake not to allow us to make our own mistakes, to learn for ourselves, to live our own lives? Must we be always working for 'the balance,' in one thing or another? I want to be myself—to get outside of this everlasting, profitable 'plan'—to let myself go, and lose myself for a while at least—to do the things that I want to do, just because I want to do them."

"My boy," said his mother, anxiously, "you are not going to do anything wrong or foolish? You know the falsehood of that old proverb about wild oats."

He threw back his head and laughed. "Yes, mother," he answered, "I know it well enough. But in California, you know, the wild oats are one of the most valuable crops. They grow all over the hillsides and keep the cattle and the horses alive. But that wasn't what I meant—to sow wild oats. Say to pick wild flowers, if you like, or even to chase wild geese—to do something that seems good to me just for its own sake, not for the sake of wages of one kind or another. I feel like a hired man, in the service of this magnificent mansion—say in training for father's place as majordomo. I'd like to get out some way, to feel free—perhaps to do something for others."

The young man's voice hesitated a little. "Yes, it sounds like cant, I know, but sometimes I feel as if I'd like to do some good in the world, if father only wouldn't insist upon God's putting it into the ledger."

His mother moved uneasily, and a slight look of bewilderment came into her face.

"Isn't that almost irreverent?" she asked. "Surely the righteous must have their reward. And your father is good. See how much he gives to all the established charities, how many things he has founded. He's always thinking of others, and planning for them. And surely, for us, he does everything. How well he has planned this trip to Europe for me and the girls—the court-presentation at Berlin, the season on the

Riviera, the visits in England with the Plumptons and the Halverstones. He says Lord Halverstone has the finest old house in Sussex, pure Elizabethan, and all the old customs are kept up, too—family prayers every morning for all the domestics. By-the-way, you know his son Bertie, I believe."

Harold smiled a little to himself as he answered: "Yes, I fished at Catalina Island last June with the Honorable Ethelbert; he's rather a decent chap, in spite of his ingrowing mind. But you?—mother, you are simply magnificent! You are father's masterpiece." The young man leaned over to kiss her, and went up to the Riding Club for his afternoon canter in the Park.

So it came to pass, early in December, that Mrs. Weightman and her two daughters sailed for Europe, on their serious pleasure trip, even as it had been written in the book of Providence; and John Weightman, who had made the entry, was left to pass the rest of the winter with his son and heir in the brownstone mansion.

They were comfortable enough. The machinery of the massive establishment ran as smoothly as a great electric dynamo. They were busy enough, too. John Weightman's plans and enterprises were complicated, though his principle of action was always simple—to get good value for every expenditure and effort. The banking-house of which he was the chief, the brain, the will, the absolutely controlling hand, was so admirably organized that the details of its direction took but little time.

But the scores of other interests that radiated from it and were dependent upon it—or perhaps it would be more accurate to say, that contributed to its solidity and success—the many investments, industrial, political, benevolent, reformatory, ecclesiastical, that had made the name of Weightman well known and potent in city, church, and state, demanded much attention and careful steering, in order that each might produce the desired result. There were board meetings of corporations and hospitals, conferences in Wall Street and at Albany, consultations and committee meetings in the brownstone mansion.

For a share in all this business and its adjuncts John Weightman had his son in training in one of the famous law firms of the city; for he held that banking itself is a simple affair, the only real difficulties of finance are on its legal side. Meantime he wished the young man to meet and know the men with whom he would have to deal when he became a partner in the house. So a couple of dinners were given in the mansion during December, after which the father called the son's attention to the fact that over a hundred million dollars had sat around the board.

But on Christmas Eve father and son were dining together without guests, and their talk across the broad table, glittering with silver and cut glass, and softly lit by shaded candles, was intimate, though a little slow at times. The elder man was in rather a rare mood, more expansive and confidential than usual; and, when the coffee was brought in and they were left alone, he talked more freely of his personal plans and hopes than he had ever done before.

"I feel very grateful to-night," said he, at last; "it must be something in the air of Christmas that gives me this feeling of thankfulness for the many divine mercies that have been bestowed upon me. All the princi-ples by which I have tried to guide my life have been justified. I have never made the value of this salted almond by anything that the courts would not uphold, at least in the long run, and yet—or wouldn't it be truer to say and therefore?—my affairs have been wonderfully pros-pered. There's a great deal in that text 'Honesty is the best'—but no, that's not from the Bible, after all, is it? Wait a moment; there is some-thing of that kind, I know."

"May I light a cigar, father," said Harold, turning away to hide a smile, "while you are remembering the text?"

"Yes, certainly," answered the elder man, rather shortly; "you know I don't dislike the smell. But it is a wasteful, useless habit, and therefore I have never practised it. Nothing useless is worth while, that's my motto—nothing that does not bring the reward. Oh, now I recall the text, 'Verily I say unto you they have their reward.' I shall ask Doctor Snodgrass to preach a sermon on that verse some day."

"Using you as an illustration?"

"Well, not exactly that; but I could give him some good materials from my own experience to prove the truth of Scripture. I can honestly say that there is not one of my charities that has not brought me in a good return, either in the increase of influence, the building up of credit, or the association with substantial people. Of course you have to be careful how you give, in order to secure the best results—no indiscriminate giving—no pennies in beggars' hats! It has been one of my principles always to use the same kind of judgment in charities that I use in my other affairs, and they have not disappointed me."

"Even the check that you put in the plate when you take the offertory up the aisle on Sunday morning?"

"Certainly; though there the influence is less direct; and I must confess that I have my doubts in regard to the collection for Foreign Missions. That always seems to me romantic and wasteful. You never hear from it in any definite way. They say the missionaries have done a good deal to open the way for trade; perhaps—but they have also gotten us into commercial and political difficulties. Yet I give to them—a little—it is a matter of conscience with me to identify myself with all the enterprises of the Church; it is the mainstay of social order and a prosperous civilization. But the best forms of benevolence are the well-established, organized ones here at home, where people can see them and know what they are doing."

"You mean the ones that have a local habitation and a name."

"Yes; they offer by far the safest return, though of course there is something gained by contributing to general funds. A public man can't afford to be without public spirit. But on the whole I prefer a building, or an endowment. There is a mutual advantage to a good name and a good institution in their connection in the public mind. It helps them both. Remember that, my boy. Of course at the beginning you will have to practise it in a small way; later, you will have larger opportunities. But try to put your gifts where they can be identified and do good all around. You'll see the wisdom of it in the long run."

"I can see it already, sir, and the way you describe it looks amazingly wise and prudent. In other words, we must cast our bread on the waters in large loaves, carried by sound ships marked with the owner's name, so that the return freight will be sure to come back to us."

The father laughed, but his eyes were frowning a little as if he suspected something irreverent under the respectful reply.

"You put it humorously, but there's sense in what you say. Why not? God rules the sea; but He expects us to follow the laws of navigation and commerce. Why not take good care of your bread, even when you give it away?"

"It's not for me to say why not—and yet I can think of cases—"

The young man hesitated for a moment. His half-finished cigar had gone out. He rose and tossed it into the fire, in front of which he remained standing—a slender, eager, restless young figure, with a touch of hunger in the fine face, strangely like and unlike the father, at whom he looked with half-wistful curiosity.

"The fact is, sir," he continued, "there is such a case in my mind now, and it is a good deal on my heart, too. So I thought of speaking to you about it to-night. You remember Tom Rollins, the Junior who was so good to me when I entered college?"

The father nodded. He remembered very well indeed the annoying incidents of his son's first escapade, and how Rollins had stood by him and helped to avoid a public disgrace, and how a close friendship had grown between the two boys, so different in their fortunes.

"Yes," he said, "I remember him. He was a promising young man. Has he succeeded?"

"Not exactly—that is not yet. His business has been going rather badly. He has a wife and little baby, you know. And now he has broken down,—something wrong with his lungs. The doctor says his only chance is a year or eighteen months in Colorado. I wish we could help him."

"How much would it cost?"

"Three or four thousand, perhaps, as a loan."

"Does the doctor say he will get well?"

"A fighting chance—the doctor says."

The face of the older man changed subtly. Not a line was altered, but it seemed to have a different substance, as if it were carved out of some firm, imperishable stuff.

"A fighting chance," he said, "may do for a speculation, but it is not a good investment. You owe something to young Rollins. Your grateful feeling does you credit. But don't overwork it. Send him three or four hundred, if you like. You'll never hear from it again, except in the letter of thanks. But for Heaven's sake don't be sentimental. Religion is not a matter of sentiment; it's a matter of principle."

The face of the younger man changed now. But instead of becoming fixed and graven, it seemed to melt into life by the heat of an inward fire. His nostrils quivered with quick breath, his lips were curled.

"Principle!" he said. "You mean principal—and interest too. Well, sir, you know best whether that is religion or not. But if it is, count me out, please. Tom saved me from going to the devil, six years ago; and I'll be damned if I don't help him to the best of my ability now."

John Weightman looked at his son steadily. "Harold," he said at last, "you know I dislike violent language, and it never has any influence with me. If I could honestly approve of this proposition of yours, I'd let you have the money; but I can't; it's extravagant and useless. But you have your Christmas check for a thousand dollars coming to you tomorrow. You can use it as you please. I never interfere with your private affairs."

"Thank you," said Harold. "Thank you very much! But there's another private affair. I want to get away from this life, this town, this house. It stifles me. You refused last summer when I asked you to let me go up to Grenfell's Mission on the Labrador. I could go now, at least as far as the Newfoundland Station. Have you changed your mind?"

"Not at all. I think it is an exceedingly foolish enterprise. It would interrupt the career that I have marked out for you."

"Well, then, here's a cheaper proposition. Algy Vanderhoof wants me to join him on his yacht with—well, with a little party—to cruise in the West Indies. Would you prefer that?"

"Certainly not! The Vanderhoof set is wild and godless—I do not wish to see you keeping company with fools who walk in the broad and easy way that leads to perdition."

"It is rather a hard choice," said the young man, with a short laugh, turning toward the door. "According to you there's very little difference—a fool's paradise or a fool's hell! Well, it's one or the other for me, and I'll toss up for it to-night: heads, I lose; tails, the devil wins. Anyway, I'm sick of this, and I'm out of it."

"Harold," said the older man (and there was a slight tremor in his voice), "don't let us quarrel on Christmas Eve. All I want is to persuade you to think seriously of the duties and responsibilities to which God has called you—don't speak lightly of heaven and hell—remember, there is another life."

The young man came back and laid his hand upon his father's shoulder.

"Father," he said, "I want to remember it. I try to believe in it. But somehow or other, in this house, it all seems unreal to me. No doubt all you say is perfectly right and wise. I don't venture to argue against it, but I can't feel it—that's all. If I'm to have a soul, either to lose or to save, I must really live. Just now neither the present nor the future means anything to me. But surely we won't quarrel. I'm very grateful to you, and we'll part friends. Good-night, sir."

The father held out his hand in silence. The heavy portiere dropped noiselessly behind the son, and he went up the wide, curving stairway to his own room.

Meantime John Weightman sat in his carved chair in the Jacobean dining-room. He felt strangely old and dull. The portraits of beautiful women by Lawrence and Reynolds and Raeburn, which had often seemed like real company to him, looked remote and uninteresting. He fancied something cold and almost unfriendly in their expression, as if they were staring through him or beyond him. They cared nothing for his principles, his hopes, his disappointments, his successes; they belonged to another world, in which he had no place. At this he felt a vague resentment, a sense of discomfort that he could not have defined or explained. He was used to being considered, respected, appreciated at his full value in every region, even in that of his own dreams.

Presently he rang for the butler, telling him to close the house and not to sit up, and walked with lagging steps into the long library, where the shaded lamps were burning. His eye fell upon the low shelves full of costly books, but he had no desire to open them. Even the carefully chosen pictures that hung above them seemed to have lost their attraction. He paused for a moment before an idyll of Corot—a dance of nymphs around some forgotten altar in a vaporous glade—and looked at it curiously. There was something rapturous and serene about the picture, a breath of spring-time in the misty trees, a harmony of joy in the dancing figures, that wakened in him a feeling of half-pleasure and half-envy. It represented something that he had never known in his calculated, orderly life. He was dimly mistrustful of it.

"It is certainly very beautiful," he thought, "but it is distinctly pagan; that altar is built to some heathen god. It does not fit into the scheme of a Christian life. I doubt whether it is consistent with the tone of my house. I will sell it this winter. It will bring three or four times what I paid for it. That was a good purchase, a very good bargain."

He dropped into the revolving chair before his big library table. It was covered with pamphlets and reports of the various enterprises in which he was interested. There was a pile of newspaper clippings in which his name was mentioned with praise for his sustaining power as a pillar of finance, for his judicious benevolence, for his support of wise and prudent reform movements, for his discretion in making permanent public gifts—"the Weightman Charities," one very complaisant editor called them, as if they deserved classification as a distinct species.

He turned the papers over listlessly. There was a description and a picture of the "Weightman Wing of the Hospital for Cripples," of which he was president; and an article on the new professor in the "Weightman Chair of Political Jurisprudence" in Jackson University, of which he was a trustee; and an illustrated account of the opening of the "Weightman Grammar-School" at Dulwich-on-the-Sound, where he had his legal residence for purposes of taxation.

This last was perhaps the most carefully planned of all the Weightman Charities. He desired to win the confidence and support of his rural neighbors. It had pleased him much when the local newspaper had spoken of him as an ideal citizen and the logical candidate for the Governorship of the State; but upon the whole it seemed to him wiser to keep out of active politics. It would be easier and better to put Harold into the running, to have him sent to the Legislature from the Dulwich district, then to the national House, then to the Senate. Why not? The Weightman interests were large enough to need a direct representative and guardian at Washington.

But to-night all these plans came back to him with dust upon them. They were dry and crumbling like forsaken habitations. The son upon whom his complacent ambition had rested had turned his back upon the mansion of his father's hopes. The break might not be final; and in any event there would be much to live for; the fortunes of the family would be secure. But the zest of it all would be gone if John Weightman had to give up the assurance of perpetuating his name and his principles in his son. It was a bitter disappointment, and he felt that he had not deserved it.

He rose from the chair and paced the room with leaden feet. For the first time in his life his age was visibly upon him. His head was heavy and hot, and the thoughts that rolled in it were confused and depressing. Could it be that he had made a mistake in the principles of his existence? There was no argument in what Harold had said—it was almost childish—and yet it had shaken the elder man more deeply than he cared to show. It held a silent attack which touched him more than open criticism.

Suppose the end of his life were nearer than he thought—the end must come some time—what if it were now? Had he not founded his house upon a rock? Had he not kept the Commandments? Was he not, "touching the law, blameless"? And beyond this, even if there were some faults in his character—and all men are sinners—yet he surely believed in the saving doctrines of religion—the forgiveness of sins, the resurrection of the body, the life everlasting. Yes, that was the true source of comfort, after all. He would read a bit in the Bible, as he did every night, and go to bed and to sleep.

He went back to his chair at the library table. A strange weight of weariness rested upon him, but he opened the book at a familiar place, and his eyes fell upon the verse at the bottom of the page.

"Lay not up for yourselves treasures upon earth."

That had been the text of the sermon a few weeks before. Sleepily, heavily, he tried to fix his mind upon it and recall it. What was it that Doctor Snodgrass had said? Ah, yes—that it was a mistake to pause here in reading the verse. We must read on without a pause—*Lay not up treasures upon earth where moth and rust do corrupt and where thieves break through and steal*—that was the true doctrine. We may have treasures upon earth, but they must not be put into unsafe places, but into safe places. A most comforting doctrine! He had always followed it. Moths and rust and thieves had done no harm to his investments.

John Weightman's drooping eyes turned to the next verse, at the top of the second column.

"But lay up for yourselves treasures in heaven."

Now what had the Doctor said about that? How was it to be understood—in what sense—treasures—in heaven?

The book seemed to float away from him. The light vanished. He wondered dimly if this could be Death, coming so suddenly, so quietly, so irresistibly. He struggled for a moment to hold himself up, and then sank slowly forward upon the table. His head rested upon his folded hands. He slipped into the unknown.

How long afterward conscious life returned to him he did not know. The blank might have been an hour or a century. He knew only that something had happened in the interval. What it was he could not tell. He found great difficulty in catching the thread of his identity again. He felt that he was himself; but the trouble was to make his connections, to verify and place himself, to know who and where he was.

At last it grew clear. John Weightman was sitting on a stone, not far from a road in a strange land.

The road was not a formal highway, fenced and graded. It was more like a great travel-trace, worn by thousands of feet passing across the open country in the same direction. Down in the valley, into which he could look, the road seemed to form itself gradually out of many minor paths; little footways coming across the meadows, winding tracks following along beside the streams, faintly marked trails emerging from the woodlands. But on the hillside the threads were more firmly woven into one clear band of travel, though there were still a few dim paths joining it here and there, as if persons had been climbing up the hill by other ways and had turned at last to seek the road.

From the edge of the hill, where John Weightman sat, he could see the travelers, in little groups or larger companies, gathering from time to time by the different paths, and making the ascent. They were all clothed in white, and the form of their garments was strange to him; it was like some old picture. They passed him, group after group, talking quietly together or singing; not moving in haste, but with a certain air of eagerness and joy as if they were glad to be on their way to an appointed place. They did not stay to speak to him, but they looked at him often and spoke to one another as they looked; and now and then one of them would smile and beckon him a friendly greeting, so that he felt they would like him to be with them.

There was quite an interval between the groups; and he followed each of them with his eyes after it had passed, blanching the long ribbon of the road for a little transient space, rising and receding across the wide, billowy upland, among the rounded hillocks of aerial green and gold and lilac, until it came to the high horizon, and stood outlined for a moment, a tiny cloud of whiteness against the tender blue, before it vanished over the hill.

For a long time he sat there watching and wondering. It was a very different world from that in which his mansion on the Avenue was built; and it looked strange to him, but most real—as real as anything he had ever seen. Presently he felt a strong desire to know what country it was and where the people were going. He had a faint premonition of what it must be, but he wished to be sure. So he rose from the stone where he was sitting, and came down through the short grass and the lavender flowers, toward a passing group of people. One of them turned to meet him, and held out his hand. It was an old man, under whose white beard and brows John Weightman thought he saw a suggestion of the face of the village doctor who had cared for him years ago, when he was a boy in the country.

"Welcome," said the old man. "Will you come with us?"

"Where are you going?"

"To the heavenly city, to see our mansions there."

"And who are these with you?"

"Strangers to me, until a little while ago; I know them better now. But you I have known for a long time, John Weightman. Don't you remember your old doctor?"

"Yes," he cried—"yes; your voice has not changed at all. I'm glad indeed to see you, Doctor McLean, especially now. All this seems very strange to me, almost oppressive. I wonder if—but may I go with you, do you suppose?"

"Surely," answered the doctor, with his familiar smile; "it will do you good. And you also must have a mansion in the city waiting for you—a fine one, too—are you not looking forward to it?"

"Yes," replied the other, hesitating a moment; "yes—I believe it must be so, although I had not expected to see it so soon. But I will go with you, and we can talk by the way."

The two men quickly caught up with the other people, and all went forward together along the road. The doctor had little to tell of his experience, for it had been a plain, hard life, uneventfully spent for others, and the story of the village was very simple. John Weightman's adventures and triumphs would have made a far richer, more imposing history, full of contacts with the great events and personages of the time. But somehow or other he did not care to speak much about it, walking on that wide heavenly moorland, under that tranquil, sunless arch of blue, in that free air of perfect peace, where the light was diffused without a shadow, as if the spirit of life in all things were luminous.

There was only one person besides the doctor in that little company whom John Weightman had known before—an old bookkeeper who had spent his life over a desk, carefully keeping accounts—a rusty, dull little man, patient and narrow, whose wife had been in the insane asylum for twenty years and whose only child was a crippled daughter, for whose comfort and happiness he had toiled and sacrificed himself without stint. It was a surprise to find him here, as care-free and joyful as the rest.

The lives of others in the company were revealed in brief glimpses as they talked together—a mother, early widowed, who had kept her little flock of children together and labored through hard and heavy years to bring them up in purity and knowledge—a Sister of Charity who had devoted herself to the nursing of poor folk who were being eaten to death by cancer—a schoolmaster whose heart and life had been poured into his quiet work of training boys for a clean and thoughtful manhood—a medical missionary who had given up a brilliant career in science to take the charge of a hospital in darkest Africa—a beautiful woman with silver hair who had resigned her dreams of love and marriage to care for an invalid father, and after his death had made her life a long, steady search for ways of doing kindnesses to others—a poet who had walked among the crowded tenements of the great city, bringing cheer and comfort not only by his songs, but by his wise and patient works of practical aid—a paralyzed woman who had lain for thirty years upon her bed, helpless but not hopeless, succeeding by a miracle of courage in her single aim, never to complain, but always to impart a bit of joy and peace to every one who came near her. All these, and other persons like them, people of little consideration in the world, but now seemingly all full of great contentment and an inward gladness that made their steps light, were in the company that passed along the road, talking together of things past and things to come, and singing now and then with clear voices from which the veil of age and sorrow was lifted.

John Weightman joined in some of the songs—which were familiar to him from their use in the church—at first with a touch of hesitation, and then more confidently. For as they went on his sense of strangeness and fear at his new experience diminished, and his thoughts began to take on their habitual assurance and complacency. Were not these people going to the Celestial City? And was not he in his right place among them? He had always looked forward to this journey. If they were sure, each one, of finding a mansion there, could not he be far more sure? His life had been more fruitful than theirs. He had been a leader, a founder of new enterprises, a pillar of Church and State, a prince of the House of Israel. Ten talents had been given him, and he had made them twenty. His reward would be proportionate. He was glad that his companions were going to find fit dwellings prepared for them; but he thought also with a certain pleasure of the surprise that some of them would feel when they saw his appointed mansion.

So they came to the summit of the moorland and looked over into the world beyond. It was a vast, green plain, softly rounded like a shallow vase, and circled with hills of amethyst. A broad, shining river flowed through it, and many silver threads of water were woven across the green; and there were borders of tall trees on the banks of the river, and orchards full of roses abloom along the little streams, and in the midst of all stood the city, white and wonderful and radiant.

When the travelers saw it they were filled with awe and joy. They passed over the little streams and among the orchards quickly and silently, as if they feared to speak lest the city should vanish.

The wall of the city was very low, a child could see over it, for it was made only of precious stones, which are never large. The gate of the city was not like a gate at all, for it was not barred with iron or wood, but only a single pearl, softly gleaming, marked the place where the wall ended and the entrance lay open.

A person stood there whose face was bright and grave, and whose robe was like the flower of the lily, not a woven fabric, but a living texture. "Come in," he said to the company of travelers; "you are at your journey's end, and your mansions are ready for you."

John Weightman hesitated, for he was troubled by a doubt. Suppose that he was not really, like his companions, at his journey's end, but only transported for a little while out of the regular course of his life into this mysterious experience? Suppose that, after all, he had not really passed through the door of death, like these others, but only through the door of dreams, and was walking in a vision, a living man among the blessed dead. Would it be right for him to go with them into the heavenly city? Would it not be a deception, a desecration, a deep and unforgivable offense? The strange, confusing question had no reason in it, as he very well knew; for if he was dreaming, then it was all a dream; but if his companions were real, then he also was with them in reality, and if they had died then he must have died too. Yet he could not rid his mind of the sense that there was a difference between them and him, and it made him afraid to go on. But, as he paused and turned, the Keeper of the Gate looked straight and deep into his eyes, and beckoned to him. Then he knew that it was not only right but necessary that he should enter.

They passed from street to street among fair and spacious dwellings, set in amaranthine gardens, and adorned with an infinitely varied beauty of divine simplicity. The mansions differed in size, in shape, in charm: each one seemed to have its own personal look of loveliness; yet all were alike in fitness to their place, in harmony with one another, in the addition which each made to the singular and tranquil splendor of the city.

As the little company came, one by one, to the mansions which were prepared for them, and their Guide beckoned to the happy inhabitant to enter in and take possession, there was a soft murmur of joy, half wonder and half recognition; as if the new and immortal dwelling were crowned with the beauty of surprise, lovelier and nobler than all the dreams of it had been; and yet also as if it were touched with the beauty of the familiar, the remembered, the long-loved. One after another the travelers were led to their own mansions, and went in gladly; and from within, through the open doorways came sweet voices of welcome, and low laughter, and song.

At last there was no one left with the Guide but the two old friends, Doctor McLean and John Weightman. They were standing in front of one of the largest and fairest of the houses, whose garden glowed softly with radiant flowers. The Guide laid his hand upon the doctor's shoulder.

"This is for you," he said. "Go in; there is no more pain here, no more death, nor sorrow, nor tears; for your old enemies are all conquered. But all the good that you have done for others, all the help that you have given, all the comfort that you have brought, all the strength and love that you have bestowed upon the suffering, are here; for we have built them all into this mansion for you."

The good man's face was lighted with a still joy. He clasped his old friend's hand closely, and whispered: "How wonderful it is! Go on, you will come to your mansion next, it is not far away, and we shall see each other again soon, very soon."

So he went through the garden, and into the music within. The Keeper of the Gate turned to John Weightman with level, quiet, searching eyes. Then he asked, gravely:

"Where do you wish me to lead you now?"

"To see my own mansion," answered the man, with half-concealed excitement. "Is there not one here for me? You may not let me enter it yet, perhaps, for I must confess to you that I am only—"

"I know," said the Keeper of the Gate—"I know it all. You are John Weightman."

"Yes," said the man, more firmly than he had spoken at first, for it gratified him that his name was known. "Yes, I am John Weightman, Senior Warden of St. Petronius' Church. I wish very much to see my mansion here, if only for a moment. I believe that you have one for me. Will you take me to it?"

The Keeper of the Gate drew a little book from the breast of his robe and turned over the pages.

"Certainly," he said, with a curious look at the man, "your name is here; and you shall see your mansion if you will follow me."

It seemed as if they must have walked miles and miles, through the vast city, passing street after street of houses larger and smaller, of gardens richer and poorer, but all full of beauty and delight. They came into a kind of suburb, where there were many small cottages, with plots of flowers, very lowly, but bright and fragrant. Finally they reached an open field, bare and lonely-looking. There were two or three little bushes in it, without flowers, and the grass was sparse and thin. In the center of the field was a tiny hut, hardly big enough for a shepherd's shelter. It looked as if it had been built of discarded things, scraps and fragments of other buildings, put together with care and pains, by some one who had tried to make the most of cast-off material. There was something pitiful and shamefaced about the hut. It shrank and drooped and faded in its barren field, and seemed to cling only by sufferance to the edge of the splendid city.

"This," said the Keeper of the Gate, standing still and speaking with a low, distinct voice—"this is your mansion, John Weightman."

An almost intolerable shock of grieved wonder and indignation choked the man for a moment so that he could not say a word. Then he turned his face away from the poor little hut and began to remonstrate eagerly with his companion.

"Surely, sir," he stammered, "you must be in error about this. There is something wrong—some other John Weightman—a confusion of names—the book must be mistaken."

"There is no mistake," said the Keeper of the Gate, very calmly; "here is your name, the record of your title and your possessions in this place."

"But how could such a house be prepared for me," cried the man, with a resentful tremor in his voice—"for me, after my long and faithful service? Is this a suitable mansion for one so well known and devoted? Why is it so pitifully small and mean? Why have you not built it large and fair, like the others?"

"That is all the material you sent us."

"What!"

"We have used all the material that you sent us," repeated the Keeper of the Gate.

"Now I know that you are mistaken," cried the man, with growing earnestness, "for all my life long I have been doing things that must have supplied you with material. Have you not heard that I have built a school-house; the wing of a hospital; two—yes, three—small churches, and the greater part of a large one, the spire of St. Petro—"

The Keeper of the Gate lifted his hand.

"Wait," he said; "we know all these things. They were not ill done. But they were all marked and used as foundation for the name and mansion of John Weightman in the world. Did you not plan them for that?"

"Yes," answered the man, confused and taken aback, "I confess that I thought often of them in that way. Perhaps my heart was set upon that too much. But there are other things—my endowment for the college—my steady and liberal contributions to all the established charities—my support of every respectable—"

"Wait," said the Keeper of the Gate again. "Were not all these carefully recorded on earth where they would add to your credit? They were not foolishly done. Verily, you have had your reward for them. Would you be paid twice?"

"No," cried the man, with deepening dismay, "I dare not claim that. I acknowledge that I considered my own interest too much. But surely not altogether. You have said that these things were not foolishly done. They accomplished some good in the world. Does not that count for something?"

"Yes," answered the Keeper of the Gate, "it counts in the world—where you counted it. But it does not belong to you here. We have saved and used everything that you sent us. This is the mansion prepared for you."

As he spoke, his look grew deeper and more searching, like a flame of fire. John Weightman could not endure it. It seemed to strip him naked and wither him. He sank to the ground under a crushing weight of shame, covering his eyes with his hands and cowering face downward upon the stones. Dimly through the trouble of his mind he felt their hardness and coldness.

"Tell me, then," he cried, brokenly, "since my life has been so little worth, how came I here at all?"

"Through the mercy of the King"—the answer was like the soft tolling of a bell.

"And how have I earned it?" he murmured.

"It is never earned; it is only given," came the clear, low reply.

"But how have I failed so wretchedly," he asked, "in all the purpose of my life? What could I have done better? What is it that counts here?"

"Only that which is truly given," answered the bell-like voice. "Only that good which is done for the love of doing it. Only those plans in which the welfare of others is the master thought. Only those labors in which the sacrifice is greater than the reward. Only those gifts in which the giver forgets himself."

The man lay silent. A great weakness, an unspeakable despondency and humiliation were upon him. But the face of the Keeper of the Gate was infinitely tender as he bent over him.

"Think again, John Weightman. Has there been nothing like that in your life?"

"Nothing," he sighed. "If there ever were such things, it must have been long ago—they were all crowded out—I have forgotten them."

There was an ineffable smile on the face of the Keeper of the Gate, and his hand made the sign of the cross over the bowed head as he spoke gently:

"These are the things that the King never forgets; and because there were a few of them in your life, you have a little place here."

The sense of coldness and hardness under John Weightman's hands grew sharper and more distinct. The feeling of bodily weariness and lassitude weighed upon him, but there was a calm, almost a lightness, in his heart as he listened to the fading vibrations of the silvery bell-tones. The chimney clock on the mantel had just ended the last stroke of seven as he lifted his head from the table. Thin, pale strips of the city morning were falling into the room through the narrow partings of the heavy curtains.

What was it that had happened to him? Had he been ill? Had he died and come to life again? Or had he only slept, and had his soul gone visiting in dreams? He sat for some time, motionless, not lost, but finding himself in thought. Then he took a narrow book from the table drawer, wrote a check, and tore it out.

He went slowly up the stairs, knocked very softly at his son's door, and, hearing no answer, entered without noise. Harold was asleep, his bare arm thrown above his head, and his eager face relaxed in peace. His father looked at him a moment with strangely shining eyes, and then tiptoed quietly to the writing-desk, found a pencil and a sheet of paper, and wrote rapidly:

"My dear boy, here is what you asked me for; do what you like with it, and ask for more if you need it. If you are still thinking of that work with Grenfell, we'll talk it over to-day after church. I want to know your heart better; and if I have made mistakes—"

A slight noise made him turn his head. Harold was sitting up in bed with wide-open eyes.

"Father!" he cried, "is that you?"

"Yes, my son," answered John Weightman; "I've come back—I mean I've come up—no, I mean come in—well, here I am, and God give us a good Christmas together."

ACRES OF DIAMONDS

Russell H. Conwell

A Baptist minister, Russell H. Conwell founded Temple University as well as Samaritan (now Temple University) Hospital. A prolific writer and speaker, he wrote forty books and lectured on the Lyceum and Chautauqua circuits. His famous address, "Acres of Diamonds" (first delivered in 1861), made him America's foremost platform orator. By the end of his life in 1925, he had delivered the lecture more than 6,000 times in town after town. It was heard by millions, live and over the radio. Today millions of others are still reading his practical, optimistic essay.

Following is the most recent and complete form of the lecture, which was published in 1890. Dr. Conwell delivered it in Philadelphia, his home city. When he says "right here in Philadelphia," he means the city, town, or village where you live.

Dr. Conwell wrote, "This lecture has been delivered under these circumstances: I visit a town or city, and try to arrive there early enough to see the postmaster, the barber, the keeper of the hotel, the principal of the schools, and the ministers of some of the churches, and then go into some of the factories and stores, and talk with the people, and get into sympathy with the local conditions of that town or city and see what has been their history, what opportunities they had, and what they had failed to do—and every town fails to do something—and then go to the lecture and talk to those people about the subjects which applied to their locality. 'Acres of Diamonds' the idea—has continuously been precisely the same. The idea is that in this country of ours every man has the opportunity to make more of himself than he does in his own environment, with his own skill, with his own energy, and with his own friends."

President James E. Faust, after recounting the story of "Acres of Diamonds," noted, "The search for truth is often not unlike Ali Hafed's search for diamonds. The truth is not in distant lands but under our feet." (*Ensign,* September 1998, 2.)

Elder Sterling W. Sill wrote of this timeless classic:

"Some of us never become aware of our greatest treasures. The most likely places to look for diamonds is under our own feet and within ourselves. In fact, God has implanted in every man the very things that he seeks. If you seek the kind of faith that moves mountains, look within yourself, for God has already implanted in your own heart the seeds of faith and power waiting only for you to make them grow. . . .

"Dr. Conwell said that the very apex of his life's thought is that people should do their best right where they are with the wonderful gifts that God has already given them. He said, "'Arise, ye millions of Americans. Trust in God and believe in your opportunities and in yourselves.'" Dr. Conwell's principle of greatness will work for everyone. Whatever you have to do, put your whole mind and soul into its doing. The greatest of all wealth is eternal life, and it also comes by this vigorous digging process. As Jesus said, ' . . . see that ye serve him with all your heart, might, mind and strength, that ye may stand blameless before God at the last day.' (D&C 4:2.)

"Ali Hafid sought for diamonds because he believed them to be the most valuable things in the world, but Jesus said, ' . . . seek ye first the kingdom of God, and his righteousness; and all these things shall be added unto you.' (Matthew 6:33.) Jesus said the kingdom of God is within you, and that is where most of the digging needs to take place. A little of the light and glory of God in our lives dwarfs into insignificance all of the brilliance that came from Ali Hafid's brook. It is a great day in our lives when we determine to dig a little deeper into the acre that God has given into our personal care." (*The Majesty of Books* [Salt Lake City: Deseret Book Co., 1974], 301, 303.)

ACRES OF DIAMONDS

When going down the Tigris and Euphrates rivers many years ago with a party of English travelers I found myself under the direction of an old Arab guide whom we hired up at Bagdad, and I have often thought how that guide resembled our barbers in certain mental characteristics. He thought that it was not only his duty to guide us down those rivers, and do what he was paid for doing, but also to entertain us with stories curious and weird, ancient and modern, strange and familiar. Many of them I have forgotten, and I am glad I have, but there is one I shall never forget.

The old guide was leading my camel by its halter along the banks of those ancient rivers, and he told me story after story until I grew weary of his story-telling and ceased to listen. I have never been irritated with that guide when he lost his temper as I ceased listening. But I remember that he took off his Turkish cap and swung it in a circle to get my attention. I could see it through the corner of my eye, but I determined not to look straight at him for fear he would tell another story. But although I am not a woman, I did finally look, and as soon as I did he went right into another story.

Said he, "I will tell you a story now which I reserve for my particular friends." When he emphasized the words "particular friends," I listened, and I have ever been glad I did. I really feel devoutly thankful, that there are 1,674 young men who have been carried through college by this lecture who are also glad that I did listen. The old guide told me that there once lived not far from the River Indus an ancient Persian by the name of Ali Hafed. He said that Ali Hafed owned a very large farm, that he had orchards, grain-fields, and gardens; that he had money at interest, and was a wealthy and contented man. He was contented because he was wealthy, and wealthy because he was contented. One day there visited that old Persian farmer one of these ancient Buddhist priests, one of the wise men of the East. He sat down by the fire and told the old farmer how this world of ours was made. He said that this world was once a mere bank of fog, and that the Almighty thrust His finger into this bank of fog, and began slowly to move His finger around, increasing the speed until at last He whirled this bank of fog into a solid ball of fire. Then it went rolling through the universe, burning its way through other banks of fog, and condensed the moisture without, until it fell in floods of rain upon its hot surface, and cooled the outward crust. Then the internal fires bursting outward through the crust threw up the mountains and hills, the valleys, the plains and prairies of this wonderful world of ours. If this internal molten mass came bursting out and cooled very quickly it became granite; less quickly copper, less quickly silver, less quickly gold, and, after gold, diamonds were made.

Said the old priest, "A diamond is a congealed drop of sunlight." Now that is literally scientifically true, that a diamond is an actual deposit of carbon from the sun. The old priest told Ali Hafed that if he had one diamond the size of his thumb he could purchase the county, and if he had a mine of diamonds he could place his children upon thrones through the influence of their great wealth.

Ali Hafed heard all about diamonds, how much they were worth, and went to his bed that night a poor man. He had not lost anything, but he was poor because he was discontented, and discontented because he feared he was poor. He said, "I want a mine of diamonds," and he lay awake all night.

Early in the morning he sought out the priest. I know by experience that a priest is very cross when awakened early in the morning, and when he shook that old priest out of his dreams, Ali Hafed said to him:

"Will you tell me where I can find diamonds?"

"Diamonds! What do you want with diamonds?" "Why, I wish to be immensely rich." "Well, then, go along and find them. That is all you have to do; go and find them, and then you have them." "But I don't know where to go." "Well, if you will find a river that runs through white sands, between high mountains, in those white sands you will always find diamonds." "I don't believe there is any such river." "Oh yes, there are plenty of them. All you have to do is to go and find them, and then you have them." Said Ali Hafed, "I will go."

So he sold his farm, collected his money, left his family in charge of a neighbor, and away he went in search of diamonds. He began his search, very properly to my mind, at the Mountains of the Moon. Afterward he came around into Palestine, then wandered on into Europe, and at last when his money was all spent and he was in rags, wretchedness, and poverty, he stood on the shore of that bay at Barcelona, in Spain, when a great tidal wave came rolling in between the pillars of Hercules, and the poor, afflicted, suffering, dying man could not resist the awful temptation to cast himself into that incoming tide, and he sank beneath its foaming crest, never to rise in this life again.

When that old guide had told me that awfully sad story he stopped the camel I was riding on and went back to fix the baggage that was coming off another camel, and I had an opportunity to muse over his story while he was gone. I remember saying to myself, "Why did he reserve that story for his 'particular friends'?" There seemed to be no beginning, no middle, no end, nothing to it. That was the first story I had ever heard told in my life, and would be the first one I ever read, in which the hero was killed in the first chapter. I had but one chapter of that story, and the hero was dead.

When the guide came back and took up the halter of my camel, he went right ahead with the story, into the second chapter, just as though there had been no break. The man who purchased Ali Hafed's farm one day led his camel into the garden to drink, and as that camel put its nose into the shallow water of that garden brook, Ali Hafed's successor noticed a curious flash of light from the white sands of the stream. He pulled out a black stone having an eye of light reflecting all the hues of the rainbow. He took the pebble into the house and put it on the mantel which covers the central fires, and forgot all about it.

A few days later this same old priest came in to visit Ali Hafed's successor, and the moment he opened that drawing-room door he saw that flash of light on the mantel, and he rushed up to it, and shouted: "Here is a diamond! Has Ali Hafed returned?" "Oh no, Ali Hafed has not returned, and that is not a diamond. That is nothing but a stone we found right out here in our own garden." "But," said the priest, "I tell you I know a diamond when I see it. I know positively that is a diamond."

Then together they rushed out into that old garden and stirred up the white sands with their fingers, and lo! there came up other more beautiful and valuable gems than the first. "Thus," said the guide to me, and, friends, it is historically true, "was discovered the diamond-mine of Golconda, the most magnificent diamond-mine in all the history of mankind, excelling the Kimberly itself. The Kohinoor, and the Orloff of the crown jewels of England and Russia, the largest on earth, came from that mine."

When that old Arab guide told me the second chapter of his story, he then took off his Turkish cap and swung it around in the air again to get my attention to the moral. Those Arab guides have morals to their stories, although they are not always moral. As he swung his hat, he said to me, "Had Ali Hafed remained at home and dug in his own cellar, or underneath his own wheatfields, or in his own garden, instead of wretchedness, starvation, and death by suicide in a strange land, he would have had 'acres of diamonds.' For every acre of that old farm, yes, every shovelful, afterward revealed gems which since have decorated the crowns of monarchs."

When he had added the moral to his story I saw why he reserved it for "his particular friends." But I did not tell him I could see it. It was that mean old Arab's way of going around a thing like a lawyer, to say indirectly what he did not dare say directly, that "in his private opinion there was a certain young man then traveling down the Tigris River that might better be at home in America." I did not tell him I could see that, but I told him his story reminded me of one, and I told it to him quick, and I think I will tell it to you.

I told him of a man out in California in 1847, who owned a ranch. He heard they had discovered gold in southern California, and so with a passion for gold he sold his ranch to Colonel Sutter, and away he went, never to come back. Colonel Sutter put a mill upon a stream that ran through that ranch, and one day his little girl brought some wet sand from the raceway into their home and sifted it through her fingers before the fire, and in that falling sand a visitor saw the first shining scales of real gold that were ever discovered in California. The man who had owned that ranch wanted gold, and he could have secured it for the mere taking. Indeed, thirty-eight millions of dollars has been taken out of a very few acres since then. About eight years ago I delivered this lecture in a city that stands on that farm, and they told me that a one-third owner for years and years had been getting one hundred and twenty dollars in gold every fifteen minutes, sleeping or waking, without taxation. You and I would enjoy an income like that—if we didn't have to pay an income tax.

But a better illustration really than that occurred here in our own Pennsylvania. If there is anything I enjoy above another on the platform, it is to get one of these German audiences in Pennsylvania before me, and fire that at them, and I enjoy it to-night. There was a man living in Pennsylvania, not unlike some Pennsylvanians you have seen, who owned a farm, and he did with that farm just what I should do with a farm if I owned one in Pennsylvania—he sold it. But before he sold it he decided to secure employment collecting coal-oil for his cousin, who was in the business in Canada, where they first discovered oil on this continent. They dipped it from the running streams at that early time. So this Pennsylvania farmer wrote to his cousin asking for employment. You see, friends, this farmer was not altogether a foolish man. No, he was not. He did not leave his farm until he had something else to do. *Of all the simpletons the stars shine on I don't know of a worse one than the man who leaves one job before he has gotten another.* That has especial reference to my profession, and has no reference whatever to a man seeking a divorce. When he wrote to his cousin for employment, his cousin replied, "I cannot engage you because you know nothing about the oil business."

Well, then the old farmer said, "I will know," and with most commendable zeal (characteristic of the students of Temple University) he set himself at the study of the whole subject. He began away back at the second day of God's creation when this world was covered thick and deep with that rich vegetation which since has turned to the primitive beds of coal. He studied the subject until he found that the drainings really of those rich beds of coal furnished the coal-oil that was worth pumping, and then he found how it came up with the living springs. He studied until he knew what it looked like, smelled like, tasted like, and how to refine it. Now said he in his letter to his cousin, "I understand the oil business." His cousin answered, "All right, come on."

So he sold his farm, according to the county record, for $833 (even money, "no cents"). He had scarcely gone from that place before the man who purchased the spot went out to arrange for the watering of the cattle. He found the previous owner had gone out years before and put a plank across the brook back of the barn, edgewise into the surface of the water just a few inches. The purpose of that plank at that sharp angle across the brook was to throw over to the other bank a dreadful-looking scum through which the cattle would not put their noses. But with that plank there to throw it all over to one side, the cattle would drink below, and thus that man who had gone to Canada had been himself damming back for twenty-three years a flood of coal-oil which the state geologists of Pennsylvania declared to us ten years later was even then worth a hundred millions of dollars to our state, and four years ago our geologist declared the discovery to be worth to our state a thousand millions of dollars. The man who owned that territory on which the city of Titusville now stands, and those Pleasantville valleys, had studied the subject from the second day of God's creation clear down to the present time. He studied it until he knew all about it, and yet he is said to have sold the whole of it for $833, and again I say, "no sense."

But I need another illustration. I found it in Massachusetts, and I am sorry I did because that is the state I came from. This young man in Massachusetts furnishes just another phase of my thought. He went to Yale College and studied mines and mining, and became such an adept as a mining engineer that he was employed by the authorities of the university to train students who were behind their classes. During his senior year he earned $15 a week for doing that work. When he graduated they raised his pay from $15 to $45 a week, and offered him a professorship, and as soon as they did he went right home to his mother. *If they had raised that boy's pay from $15 to $15.60 he would have stayed and been proud of the place, but when they put it up to $45 at one leap, he said, "Mother, I won't work for $45 a week. The idea of a man with a brain like* *mine working for $45 a week!* Let's go out in California and stake out gold-mines and silver-mines, and be immensely rich."

Said his mother, "Now, Charlie, it is just as well to be happy as it is to be rich."

"Yes," said Charlie, "but it is just as well to be rich and happy, too." And they were both right about it. As he was an only son and she a widow, of course he had his way. They always do.

They sold out in Massachusetts, and instead of going to California they went to Wisconsin, where he went into the employ of the Superior Copper Mining Company at $15 a week again, but with the proviso in his contract that he should have an interest in any mines he should discover for the company. I don't believe he ever discovered a mine, and if I am looking in the face of any stockholder of that copper company you wish he had discovered something or other. I have friends who are not here because they could not afford a ticket, who did have stock in that company at the time this young man was employed there. This young man went out there, and I have not heard a word from him. I don't know what became of him, and I don't know whether he found any mines or not, but I don't believe he ever did.

But I do know the other end of the line. He had scarcely gotten out of the old homestead before the succeeding owner went out to dig potatoes. The potatoes were already growing in the ground when he bought the farm, and as the old farmer was bringing in a basket of potatoes it hugged very tight between the ends of the stone fence. You know in Massachusetts our farms are nearly all stone wall. There you are obliged to be very economical of front gateways in order to have some place to put the stone. When that basket hugged so tight he set it down on the ground, and then dragged on one side, and pulled on the other side, and as he was dragging that basket through this farmer noticed in the upper and outer corner of that stone wall, right next to the gate, a block of native silver eight inches square. That professor of mines, mining, and mineralogy who knew so much about the subject that he would not work for $45 a week, when he sold that homestead in Massachusetts sat right on that silver to make the bargain. He was born on that homestead, was brought up there, and had gone back and forth rubbing the stone with his sleeve until it reflected his countenance, and seemed to say, "Here is a hundred thousand dollars right down here just for the taking." But he would not take it. It was in a home in Newburyport, Massachusetts, and there was no silver there, all away off—well, I don't know where, and he did not, but somewhere else, and he was a professor of mineralogy.

My friends, that mistake is very universally made, and why should we even smile at him. I often wonder what has become of him. I do not know at all, but I will tell you what I "guess" as a Yankee. I guess that he sits out there by his fireside to-night with his friends gathered around him, and he is saying to them something like this: "Do you know that man Conwell who lives in Philadelphia?" "Oh yes, I have heard of him." "Do you know that man Jones that lives in Philadelphia?" "Yes, I have heard of him, too."

Then he begins to laugh, and shakes his sides and says to his friends, "Well, they have done just the same thing I did, precisely"—and that spoils the whole joke, for you and I have done the same thing he did, and while we sit here and laugh at him he has a better right to sit out there and laugh at us. I know I have made the same mistakes, but, of course, that does not make any difference, because we don't expect the same man to preach and practise, too.

As I come here to-night and look around this audience I am seeing again what through these fifty years I have continually seen—men that are making precisely that same mistake. I often wish I could see the younger people, and would that the Academy had been filled to-night with our high-school scholars and our grammar-school scholars, that I could have them to talk to. While I would have preferred such an audience as that, because they are most susceptible, as they have not grown up into their prejudices as we have, they have not gotten into any custom that they cannot break, they have not met with any failures as we have; and while I could perhaps do such an audience as that more good than I can do grownup people, yet I will do the best I can with the material I have. I say to you that you have "acres of diamonds" in Philadelphia right where you now live. "Oh," but you will say, "you cannot know much about your city if you think there are any 'acres of diamonds' here."

I was greatly interested in that account in the newspaper of the young man who found that diamond in North Carolina. It was one of the purest diamonds that has ever been discovered, and it has several predecessors near the same locality. I went to a distinguished professor in mineralogy and asked him where he thought those diamonds came from. The professor secured the map of the geologic formations of our continent, and traced it. He said it went either through the underlying carboniferous strata adapted for such production, westward through Ohio and the Mississippi, or in more probability came eastward through Virginia and up the shore of the Atlantic Ocean. It is a fact that the diamonds were there, for they have been discovered and sold; and that they were carried down there during the drift period, from some northern locality. Now who can say but some person going down with his drill in Philadelphia will find some trace of a diamond-mine yet down here? Oh, friends! you cannot say that you are not over one of the greatest diamond-mines in the world, for such a diamond as that only comes from the most profitable mines that are found on earth.

But it serves simply to illustrate my thought, which I emphasize by saying if you do not have the actual diamond-mines literally you have all that they would be good for to you. Because now that the Queen of England has given the greatest compliment ever conferred upon American woman for her attire because she did not appear with any jewels at all at the late reception in England, it has almost done away with the use of diamonds anyhow. All you would care for would be the few you would wear if you wish to be modest, and the rest you would sell for money.

Now then, I say again that the opportunity to get rich, to attain unto great wealth, is here in Philadelphia now, within the reach of almost every man and woman who hears me speak tonight, and I mean just what I say. I have not come to this platform even under these circumstances to recite something to you. I have come to tell you what in God's sight I believe to be the truth, and if the years of life have been of any value to me in the attainment of common sense, I know I am right;

that the men and women sitting here, who found it difficult perhaps to buy a ticket to this lecture or gathering to-night, have within their reach "acres of diamonds," opportunities to get largely wealthy. There never was a place on earth more adapted than the city of Philadelphia to-day, and never in the history of the world did a poor man without capital have such an opportunity to get rich quickly and honestly as he has now in our city. I say it is the truth, and I want you to accept it as such; for if you think I have come to simply recite something, then I would better not be here. I have no time to waste in any such talk, but to say the things I believe, and unless some of you get richer for what I am saying to-night my time is wasted.

I say that you ought to get rich, and it is your duty to get rich. How many of my pious brethren say to me, "Do you, a Christian minister, spend your time going up and down the country advising young people to get rich, to get money?" "Yes, of course I do." They say, "Isn't that awful! Why don't you preach the gospel instead of preaching about man's making money?" "Because to make money honestly is to preach the gospel." That is the reason. The men who get rich may be the most honest men you find in the community.

"Oh," but says some young man here to-night, "I have been told all my life that if a person has money he is very dishonest and dishonorable and mean and contemptible." My friend, that is the reason why you have none, because you have that idea of people. The foundation of your faith is altogether false. Let me say here clearly, and say it briefly, though subject to discussion which I have not time for here, ninety-eight out of one hundred of the rich men of America are honest. That is why they are rich. That is why they are trusted with money. That is why they carry on great enterprises and find plenty of people to work with them. It is because they are honest men.

Says another young man, "I hear sometimes of men that get millions of dollars dishonestly." Yes, of course you do, and so do I. But they are so rare a thing in fact that the newspapers talk about them all the time as a matter of news until you get the idea that all the other rich men got rich dishonestly.

My friend, you take and drive me—if you furnish the auto—out into the suburbs of Philadelphia, and introduce me to the people who own their homes around this great city, those beautiful homes with gardens and flowers, those magnificent homes so lovely in their art, and I will introduce you to the very best people in character as well as in enterprise in our city, and you know I will. A man is not really a true man until he owns his own home, and they that own their homes are made more honorable and honest and pure, and true and economical and careful, by owning the home.

For a man to have money, even in large sums, is not an inconsistent thing. We preach against covetousness, and you know we do, in the pulpit, and oftentimes preach against it so long and use the terms about "filthy lucre" so extremely that Christians get the idea that when we stand in the pulpit we believe it is wicked for any man to have money— until the collection-basket goes around, and then we almost swear at the people because they don't give more money. Oh, the inconsistency of such doctrines as that!

Money is power, and you ought to be reasonably ambitious to have it. You ought because you can do more good with it than you could without it. Money printed your Bible, money builds your churches, money sends your missionaries, and money pays your preachers, and you would not have many of them, either, if you did not pay them. I am always willing that my church should raise my salary, because the church that pays the largest salary always raises it the easiest. You never knew an exception to it in your life. The man who gets the largest salary can do the most good with the power that is furnished to him. Of course he can if his spirit be right to use it for what it is given to him.

I say, then, you ought to have money. If you can honestly attain unto riches in Philadelphia, it is your Christian and godly duty to do so. It is an awful mistake of these pious people to think you must be awfully poor in order to be pious.

Some men say, "Don't you sympathize with the poor people?" Of course I do, or else I would not have been lecturing these years. I won't give in but what I sympathize with the poor, but the number of poor who are to be sympathized with is very small. To sympathize with a man whom God has punished for his sins, thus to help him when God would still continue a just punishment, is to do wrong, no doubt about it, and we do that more than we help those who are deserving. While we should sympathize with God's poor—that is, those who cannot help themselves—let us remember there is not a poor person in the United States who was not made poor by his own shortcomings, or by the shortcomings of some one else. It is all wrong to be poor, anyhow. Let us give in to that argument and pass that to one side.

A gentleman gets up back there, and says, "Don't you think there are some things in this world that are better than money?" Of course I do, but I am talking about money now. Of course there are some things higher than money. Oh yes, I know by the grave that has left me standing alone that there are some things in this world that are higher and sweeter and purer than money. Well do I know there are some things higher and grander than gold. Love is the grandest thing on God's earth, but fortunate the lover who has plenty of money. Money is power, money is force, money will do good as well as harm. In the hands of good men and women it could accomplish, and it has accomplished, good.

I hate to leave that behind me. I heard a man get up in a prayer-meeting in our city and thank the Lord he was "one of God's poor." Well, I wonder what his wife thinks about that? She earns all the money that comes into that house, and he smokes a part of that on the veranda. I don't want to see any more of the Lord's poor of that kind, and I don't believe the Lord does. And yet there are some people who think in order to be pious you must be awfully poor and awfully dirty. That does not follow at all. While we sympathize with the poor, let us not teach a doctrine like that.

Yet the age is prejudiced against advising a Christian man (or, as a Jew would say, a godly man) from attaining unto wealth. The prejudice is so universal and the years are far enough back, I think, for me to safely mention that years ago up at Temple University there was a young man in our theological school who thought he was the only pious student in that department. He came into my office one evening and sat down by my desk, and said to me: "Mr. President, I think it is my duty sir, to come in and labor with you." "What has happened now?" Said he, "I heard you say at the Academy, at the Peirce School commencement, that you thought it was an honorable ambition for a young man to desire to have wealth, and that you thought it made him temperate, made him anxious to have a good name, and made him industrious. You spoke about man's ambition to have money helping to make him a good man. Sir, I have come to tell you the Holy Bible says that 'money is the root of all evil.'"

I told him I had never seen it in the Bible, and advised him to go out into the chapel and get the Bible, and show me the place. So out he went for the Bible, and soon he stalked into my office with the Bible open, with all the bigoted pride of the narrow sectarian, or of one who founds his Christianity on some misinterpretation of Scripture. He flung the Bible down on my desk, and fairly squealed into my ear: "There it is, Mr. President; you can read it for yourself." I said to him: "Well, young man, you will learn when you get a little older that you cannot trust another denomination to read the Bible for you. You belong to another denomination. You are taught in the theological school, however, that emphasis is exegesis. Now, will you take that Bible and read it yourself, and give the proper emphasis to it?"

He took the Bible, and proudly read, "'The love of money is the root of all evil.'"

Then he had it right, and when one does quote aright from that same old Book he quotes the absolute truth. I have lived through fifty years of the mightiest battle that old Book has ever fought, and I have lived to see its banners flying free; for never in the history of this world did the great minds of earth so universally agree that the Bible is true—all true—as they do at this very hour.

So I say that when he quoted right, of course he quoted the absolute truth. "The love of money is the root of all evil." He who tries to attain unto it too quickly, or dishonestly, will fall into many snares, no doubt about that. The love of money. What is that? It is making an idol of money, and idolatry pure and simple everywhere is condemned by the Holy Scriptures and by man's common sense. The man that worships the dollar instead of thinking of the purposes for which it ought to be used, the man who idolizes simply money, the miser that hordes his money in the cellar, or hides it in his stocking, or refuses to invest it where it will do the world good, that man who hugs the dollar until the eagle squeals has in him the root of all evil.

I think I will leave that behind me now and answer the question of nearly all of you who are asking, "Is there opportunity to get rich in Philadelphia?" Well, now, how simple a thing it is to see where it is, and the instant you see where it is it is yours. Some old gentleman gets up back there and says, "Mr. Conwell, have you lived in Philadelphia for thirty-one years and don't know that the time has gone by when you can make anything in this city?" "No, I don't think it is." "Yes, it is; I have tried it." "What business are you in?" "I kept a store here for twenty years, and never made over a thousand dollars in the whole twenty years."

"Well, then, you can measure the good you have been to this city by what this city has paid you, because a man can judge very well what he is worth by what he receives; that is, in what he is to the world at this time. If you have not made over a thousand dollars in twenty years in Philadelphia, it would have been better for Philadelphia if they had kicked you out of the city nineteen years and nine months ago. A man has no right to keep a store in Philadelphia twenty years and not make at least five hundred thousand dollars even though it be a corner grocery up-town." You say, "You cannot make five thousand dollars in a store now." Oh, my friends, if you will just take only four blocks around you, and find out what the people want and what you ought to supply and set them down with your pencil and figure up the profits you would make if you did supply them, you would very soon see it. There is wealth right within the sound of your voice.

Some one says: "You don't know anything about business. A preacher never knows a thing about business." Well, then, I will have to prove that I am an expert. I don't like to do this, but I have to do it because my testimony will not be taken if I am not an expert. My father kept a country store, and if there is any place under the stars where a man gets all sorts of experience in every kind of mercantile transactions, it is in the country store. I am not proud of my experience, but sometimes when my father was away he would leave me in charge of the store, though fortunately for him that was not very often. But this did occur many times, friends: A man would come in the store, and say to me, "Do you keep jack-knives?" "No, we don't keep jack-knives," and I went off whistling a tune. What did I care about that man, anyhow? Then another farmer would come in and say, "Do you keep jack-knives?" "No, we don't keep jack-knives." Then I went away and whistled another tune. Then a third man came right in the same door and said, "Do you keep jack-knives?" "No. Why is every one around here asking for jack-knives? Do you suppose we are keeping this store to supply the whole neighborhood with jack-knives?" Do you carry on your store like that in Philadelphia? The difficulty was I had not then learned that the foundation of godliness and the foundation principle of success in business are both the same precisely. The man who says, "I cannot carry my religion into business" advertises himself either as being an imbecile in business, or on the road to bankruptcy, or a thief, one of the three, sure. He will fail within a very few years. He certainly will if he doesn't carry his religion into business. If I had been carrying on my father's store on a Christian plan, godly plan, I would have had a jack-knife for the third man when he called for it. Then I would have actually done him a kindness, and I would have received a reward myself, which it would have been my duty to take.

There are some over-pious Christian people who think if you take any profit on anything you sell that you are an unrighteous man. On the contrary, you would be a criminal to sell goods for less than they cost. You have no right to do that. You cannot trust a man with your money who cannot take care of his own. You cannot trust a man in your family that is not true to his own wife. You cannot trust a man in the world that does not begin with his own heart, his own character, and his own life. It would have been my duty to have furnished a jack-knife to the third man, or the second, and to have sold it to him and actually profited myself. I have no more right to sell goods without making a profit on them than I have to overcharge him dishonestly beyond what they are worth. But I should so sell each bill of goods that the person to whom I sell shall make as much as I make.

To live and let live is the principle of the gospel, and the principle of every-day common sense. Oh, young man, hear me; live as you go along. Do not wait until you have reached my years before you begin to enjoy anything of this life. If I had the millions back, or fifty cents of it, which I have tried to earn in these years, it would not do me anything like the good that it does me now in this almost sacred presence tonight. Oh, yes, I am paid over and over a hundredfold to-night for dividing as I have tried to do in some measure as I went along through the years. I ought not speak that way, it sounds egotistic, but I am old enough now to be excused for that. I should have helped my fellow-men, which I have tried to do, and every one should try to do, and get the happiness of it. The man who goes home with the sense that he has stolen a dollar that day, that he has robbed a man of what was his honest due, is not going to sweet rest. He arises tired in the morning, and goes with an unclean conscience to his work the next day. He is not a successful man at all, although he may have laid up millions. But the man who has gone through life dividing always with his fellow-men, making and demanding his own rights and his own profits, and giving to every other man his rights and profits, lives every day, and not only that, but it is the royal road to great wealth. The history of the thousands of millionaires shows that to be the case.

The man over there who said he could not make anything in a store in Philadelphia has been carrying on his store on the wrong principle. Suppose I go into your store to-morrow morning and ask, "Do you know neighbor A, who lives one square away, at house No. 1240?" "Oh yes, I have met him. He deals here at the corner store." "Where did he come from?" "I don't know." "How many does he have in his family?" "I don't know." "What ticket does he vote?" "I don't know." "What church does he go to?" "I don't know, and don't care. What are you asking all these questions for?"

If you had a store in Philadelphia would you answer me like that? If so, then you are conducting your business just as I carried on my father's business in Worthington, Massachusetts. You don't know where your neighbor came from when he moved to Philadelphia, and you don't care. If you had cared you would be a rich man now. If you had cared enough about him to take an interest in his affairs, to find out what he needed, you would have been rich. But you go through the world saying, "No opportunity to get rich," and there is the fault right at your own door.

But another young man gets up over there and says, "I cannot take up the mercantile business." (While I am talking of trade it applies to every occupation.) "Why can't you go into the mercantile business?" "Because I haven't any capital." Oh, the weak and dudish creature that can't see over its collar! It makes a person weak to see these little dudes standing around the corners and saying, "Oh, if I had plenty of capital, how rich I would get." "Young man, do you think you are going to get rich on capital?" "Certainly." Well, I say, "Certainly not." If your mother has plenty of money, and she will set you up in business, you will "set her up in business," supplying you with capital.

The moment a young man or woman gets more money than he or she has grown to by practical experience, that moment he has gotten a curse. It is no help to a young man or woman to inherit money. It is no help to your children to leave them money, but if you leave them education, if you leave them Christian and noble character, if you leave them a wide circle of friends, if you leave them an honorable name, it is far better than that they should have money. It would be worse for them, worse for the nation, that they should have any money at all. Oh, young man, if you have inherited money, don't regard it as a help. It will curse you through your years, and deprive you of the very best things of human life. There is no class of people to be pitied so much as the inexperienced sons and daughters of the rich of our generation. I pity the rich man's son. He can never know the best things in life.

One of the best things in our life is when a young man has earned his own living, and when he becomes engaged to some lovely young woman, and makes up his mind to have a home of his own. Then with that same love comes also that divine inspiration toward better things, and he begins to save his money. He begins to leave off his bad habits and put money in the bank. When he has a few hundred dollars he goes out in the suburbs to look for a home. He goes to the savings-bank, perhaps, for half of the value, and then goes for his wife, and when he takes his bride over the threshold of that door for the first time he says in words of eloquence my voice can never touch: "I have earned this home myself. It is all mine, and I divide with thee." That is the grandest moment a human heart may ever know.

But a rich man's son can never know that. He takes his bride into a finer mansion, it may be, but he is obliged to go all the way through it and say to his wife, "My mother gave me that, my mother gave me that, and my mother gave me this," until his wife wishes she had married his mother. I pity the rich man's son.

The statistics of Massachusetts showed that not one rich man's son out of seventeen ever dies rich. I pity the rich man's sons unless they have the good sense of the elder Vanderbilt, which sometimes happens. He went to his father and said, "Did you earn all your money?" "I did, my son. I began to work on a ferry-boat for twenty-five cents a day." "Then," said his son, "I will have none of your money," and he, too, tried to get employment on a ferry-boat that Saturday night. He could not get one there, but he did get a place for three dollars a week. Of course, if a rich man's son will do that, he will get the discipline of a poor boy that is worth more than a university education to any man. He would then be able to take care of the millions of his father. But as a rule the rich men will not let their sons do the very thing that made them great. As a rule, the rich man will not allow his son to work—and his mother! Why, she would think it was a social disgrace if her poor, weak, little lily-fingered, sissy sort of a boy had to earn his living with honest toil. I have no pity for such rich men's sons.

I remember one at Niagara Falls. I think I remember one a great deal nearer. I think there are gentlemen present who were at a great banquet, and I beg pardon of his friends. At a banquet here in Philadelphia there sat beside me a kind-hearted young man, and he said, "Mr. Conwell, you have been sick for two or three years. When you go out, take my limousine, and it will take you up to your house on Broad Street." I thanked him very much, and perhaps I ought not to mention the incident in this way, but I follow the facts. I got on to the seat with the driver of that limousine, outside, and when we were going up I asked the driver, "How much did this limousine cost?" "Six thousand eight hundred, and he had to pay the duty on it." "Well," I said, "does the owner of this machine ever drive it himself?" At that the chauffeur laughed so heartily that he lost control of his machine. He was so surprised at the question that he ran up on the sidewalk, and around a corner lamp-post out into the street again. And when he got out into the street he laughed till the whole machine trembled. He said: "He drive this machine! Oh, he would be lucky if he knew enough to get out when we get there."

I must tell you about a rich man's son at Niagara Falls. I came in from the lecture to the hotel, and as I approached the desk of the clerk there stood a millionaire's son from New York. He was an indescribable specimen of anthropologic potency. He had a skull-cap on one side of his head, with a gold tassel in the top of it, and a gold-headed cane under his arm with more in it than in his head. It is a very difficult thing to describe that young man. He wore an eye-glass that he could not see through, patent-leather boots that he could not walk in, and pants that he could not sit down in—dressed like a grasshopper. This human cricket came up to the clerk's desk just as I entered, adjusted his unseeing eye-glass, and spake in this wise to the clerk. You see, he thought it was "Hinglish, you know," to lisp. "Thir, will you have the kindness to supply me with thome papah and enwelophs!" The hotel clerk measured that man quick, and he pulled the envelopes and paper out of a drawer, threw them across the counter toward the young man, and then turned away to his books. You should have seen that young man when those envelopes came across that counter. He swelled up like a gobbler turkey, adjusted his unseeing eye-glass, and yelled: "Come right back here. Now thir, will you order a thervant to take that papah and enwelophs to yondah dethk." Oh, the poor, miserable, contemptible American monkey! He could not carry paper and envelopes twenty feet. I suppose he could not get his arms down to do it. I have no pity for such travesties upon human nature. If you have not capital, young man, I am glad of it. What you need is common sense, not copper cents.

The best thing I can do is to illustrate by actual facts well-known to you all. A. T. Stewart, a poor boy in New York, had $1.50 to begin life on. He lost 87 1/2 cents of that on the very first venture. How fortunate that young man who loses the first time he gambles. That boy said, "I will never gamble again in business," and he never did. How came he to lose 87 1/2 cents? You probably all know the story how he lost it—because he bought some needles, threads, and buttons to sell which people did not want, and had them left on his hands, a dead loss. Said the boy, "I will not lose any more money in that way." Then he went around first to the doors and asked the people what they did want. Then when he had found out what they wanted he invested his 62 1/2 cents to supply a known demand. Study it wherever you choose—in business, in your profession, in your housekeeping, whatever your life, that one thing is the secret of success. You must first know the demand. You must first know what people need, and then invest yourself where you are most needed. A. T. Stewart went on that principle until he was worth what amounted afterward to forty millions of dollars, owning the very store in which Mr. Wanamaker carries on his great work in New York. His fortune was made by his losing something, which taught him the great lesson that he must only invest himself or his money in something that people need. When will you salesmen learn it? When will you manufacturers learn that you must know the changing needs of humanity if you would succeed in life? Apply yourselves, all you Christian people, as manufacturers or merchants or workmen to supply that human need. It is a great principle as broad as humanity and as deep as the Scripture itself.

The best illustration I ever heard was of John Jacob Astor. You know that he made the money of the Astor family when he lived in New York. He came across the sea in debt for his fare. But that poor boy with nothing in his pocket made the fortune of the Astor family on one principle. Some young man here to-night will say, "Well they could make those fortunes over in New York, but they could not do it in Philadelphia!" My friends, did you ever read that wonderful book of Riis (his memory is sweet to us because of his recent death), wherein is given his statistical account of the records taken in 1889 of 107 millionaires of New York. If you read the account you will see that out of the 107 millionaires only seven made their money in New York. Out of the 107 millionaires worth ten million dollars in real estate then, 67 of them made their money in towns of less than 3,500 inhabitants. The richest man in this country to-day, if you read the real-estate values, has never moved away from a town of 3,500 inhabitants. It makes not so much difference where you are as who you are. But if you cannot get rich in Philadelphia you certainly cannot do it in New York.

Now John Jacob Astor illustrated what can be done anywhere. He had a mortgage once on a millinery-store, and they could not sell bonnets enough to pay the interest on his money. So he foreclosed that mortgage, took possession of the store, and went into partnership with the very same people, in the same store, with the same capital. He did not give them a dollar of capital. They had to sell goods to get any money. Then he left them alone in the store just as they had been before, and he went out and sat down on a bench in the park in the shade. What was John Jacob Astor doing out there, and in partnership with people who had failed on his own hands? He had the most important and, to my mind, the most pleasant part of that partnership on his hands. For as John Jacob Astor sat on that bench he was watching the ladies as they went by; and where is the man who would not get rich at that business? As he sat on the bench if a lady passed him with her shoulders back and head up, and looked straight to the front, as if she did not care if all the world did gaze on her, then he studied her bonnet, and by the time it was out of sight he knew the shape of the frame, the color of the trimmings, and the crinklings in the feather. I sometimes try to describe a bonnet, but not always. I would not try to describe a modern bonnet. Where is the man that could describe one? This aggregation of all sorts of driftwood stuck on the back of the head, or the side of the neck, like a rooster with only one tail feather left. But in John Jacob Astor's day there was some art about the millinery business, and he went to the millinery-store and said to them: "Now put into the show-window just such a bonnet as I describe to you, because I have already seen a lady who likes such a bonnet. Don't make up any more until I come back." Then he went out and sat down again, and another lady passed him of a different form, of different complexion, with a different shape and color of bonnet. "Now," said he, "put such a bonnet as that in the show-window." He did not fill his show-window up town with a lot of hats and bonnets to drive people away, and then sit on the back stairs and bawl because people went to Wanamaker's to trade. He did not have a hat or a bonnet in that show-window but what some lady liked before it was made up. The tide of custom began immediately to turn in, and that has been the foundation of the greatest store in New York in that line, and still exists as one of three stores. Its fortune was made by John Jacob Astor after they had failed in business, not by giving them any more money, but by finding out what the ladies liked for bonnets before they wasted any material in making them up. I tell you if a man could foresee the millinery business he could foresee anything under heaven!

Suppose I were to go through this audience to-night and ask you in this great manufacturing city if there are not opportunities to get rich in manufacturing. "Oh yes," some young man says, "there are opportunities here still if you build with some trust and if you have two or three millions of dollars to begin with as capital." Young man, the history of the breaking up of the trusts by that attack upon "big business" is only illustrating what is now the opportunity of the smaller man. The time never came in the history of the world when you could get rich so quickly manufacturing without capital as you can now.

But you will say, "You cannot do anything of the kind. You cannot start without capital." Young man, let me illustrate for a moment. I must do it. It is my duty to every young man and woman, because we are all going into business very soon on the same plan. Young man, remember if you know what people need you have gotten more knowledge of a fortune than any amount of capital can give you.

There was a poor man out of work living in Hingham, Massachusetts. He lounged around the house until one day his wife told him to get out and work, and, as he lived in Massachusetts, he obeyed his wife. He went out and sat down on the shore of the bay, and whittled a soaked shingle into a wooden chain. His children that evening quarreled over it, and he whittled a second one to keep peace. While he was whittling the second one a neighbor came in and said: "Why don't you whittle toys and sell them? You could make money at that." "Oh," he said, "I would not know what to make." "Why don't you ask your own children right here in your own house what to make?" "What is the use of trying that?" said the carpenter. "My children are different from other people's children." (I used to see people like that when I taught school.) But he acted upon the hint, and the next morning when Mary came down the stairway, he asked, "What do you want for a toy?" She began to tell him she would like a doll's bed, a doll's washstand, a doll's carriage, a little doll's umbrella, and went on with a list of things that would take him a lifetime to supply. So, consulting his own children, in his own house, he took the firewood, for he had no money to buy lumber, and whittled those strong, unpainted Hingham toys that were for so many years known all over the world. That man began to make those toys for his own children, and then made copies and sold them through the boot-and-shoe store next door. He began to make a little money, and then a little more, and Mr. Lawson, in his *Frenzied Finance* says that man is the richest man in old Massachusetts, and I think it is the truth. And that man is worth a hundred millions of dollars to-day, and has been only thirty-four years making it on that one principle—that one must judge that what his own children like at home other people's children would like in their homes, too; to judge the human heart by oneself, by one's wife or by one's children. It is the royal road to success in manufacturing. "Oh," but you say, "didn't he have any capital?" Yes, a penknife, but I don't know that he had paid for that.

I spoke thus to an audience in New Britain, Connecticut, and a lady four seats back went home and tried to take off her collar, and the collar-button stuck in the buttonhole. She threw it out and said, "I am going to get up something better than that to put on collars." Her husband said: "After what Conwell said to-night, you see there is a need of an improved collar-fastener that is easier to handle. There is a human need; there is a great fortune. Now, then, get up a collar-button and get rich." He made fun of her, and consequently made fun of me, and that is one of the saddest things which comes over me like a deep cloud of midnight sometimes—although I have worked so hard for more than half a century, yet how little I have ever really done. Notwithstanding the greatness and the handsomeness of your compliment to-night, I do not believe there is one in ten of you that is going to make a million of dollars because you are here to-night; but it is not my fault, it is yours. I say that sincerely. What is the use of my talking if people never do what I advise them to do? When her husband ridiculed her, she made up her mind she would make a better collar-button, and when a woman makes up her mind "she will," and does not say anything about it, she does it. It was that New England woman who invented the snap button which you can find anywhere now. It was first a collar-button with a spring cap attached to the outer side. Any of you who wear modern waterproofs know the button that simply pushes together, and when you unbutton it you simply pull it apart. That is the button to which I refer, and which she invented. She afterward invented several other buttons, and then invested in more, and then was taken into partnership with great factories. Now that woman goes over the sea every summer in her private steamship—yes, and takes her husband with her! If her husband were to die, she would have money enough left now to buy a foreign duke or count or some such title as that at the latest quotations.

Now what is my lesson in that incident? It is this: I told her then, though I did not know her, what I now say to you, "Your wealth is too near to you. You are looking right over it"; and she had to look over it because it was right under her chin.

I have read in the newspaper that a woman never invented anything. Well, that newspaper ought to begin again. Of course, I do not refer to gossip—I refer to machines—and if I did I might better include the men. That newspaper could never appear if women had not invented something. Friends, think. Ye women, think! You say you cannot make a fortune because you are in some laundry, or running a sewing-machine, it may be, or walking before some loom, and yet you can be a millionaire if you will but follow this almost infallible direction.

When you say a woman doesn't invent anything, I ask, Who invented the Jacquard loom that wove every stitch you wear? Mrs. Jacquard. The printer's roller, the printing-press, were invented by farmers' wives. Who invented the cotton-gin of the South that enriched our country so amazingly? Mrs. General Greene invented the cotton-gin and showed the idea to Mr. Whitney, and he, like a man, seized it. Who was it that invented the sewing-machine? If I would go to school to-morrow and ask your children they would say, "Elias Howe."

He was in the Civil War with me, and often in my tent, and I often heard him say that he worked fourteen years to get up that sewing-machine. But his wife made up her mind one day that they would starve to death if there wasn't something or other invented pretty soon, and so in two hours she invented the sewing-machine. Of course he took out the patent in his name. Men always do that. Who was it that invented the mower and the reaper? According to Mr. McCormick's confidential communication, so recently published, it was a West Virginia woman, who, after his father and he had failed altogether in making a reaper and gave it up, took a lot of shears and nailed them together on the edge of a board, with one shaft of each pair loose, and then wired them so that when she pulled the wire one way it closed them, and when she pulled the wire the other way it opened them, and there she had the principle of the mowing-machine. If you look at a mowing-machine, you will see it is nothing but a lot of shears. If a woman can invent a mowing-machine, if a woman can invent a Jacquard loom, if a woman can invent a cotton-gin, if a woman can invent a trolley switch—as she did and made the trolleys possible; if a woman can invent, as Mr. Carnegie said, the great iron squeezers that laid the foundation of all the steel millions of the United States, "we men" can invent anything under the stars! I say that for the encouragement of the men.

Who are the great inventors of the world? Again this lesson comes before us. The great inventor sits next to you, or you are the person yourself. "Oh," but you will say, "I have never invented anything in my life." Neither did the great inventors until they discovered one great secret. Do you think it is a man with a head like a bushel measure or a man like a stroke of lightning? It is neither. The really great man is a plain, straightforward, every-day, common-sense man. You would not dream that he was a great inventor if you did not see something he had actually done. His neighbors do not regard him so great. You never see anything great over your back fence. You say there is no greatness among your neighbors. It is all away off somewhere else. Their greatness is ever so simple, so plain, so earnest, so practical, that the neighbors and friends never recognize it.

True greatness is often unrecognized. That is sure. You do not know anything about the greatest men and women. I went out to write the life of General Garfield, and a neighbor, knowing I was in a hurry, and as there was a great crowd around the front door, took me around to General Garfield's back door and shouted, "Jim! Jim!" And very soon "Jim" came to the door and let me in, and I wrote the biography of one of the grandest men of the nation, and yet he was just the same old "Jim" to his neighbor. If you know a great man in Philadelphia and you should meet him to-morrow, you would say, "How are you, Sam?" or "Good morning, Jim." Of course you would. That is just what you would do.

One of my soldiers in the Civil War had been sentenced to death, and I went up to the White House in Washington—sent there for the first time in my life to see the President. I went into the waiting-room and sat down with a lot of others on the benches, and the secretary asked one after another to tell him what they wanted. After the secretary had been through the line, he went in, and then came back to the door and motioned for me. I went up to that anteroom, and the secretary said: "That is the President's door right over there. Just rap on it and go right in." I never was so taken aback, friends, in all my life, never. The secretary himself made it worse for me, because he had told me how to go in and then went out another door to the left and shut that. There I was, in the hallway by myself before the President of the United States of America's door. I had been on fields of battle, where the shells did sometimes shriek and the bullets did sometimes hit me, but I always wanted to run. I have no sympathy with the old man who says, "I would just as soon march up to the cannon's mouth as eat my dinner." I have no faith in a man who doesn't know enough to be afraid when he is being shot at. I never was so afraid when the shells came around us at Antietam as I was when I went into that room that day; but I finally mustered the courage—I don't know how I ever did—and at arm's-length tapped on the door. The man inside did not help me at all, but yelled out, "Come in and sit down!"

Well, I went in and sat down on the edge of a chair, and wished I were in Europe, and the man at the table did not look up. He was one of the world's greatest men, and was made great by one single rule. Oh, that all the young people of Philadelphia were before me now and I could say just this one thing, and that they would remember it. I would give a lifetime for the effect it would have on our city and on civilization. Abraham Lincoln's principle for greatness can be adopted by nearly all. This was his rule: Whatsoever he had to do at all, he put his whole mind into it and held it all there until that was all done. That makes men great almost anywhere. He stuck to those papers at that table and did not look up at me, and I sat there trembling. Finally, when he had put the string around his papers, he pushed them over to one side and looked over to me, and a smile came over his worn face. He said: "I am a very busy man and have only a few minutes to spare. Now tell me in the fewest words what it is you want." I began to tell him, and mentioned the case, and he said: "I have heard all about it and you do not need to say any more. Mr. Stanton was talking to me only a few days ago about that. You can go to the hotel and rest assured that the President never did sign an order to shoot a boy under twenty years of age, and never will. You can say that to his mother anyhow."

Then he said to me, "How is it going in the field?" I said, "We sometimes get discouraged." And he said: "It is all right. We are going to win out now. We are getting very near the light. No man ought to wish to be President of the United States, and I will be glad when I get through; then Tad and I are going out to Springfield, Illinois. I have bought a farm out there and I don't care if I again earn only twenty-five cents a day. Tad has a mule team, and we are going to plant onions."

Then he asked me, "Were you brought up on a farm?" I said, "Yes; in the Berkshire Hills of Massachusetts." He then threw his leg over the corner of the big chair and said, "I have heard many a time, ever since I was young, that up there in those hills you have to sharpen the noses of the sheep in order to get down to the grass between the rocks." He was so familiar, so everyday, so farmer-like, that I felt right at home with him at once.

He then took hold of another roll of paper, and looked up at me and said, "Good morning." I took the hint then and got up and went out. After I had gotten out I could not realize I had seen the President of the United States at all. But a few days later, when still in the city, I saw the crowd pass through the East Room by the coffin of Abraham Lincoln, and when I looked at the upturned face of the murdered President I felt then that the man I had seen such a short time before, who, so simple a man, so plain a man, was one of the greatest men that God ever raised up to lead a nation on to ultimate liberty. Yet he was only "Old Abe" to his neighbors. When they had the second funeral, I was invited among others, and went out to see that same coffin put back in the tomb at Springfield. Around the tomb stood Lincoln's old neighbors, to whom he was just "Old Abe." Of course that is all they would say.

Did you ever see a man who struts around altogether too large to notice an ordinary working mechanic? Do you think he is great? He is nothing but a puffed-up balloon, held down by his big feet. There is no greatness there.

Who are the great men and women? My attention was called the other day to the history of a very little thing that made the fortune of a very poor man. It was an awful thing, and yet because of that experience he—not a great inventor or genius—invented the pin that now is called the safety-pin, and out of that safety-pin made the fortune of one of the great aristocratic families of this nation.

A poor man in Massachusetts who had worked in the nail-works was injured at thirty-eight, and he could earn but little money. He was employed in the office to rub out the marks on the bills made by pencil memorandums, and he used a rubber until his hand grew tired. He then tied a piece of rubber on the end of a stick and worked it like a plane. His little girl came and said, "Why, you have a patent, haven't you?" The father said afterward, "My daughter told me when I took that stick and put the rubber on the end that there was a patent, and that was the first thought of that." He went to Boston and applied for his patent, and every one of you that has a rubber-tipped pencil in your pocket is now paying tribute to the millionaire. No capital, not a penny did he invest in it. All was income, all the way up into the millions.

But let me hasten to one other greater thought. "Show me the great men and women who live in Philadelphia." A gentleman over there will get up and say: "We don't have any great men in Philadelphia. They don't live here. They live away off in Rome or St. Petersburg or London or Manayunk, or anywhere else but here in our town." I have come now to the apex of my thought. I have come now to the heart of the whole matter and to the center of my struggle: Why isn't Philadelphia a greater city in its greater wealth? Why does New York excel Philadelphia? People say, "Because of her harbor." Why do many other cities of the United States get ahead of Philadelphia now? There is only one answer, and that is because our own people talk down their own city. If there ever was a community on earth that has to be forced ahead, it is the city of Philadelphia. If we are to have a boulevard, talk it down; if we are going to have better schools, talk them down; if you wish to have wise legislation, talk it down; talk all the proposed improvements down. That is the only great wrong that I can lay at the feet of the magnificent Philadelphia that has been so universally kind to me. I say it is time we turn around in our city and begin to talk up the things that are in our city, and begin to set them before the world as the people of Chicago, New York, St. Louis, and San Francisco do. Oh, if we only could get that spirit out among our people, that we can do things in Philadelphia and do them well!

Arise, ye millions of Philadelphians, trust in God and man, and believe in the great opportunities that are right here not over in New York or Boston, but here—for business, for everything that is worth living for on earth. There was never an opportunity greater. Let us talk up our own city.

But there are two other young men here to-night, and that is all I will venture to say, because it is too late. One over there gets up and says, "There is going to be a great man in Philadelphia, but never was one." "Oh, is that so? When are you going to be great?" "When I am elected to some political office." Young man, won't you learn a lesson in the primer of politics that it is a *prima facie* evidence of littleness to hold office under our form of government? Great men get into office sometimes, but what this country needs is men that will do what we tell them to do. This nation—where the people rule—is governed by the people, for the people, and so long as it is, then the office-holder is but the servant of the people, and the Bible says the servant cannot be greater than the master. The Bible says, "He that is sent cannot be greater than Him who sent Him." The people rule, or should rule, and if they do, we do not need the greater men in office. If the great men in America took our offices, we would change to an empire in the next ten years.

I know of a great many young women, now that woman's suffrage is coming, who say, "I am going to be President of the United States some day." I believe in woman's suffrage, and there is no doubt but what it is coming, and I am getting out of the way, anyhow. I may want an office by and by myself; but if the ambition for an office influences the women in their desire to vote, I want to say right here what I say to the young men, that if you only get the privilege of casting one vote, you don't get anything that is worth while. Unless you can control more than one vote, you will be unknown, and your influence so dissipated as practically not to be felt. This country is not run by votes. Do you think it is? It is governed by influence. It is governed by the ambitions and the enterprises which control votes. The young woman that thinks she is going to vote for the sake of holding an office is making an awful blunder.

That other young man gets up and says, "There are going to be great men in this country and in Philadelphia." "Is that so? When?" "When there comes a great war, when we get into difficulty through watchful waiting in Mexico; when we get into war with England over some frivolous deed, or with Japan or China or New Jersey or some distant country. Then I will march up to the cannon's mouth; I will sweep up among the glistening bayonets; I will leap into the arena and tear down the flag and bear it away in triumph. I will come home with stars on my shoulder, and hold every office in the gift of the nation, and I will be great." No, you won't. You think you are going to be made great by an office, but remember that if you are not great before you get the office, you won't be great when you secure it. It will only be a burlesque in that shape.

We had a Peace Jubilee here after the Spanish War. Out West they don't believe this, because they said, "Philadelphia would not have heard of any Spanish War until fifty years hence." Some of you saw the procession go up Broad Street. I was away, but the family wrote to me that the tally-ho coach with Lieutenant Hobson upon it stopped right at the front door and the people shouted, "Hurrah for Hobson!" and if I had been there I would have yelled too, because he deserves much more of his country than he has ever received. But suppose I go into school and say, "Who sunk the *Merrimac* at Santiago?" and if the boys answer me, "Hobson," they will tell me seven-eighths of a lie. There were seven other heroes on that steamer, and they, by virtue of their position, were continually exposed to the Spanish fire, while Hobson, as an officer, might reasonably be behind the smoke-stack. You have gathered in this house your most intelligent people, and yet, perhaps, not one here can name the other seven men.

We ought not to so teach history. We ought to teach that, however humble a man's station may be, if he does his full duty in that place he is just as much entitled to the American people's honor as is the king upon his throne. But we do not so teach. We are now teaching everywhere that the generals do all the fighting.

I remember that, after the war, I went down to see General Robert E. Lee, that magnificent Christian gentleman of whom both North and South are now proud as one of our great Americans. The general told me about his servant, "Rastus," who was an enlisted colored soldier. He called him in one day to make fun of him, and said, "Rastus, I hear that all the rest of your company are killed, and why are you not killed?" Rastus winked at him and said, "'Cause when there is any fightin' goin' on I stay back with the generals."

I remember another illustration. I would leave it out but for the fact that when you go to the library to read this lecture, you will find this has been printed in it for twenty-five years. I shut my eyes—shut them close—and lo! I see the faces of my youth. Yes, they sometimes say to me, "Your hair is not white; you are working night and day without seeming ever to stop; you can't be old." But when I shut my eyes, like any other man of my years, oh, then come trooping back the faces of the loved and lost of long ago, and I know, whatever men may say, it is evening-time.

I shut my eyes now and look back to my native town in Massachusetts, and I see the cattle-show ground on the mountain-top; I can see the horse-sheds there. I can see the Congregational church; see the town hall and mountaineers' cottages; see a great assembly of people turning out, dressed resplendently, and I can see flags flying and hand-kerchiefs waving and hear bands playing. I can see that company of soldiers that had re-enlisted marching up on that cattle-show ground. I was but a boy, but I was captain of that company and puffed out with pride. A cambric needle would have burst me all to pieces. Then I thought it was the greatest event that ever came to man on earth. If you have ever thought you would like to be a king or queen, you go and be received by the mayor.

The bands played, and all the people turned out to receive us. I marched up that Common so proud at the head of my troops, and we turned down into the town hall. Then they seated my soldiers down the center aisle and I sat down on the front seat. A great assembly of people a hundred or two—came in to fill the town hall, so that they stood up all around. Then the town officers came in and formed a half-circle. The mayor of the town sat in the middle of the platform. He was a man who had never held office before; but he was a good man, and his friends have told me that I might use this without giving them offense. He was a good man, but he thought an office made a man great. He came up and took his seat, adjusted his powerful spectacles, and looked around, when he suddenly spied me sitting there on the front seat. He came right forward on the platform and invited me up to sit with the town officers. No town officer ever took any notice of me before I went to war, except to advise the teacher to thrash me, and now I was invited up on the stand with the town officers. Oh my! the town mayor was then the emperor, the king of our day and our time. As I came up on the platform they gave me a chair about this far, I would say, from the front.

When I had got seated, the chairman of the Selectmen arose and came forward to the table, and we all supposed he would introduce the Congregational minister, who was the only orator in town, and that he would give the oration to the returning soldiers. But, friends, you should have seen the surprise which ran over the audience when they discovered that the old fellow was going to deliver that speech himself. He had never made a speech in his life, but he fell into the same error that hundreds of other men have fallen into. It seems so strange that a man won't learn he must speak his piece as a boy if he intends to be an orator when he is grown, but he seems to think all he has to do is to hold an office to be a great orator.

So he came up to the front, and brought with him a speech which he had learned by heart walking up and down the pasture, where he had frightened the cattle. He brought the manuscript with him and spread it out on the table so as to be sure he might see it. He adjusted his spectacles and leaned over it for a moment and marched back on that platform, and then came forward like this—tramp, tramp, tramp. He must have studied the subject a great deal, when you come to think of it, because he assumed an "elocutionary" attitude. He rested heavily upon his left heel, threw back his shoulders, slightly advanced the right foot, opened the organs of speech, and advanced his right foot at an angle of forty-five. As he stood in that elocutionary attitude, friends, this is just the way that speech went. Some people say to me, "Don't you exaggerate?" That would be impossible. But I am here for the lesson and not for the story, and this is the way it went:

"Fellow-citizens—" As soon as he heard his voice his fingers began to go like that, his knees began to shake, and then he trembled all over. He choked and swallowed and came around to the table to look at the manuscript. Then he gathered himself up with clenched fists and came back: "Fellow-citizens, we are Fellow-citizens, we are—we are—we are—we are—we are—we are very happy—we are very happy—we are very happy. We are very happy to welcome back to their native town these soldiers who have fought and bled—and come back again to their native town. We are especially—we are especially—we are especially. We are especially pleased to see with us to-day this young hero" (that meant me)—"this young hero who in imagination" (friends, remember he said that; if he had not said "in imagination" I would not be egotistic enough to refer to it at all)—"this young hero who in imagination we have seen leading—we have seen leading—leading. We have seen leading his troops on to the deadly breach. We have seen his shining—we have seen his shining—his shining—his shining sword—flashing. Flashing in the sunlight, as he shouted to his troops, 'Come on'!"

Oh dear, dear, dear! how little that good man knew about war. If he had known anything about war at all he ought to have known what any of my G. A. R. comrades here to-night will tell you is true, that it is next to a crime for an officer of infantry ever in time of danger to go ahead of his men. "I, with my shining sword flashing in the sunlight, shouting to my troops, 'Come on'!" I never did it. Do you suppose I would get in front of my men to be shot in front by the enemy and in the back by my own men? That is no place for an officer. The place for the officer in actual battle is behind the line. How often, as a staff officer, I rode down the line, when our men were suddenly called to the line of battle, and the Rebel yells were coming out of the woods, and shouted: "Officers to the rear! Officers to the rear!" Then every officer gets behind the line of private soldiers, and the higher the officer's rank the farther behind he goes. Not because he is any the less brave, but because the laws of war require that. And yet he shouted, "I, with my shining sword—" In that house there sat the company of my soldiers who had carried that boy across the Carolina rivers that he might not wet his feet. Some of them had gone far out to get a pig or a chicken. Some of them had gone to death under the shell-swept pines in the mountains of Tennessee, yet in the good man's speech they were scarcely known. He did refer to them, but only incidentally. The hero of the hour was this boy. Did the nation owe him anything? No, nothing then and nothing now. Why was he the hero? Simply because that man fell into that same human error—that this boy was great because he was an officer and these were only private soldiers.

Oh, I learned the lesson then that I will never forget so long as the tongue of the bell of time continues to swing for me. Greatness consists not in the holding of some future office, but really consists in doing great deeds with little means and the accomplishment of vast purposes from the private ranks of life. To be great at all one must be great here, now, in Philadelphia. He who can give to this city better streets and better sidewalks, better schools and more colleges, more happiness and more civilization, more of God, he will be great anywhere. Let every man or woman here, if you never hear me again, remember this, that if you wish to be great at all, you must begin where you are and what you are, in Philadelphia, now. He that can give to his city any blessing, he who can be a good citizen while he lives here, he that can make better homes, he that can be a blessing whether he works in the shop or sits behind the counter or keeps house, whatever be his life, he who would be great anywhere must first be great in his own Philadelphia.

A Message to Garcia

Elbert Hubbard

Elbert Hubbard—writer, philosopher, and publisher—called "A Message to Garcia" a "literary trifle, written one evening after supper in a single hour." He explained, "It was on the twenty-second of February, eighteen hundred ninety-nine, Washington's birthday, and we were just going to press with the March *Philistine*. The thing leaped hot from my heart, written after a trying day, when I had been endeavoring to train some rather delinquent villagers to abandon the comatose state and get radioactive."

The article was inspired by an argument with Hubbard's son, Bert, who suggested that "an obscure lieutenant named Rowan was the real hero of the Cuban War" (now known as the Spanish-American War) because Rowan had "gone alone and done the thing—carried the message to Garcia."

Hubbard recorded, "I then got up from the table and wrote 'A Message to Garcia.' I thought so little of it that we ran it [as a newspaper filler] without a heading. The edition went out, and soon orders began to come for extra copies. A dozen, fifty, a hundred, and when the American News Company ordered a thousand, I asked one of my helpers which article it was that had stirred up the cosmic dust.

" 'It's the stuff about Garcia,' he said.

"The next day a telegram came from George H. Daniels, of the New York Central Railroad: 'Give price on one hundred thousand Rowan article in pamphlet form—Empire State Express advertisement on back—also how soon can ship?'

"I replied giving price, and stated we could supply the pamphlets in two years. Our facilities were small and a hundred thousand booklets looked like an awful undertaking."

Needing the pamphlets immediately, Mr. Daniels obtained permission to print them himself as needed, which turned out to be multiple editions of 500,000 copies each. The article was also reprinted in more than two hundred magazines and newspapers, and within fourteen years it had been translated into dozens of languages.

On December 1, 1913, more than fourteen years after writing the piece, Hubbard noted, "Over forty million copies of 'A Message to Garcia' have now been printed. This is said to be a larger circulation than any other literary venture has ever attained during the lifetime of the author, in all history—thanks to a series of lucky accidents!"

This little piece brings powerfully to mind these words of the Savior: "Not every one that saith unto me, Lord, Lord, shall enter into the kingdom of heaven; but he that doeth the will of my Father which is in heaven." (Matthew 7:21.)

A MESSAGE TO GARCIA

In all this Cuban business there is one man stands out on the horizon of my memory like Mars at perihelion.

When war broke out between Spain and the United States, it was very necessary to communicate quickly with the leader of the Insurgents. Garcia was somewhere in the mountain fastnesses of Cuba—no one knew where. No mail or telegraph could reach him. The President must secure his co-operation, and quickly.

What to do!

Some one said to the President, "There's a fellow by the name of Rowan will find Garcia for you, if anybody can."

Rowan was sent for and given a letter to be delivered to Garcia.

How "the fellow by name of Rowan" took the letter, sealed it up in an oil-skin pouch, strapped it over his heart, in four days landed by night off the coast of Cuba from an open boat, disappeared into the jungle, and in three weeks came out on the other side of the Island, having traversed a hostile country on foot, and having delivered his letter to Garcia, are things I have no special desire now to tell in detail. The point I wish to make is this: McKinley gave Rowan a letter to be delivered to Garcia; Rowan took the letter and did not ask, "Where is he at!"

By the Eternal! There is a man whose form should be cast in death-less bronze and the statue placed in every college in the land. It is not book-learning young men need, nor instruction about this or that, but a stiffening of the vertebrae which will cause them to be loyal to a trust, to act promptly, concentrate their energies; do the thing—"carry a message to Garcia!"

General Garcia is dead now, but there are other Garcias. No man, who has endeavored to carry out an enterprise where many hands were needed, but has been well-nigh appalled at times by the imbecility of the average man—the inability or unwillingness to concentrate on a thing and do it.

Slip-shod assistance, foolish inattention, dowdy indifference, and half-hearted work seem the rule; and no man succeeds, unless by hook or crook, or threat, he forces or bribes other men to assist him; or mayhap, God in His goodness performs a miracle, and sends him an Angel of Light for an assistant.

You, reader, put this matter to a test: You are sitting now in your office—six clerks are within your call. Summon any one and make this request: "Please look in the encyclopedia and make a brief memorandum for me concerning the life of Corregio."

Will the clerk quietly say, "Yes, sir," and go do the task?

On your life, he will not. He will look at you out of a fishy eye, and ask one or more of the following questions:

Who was he?

Which encyclopedia?

Where is the encyclopedia?

Was I hired for that?

Don't you mean Bismarck?

What's the matter with Charlie doing it?

Is he dead?

Is there any hurry?

Shan't I bring you the book and let you look it up yourself?

What do you want to know for?

And I will lay you ten to one that after you have answered the questions, & explained how to find the information, and why you want it, the clerk will go off and get one of the other clerks to help him find Garcia—and then come back and tell you there is no such man. Of course I may lose my bet, but according to the Law of Average, I will not.

Now if you are wise you will not bother to explain to your "assistant" that Corregio is indexed under the C's, not in the K's, but you will smile sweetly & say, "Never mind," and go look it up yourself.

And this incapacity for independent action, this moral stupidity, this infirmity of the will, this unwillingness to cheerfully catch hold and lift, are the things that put pure Socialism so far into the future. If men will not act for themselves, what will they do when the benefit of their effort is for all?

A first-mate with knotted club seems necessary; and the dread of getting "the bounce" Saturday night, holds many a worker in his place.

Advertise for a stenographer, and nine out of ten who apply can neither spell nor punctuate—and do not think it necessary to.

Can such a one write a letter to Garcia?

"You see that book-keeper," said the foreman to me in a large factory.

"Yes, what about him?"

"Well, he's a fine accountant, but if I'd send him up town on an errand, he might accomplish the errand all right, and, on the other hand, might stop at four saloons on the way, and when he got to Main Street, would forget what he had been sent for."

Can such a man be entrusted to carry a message to Garcia?

We have recently been hearing much maudlin sympathy expressed for the "down-trodden denizen of the sweat-shop" and the "homeless wanderer searching for honest employment," and with it all often go many hard words for the men in power.

Nothing is said about the employer who grows old before his time in a vain attempt to get frowsy ne'er-do-wells to do intelligent work; and his long patient striving with "help" that does nothing but loaf when his back is turned. In every store and factory there is a constant weeding-out process going on. The employer is constantly sending away "help" that have shown their incapacity to further the interests of the business, and others are being taken on. No matter how good times are, this sorting continues, only if times are hard and work is scarce, this sorting is done finer—but out and forever out, the incompetent and unworthy go. It is the survival of the fittest. Self-interest prompts every employer to keep the best—those who can carry a message to Garcia.

I know one man of really brilliant parts who has not the ability to manage a business of his own, and yet who is absolutely worthless to anyone else, because he carries with him constantly the insane suspicion that his employer is oppressing, or intending to oppress, him. He cannot give orders, and he will not receive them. Should a message be given him to take to Garcia, his answer would probably be, "Take it yourself."

To-night this man walks the streets looking for work, the wind whistling through his thread-bare coat. No one who knows him dare employ him, for he is a regular fire-brand of discontent. He is impervious to reason, and the only thing that can impress him is the toe of a thick-soled No. 9 boot.

Of course I know that one so morally deformed is no less to be pitied than a physical cripple; but in your pitying, let us drop a tear, too, for the men who are striving to carry on a great enterprise, whose working hours are not limited by the whistle, and whose hair is fast turning white through the struggle to hold the line in dowdy indifference, slipshod imbecility, and the heartless ingratitude which, but for their enterprise, would be both hungry and homeless.

Have I put the matter too strongly? Possibly I have; but when all the world has gone a-slumming I wish to speak a word of sympathy for the man who succeeds—the man who, against great odds, has directed the efforts of others, and, having succeeded, finds there's nothing in it: nothing but bare board and clothes. I have carried a dinner pail and worked for a day's wages, and I have also been an employer of labor, and I know there is something to be said on both sides. There is no excellence, *per se,* in poverty; rags are no recommendation; and all employers are not rapacious and high-handed, any more than all poor men are virtuous. My heart goes out to the man who does his work when the "boss" is away, as well as when he is home. And the man, who, when given a letter for Garcia, quietly takes the missive, without asking any idiotic questions, and with no lurking intention of chucking it into the nearest sewer, or of doing aught else but deliver it, never gets "laid off," nor has to go on strike for higher wages. Civilization is one long anxious search for just such individuals. Anything such a man asks will be granted; his kind is so rare that no employer can afford to let him go. He is wanted in every city, town, & village—in every office, shop, store and factory. The world cries out for such; he is needed, & needed badly—the man who can carry a message to Garcia.

SELF-RELIANCE

Ralph Waldo Emerson

Ralph Waldo Emerson, born just two years before Joseph Smith in 1803, was one of America's most influential authors, thinkers, and lecturers. A Unitarian minister, he left his only pastorate, Boston's Old North Church, because of doctrinal disputes. Traveling to Europe, Emerson met Thomas Carlyle, Samuel Taylor Coleridge, and William Wordsworth, all important literary figures of the day. Their ideas strongly influenced his philosophy, and upon his return to the United States in 1835, he became a leader in the Transcendentalist movement in American literature. This movement stressed God's presence in human life and in nature, and it emphasized individualism and independence. Its ideas were most eloquently expressed in *Walden,* by Henry David Thoreau, and, of course, in the essays of Emerson, who died in 1882.

Among the best known of these essays are "Compensation" and "Self-Reliance," both of which are included in this volume. "Self-Reliance," published in 1841, discusses a subject that has often been emphasized by General Authorities of the Church. As President Brigham Young said, "My faith does not lead me to think the Lord will provide us with roast pigs, bread already buttered, etc.; he will give us the ability to raise the grain, to obtain the fruits of the earth, to make habitations, to procure a few boards to make a box, and when harvest comes, giving us the grain, it is for us to preserve it." He also noted, "Instead of searching after what the Lord is going to do for us, let us inquire what we can do for ourselves." (*Discourses of Brigham Young* [Salt Lake City: Deseret Book Co., 1954], 291–93.)

The principle of self-reliance also applies to spiritual matters. As the

Lord instructed the Saints in 1831, "It is not meet that I should command in all things; for he that is compelled in all things, the same is a slothful and not a wise servant; wherefore he receiveth no reward. Verily I say, men should be anxiously engaged in a good cause, and do many things of their own free will, and bring to pass much righteousness; for the power is in them, wherein they are agents unto themselves. And inasmuch as men do good they shall in nowise lose their reward." (D&C 58:26–28.)

SELF-RELIANCE

"Ne te quaesiveris extra."

"Man is his own star; and the soul that can
Render an honest and a perfect man,
  Commands all light, all influence, all fate;
Nothing to him falls early or too late.
  Our acts our angels are, or good or ill,
  Our fatal shadows that walk by us still."
— Epilogue to Beaumont and
Fletcher's *Honest Man's Fortune*

Cast the bantling on the rocks,
  Suckle him with the she-wolf's teat,
Wintered with the hawk and fox,
  Power and speed be hands and feet.

I read the other day some verses written by an eminent painter which were original and not conventional. The soul always hears an admonition in such lines, let the subject be what it may. The sentiment they instil is of more value than any thought they may contain. To believe your own thought, to believe that what is true for you in your private heart is true for all men,—that is genius. Speak your latent conviction, and it shall be the universal sense; for the inmost in due time becomes the outmost,—and our first thought is rendered back to us by the trumpets of the Last Judgment. Familiar as the voice of the mind is to each, the highest merit we ascribe to Moses, Plato, and Milton is that they set at naught books and traditions, and spoke not what men, but what they thought. A man should learn to detect and watch that gleam of light which flashes across his mind from within, more than the lustre of the firmament of bards and sages. Yet he dismisses without notice his thought, because it is his. In every work of genius we recognize our own rejected thoughts: they come back to us with a certain alienated majesty. Great works of art have no more affecting lesson for us than this. They teach us to abide by our spontaneous impression with good-humored inflexibility then most when the whole cry of voices is on the other side.

Else, to-morrow a stranger will say with masterly good sense precisely what we have thought and felt all the time, and we shall be forced to take with shame our own opinion from another.

There is a time in every man's education when he arrives at the conviction that envy is ignorance; that imitation is suicide; that he must take himself for better, for worse, as his portion; that though the wide universe is full of good, no kernel of nourishing corn can come to him but through his toil bestowed on that plot of ground which is given to him to till. The power which resides in him is new in nature, and none but he knows what that is which he can do, nor does he know until he has tried. Not for nothing one face, one character, one fact, makes much impression on him, and another none. This sculpture in the memory is not without preëstablished harmony. The eye was placed where one ray should fall, that it might testify of that particular ray. We but half express ourselves, and are ashamed of that divine idea which each of us represents. It may be safely trusted as proportionate and of good issues, so it be faithfully imparted, but God will not have his work made manifest by cowards. A man is relieved and gay when he has put his heart into his work and done his best; but what he has said or done otherwise shall give him no peace. It is a deliverance which does not deliver. In the attempt his genius deserts him; no muse befriends; no invention, no hope.

Trust thyself: every heart vibrates to that iron string. Accept the place the divine providence has found for you, the society of your contemporaries, the connection of events. Great men have always done so, and confided themselves childlike to the genius of their age, betraying their perception that the absolutely trustworthy was seated at their heart, working through their hands, predominating in all their being. And we are now men, and must accept in the highest mind the same transcendent destiny; and not minors and invalids in a protected corner, not cowards fleeing before a revolution, but guides, redeemers, and benefactors, obeying the Almighty effort, and advancing on Chaos and the Dark.

What pretty oracles nature yields us on this text, in the face and behaviour of children, babes, and even brutes! That divided and rebel mind, that distrust of a sentiment because our arithmetic has computed the strength and means opposed to our purpose, these have not. Their mind being whole, their eye is as yet unconquered, and when we look in their faces, we are disconcerted. Infancy conforms to nobody: all conform to it, so that one babe commonly makes four or five out of the adults who prattle and play to it. So God has armed youth and puberty and manhood no less with its own piquancy and charm, and made it enviable and gracious and its claims not to be put by, if it will stand by itself. Do not think the youth has no force, because he cannot speak to you and me. Hark! in the next room his voice is sufficiently clear and emphatic. It seems he knows how to speak to his contemporaries. Bashful or bold, then, he will know how to make us seniors very unnecessary.

The nonchalance of boys who are sure of a dinner, and would disdain as much as a lord to do or say aught to conciliate one, is the healthy attitude of human nature. A boy is in the parlour what the pit is in the playhouse; independent, irresponsible, looking out from his corner on such people and facts as pass by, he tries and sentences them on their merits, in the swift, summary ways of boys, as good, bad, interesting, silly, eloquent, troublesome. He cumbers himself never about consequences, about interests: he gives an independent, genuine verdict. You must court him: he does not court you. But the man is, as it were, clapped into jail by his consciousness. As soon as he has once acted or spoken with *éclat* he is a committed person, watched by the sympathy or the hatred of hundreds, whose affections must now enter into his account. There is no Lethe for this. Ah, that he could pass again into his neutrality! Who can thus avoid all pledges, and having observed, observe again from the same unaffected, unbiased, unbribable, unaffrighted innocence, must always be formidable. He would utter opinions on all passing affairs, which being seen to be not private, but necessary, would sink like darts into the ear of men, and put them in fear.

These are the voices which we hear in solitude, but they grow faint and inaudible as we enter into the world. Society everywhere is in conspiracy against the manhood of every one of its members. Society is a joint-stock company, in which the members agree, for the better securing of his bread to each shareholder, to surrender the liberty and culture of the eater. The virtue in most request is conformity. Self-reliance is its aversion. It loves not realities and creators, but names and customs.

Whoso would be a man, must be a nonconformist. He who would gather immortal palms must not be hindered by the name of goodness, but must explore if it be goodness. Nothing is at last sacred but the integrity of your own mind. Absolve you to yourself, and you shall have the suffrage of the world. I remember an answer which when quite young I was prompted to make to a valued adviser, who was wont to importune me with the dear old doctrines of the church. On my saying, What have I to do with the sacredness of traditions, if I live wholly from within? my friend suggested,—"But these impulses may be from below, not from above." I replied, "They do not seem to me to be such; but if I am the Devil's child, I will live then from the Devil." No law can be sacred to me but that of my nature. Good and bad are but names very readily transferable to that or this; the only right is what is after my constitution, the only wrong what is against it.[1] A man is to carry himself in the presence of all opposition as if everything were titular and ephemeral but he. I am ashamed to think how easily we capitulate to badges and names, to large societies and dead institutions. Every decent and well-spoken individual affects and sways me more than is right. I ought to go upright and vital, and speak the rude truth in all ways. If malice and vanity wear the coat of philanthropy, shall that pass? If an angry bigot assumes this bountiful cause of Abolition, and comes to me with his last news from Barbadoes, why should I not say to him, "Go love thy infant; love thy wood-chopper: be good-natured and modest: have that grace; and never varnish your hard, uncharitable ambition with this incredible tenderness for black folk a thousand miles off. Thy love afar is spite at home." Rough and graceless would be such greeting, but truth is handsomer than the affectation of love. Your goodness must have some edge to it,—else it is none. The doctrine of hatred must be

---

1.   Emerson is not saying here that we should follow the devil. He is saying (a bit dramatically, perhaps) that we should be true to our own convictions—our own testimonies, if you will—of what is right, and that no one can stand on borrowed light. Compare his experience with that of the young Joseph Smith in Joseph Smith—History 1:21.

preached as the counteraction of the doctrine of love when that pules and whines. I shun father and mother and wife and brother, when my genius calls me. I would write on the lintels of the door-post, *Whim.* I hope it is somewhat better than whim at last, but we cannot spend the day in explanation. Expect me not to show cause why I seek or why I exclude company. Then, again, do not tell me, as a good man did to-day, of my obligation to put all poor men in good situations. Are they *my* poor? I tell thee, thou foolish philanthropist, that I grudge the dollar, the dime, the cent, I give to such men as do not belong to me and to whom I do not belong. There is a class of persons to whom by all spiritual affinity I am bought and sold; for them I will go to prison, if need be; but your miscellaneous popular charities; the education at college of fools; the building of meeting-houses to the vain end to which many now stand; alms to sots; and the thousandfold Relief Societies;—though I confess with shame I sometimes succumb and give the dollar, it is a wicked dollar which by and by I shall have the manhood to withhold.

Virtues are, in the popular estimate, rather the exception than the rule. There is the man *and* his virtues. Men do what is called a good action, as some piece of courage or charity, much as they would pay a fine in expiation of daily non-appearance on parade. Their works are done as an apology or extenuation of their living in the world,—as invalids and the insane pay a high board. Their virtues are penances. I do not wish to expiate, but to live. My life is for itself and not for a spectacle. I much prefer that it should be of a lower strain, so it be genuine and equal, than that it should be glittering and unsteady. I wish it to be sound and sweet, and not to need diet and bleeding. I ask primary evidence that you are a man, and refuse this appeal from the man to his actions. I know that for myself it makes no difference whether I do or forbear those actions which are reckoned excellent. I cannot consent to pay for a privilege where I have intrinsic right. Few and mean as my gifts may be, I actually am, and do not need for my own assurance or the assurance of my fellows any secondary testimony.

What I must do is all that concerns me, not what the people think. This rule, equally arduous in actual and in intellectual life, may serve for the whole distinction between greatness and meanness. It is the harder, because you will always find those who think they know what is your duty better than you know it. It is easy in the world to live after the world's opinion; it is easy in solitude to live after our own; but the great man is he who in the midst of the crowd keeps with perfect sweetness the independence of solitude.

The objection to conforming to usages that have become dead to you is, that it scatters your force. It loses your time and blurs the impression of your character. If you maintain a dead church, contribute to a dead Bible-society, vote with a great party either for the government or against it, spread your table like base housekeepers,—under all these screens I have difficulty to detect the precise man you are. And, of course, so much force is withdrawn from your proper life. But do your work, and I shall know you. Do your work, and you shall reinforce yourself. A man must consider what a blind man's-buff is this game of conformity. If I know your sect, I anticipate your argument. I hear a preacher announce for his text and topic the expediency of one of the institutions of his church. Do I not know beforehand that not possibly can he say a new and spontaneous word? Do I not know that, with all this ostentation of examining the grounds of the institution, he will do no such thing? Do I not know that he is pledged to himself not to look but at one side,—the permitted side, not as a man, but as a parish minister? He is a retained attorney, and these airs of the bench are the emptiest affectation. Well, most men have bound their eyes with one or another handkerchief, and attached themselves to some one of these communities of opinion. This conformity makes them not false in a few particulars, authors of a few lies, but false in all particulars. Their every truth is not quite true. Their two is not the real two, their four not the real four; so that every word they say chagrins us, and we know not where to begin to set them right. Meantime nature is not slow to equip us in the prison-uniform of the party to which we adhere. We come to wear one cut of face and figure, and acquire by degrees the gentlest asinine expression. There is a mortifying experience in particular, which does not fail to wreak itself also in the general history; I mean "the foolish face of praise," the forced smile which we put on in company where we do not feel at ease in answer to conversation which does not interest us. The muscles, not spontaneously moved, but moved by a low usurping wilfulness, grow tight about the outline of the face with the most disagreeable sensation.

For nonconformity the world whips you with its displeasure. And therefore a man must know how to estimate a sour face. The by-standers look askance on him in the public street or in the friend's parlour. If this aversion had its origin in contempt and resistance like his own, he might well go home with a sad countenance; but the sour faces of the multitude, like their sweet faces, have no deep cause, but are put on and off as the wind blows and a newspaper directs. Yet is the discontent of the multitude more formidable than that of the senate and the college. It is easy enough for a firm man who knows the world to brook the rage of the cultivated classes. Their rage is decorous and prudent, for they are timid as being very vulnerable themselves. But when to their feminine rage the indignation of the people is added, when the ignorant and the poor are aroused, when the unintelligent brute force that lies at the bottom of society is made to growl and mow, it needs the habit of magnanimity and religion to treat it godlike as a trifle of no concernment.

The other terror that scares us from self-trust is our consistency; a reverence for our past act or word, because the eyes of others have no other data for computing our orbit than our past acts, and we are loth to disappoint them.

But why should you keep your head over your shoulder? Why drag about this corpse of your memory, lest you contradict somewhat you have stated in this or that public place? Suppose you should contradict yourself; what then? It seems to be a rule of wisdom never to rely on your memory alone, scarcely even in acts of pure memory, but to bring the past for judgment into the thousand-eyed present, and live ever in a new day. In your metaphysics you have denied personality to the Deity: yet when the devout motions of the soul come, yield to them heart and life, though they should clothe God with shape and color. Leave your theory, as Joseph his coat in the hand of the harlot, and flee.

A foolish consistency is the hobgoblin of little minds, adored by little statesmen and philosophers and divines. With consistency a great soul has simply nothing to do. He may as well concern himself with his shadow on the wall. Speak what you think now in hard words, and to-morrow speak what to-morrow thinks in hard words again, though it contradict every thing you said to-day.—"Ah, so you shall be sure to be misunderstood."—Is it so bad, then, to be misunderstood? Pythagoras was misunderstood, and Socrates, and Jesus, and Luther, and Copernicus, and Galileo, and Newton, and every pure and wise spirit that ever took flesh. To be great is to be misunderstood.

I suppose no man can violate his nature. All the sallies of his will are rounded in by the law of his being, as the inequalities of Andes and Himmaleh are insignificant in the curve of the sphere. Nor does it matter how you gauge and try him. A character is like an acrostic or Alexandrian stanza;—read it forward, backward, or across, it still spells the same thing. In this pleasing, contrite wood-life which God allows me, let me record day by day my honest thought without prospect or retrospect, and, I cannot doubt, it will be found symmetrical, though I mean it not, and see it not. My book should smell of pines and resound with the hum of insects. The swallow over my window should interweave that thread or straw he carries in his bill into my web also. We pass for what we are. Character teaches above our wills. Men imagine that they communicate their virtue or vice only by overt actions, and do not see that virtue or vice emit a breath every moment.

There will be an agreement in whatever variety of actions, so they be each honest and natural in their hour. For of one will, the actions will be harmonious, however unlike they seem. These varieties are lost sight of at a little distance, at a little height of thought. One tendency unites them all. The voyage of the best ship is a zigzag line of a hundred tacks. See the line from a sufficient distance, and it straightens itself to the average tendency. Your genuine action will explain itself, and will explain your other genuine actions. Your conformity explains nothing. Act singly, and what you have already done singly will justify you now. Greatness appeals to the future. If I can be firm enough to-day to do right, and scorn eyes, I must have done so much right before as to defend me now. Be it how it will, do right now. Always scorn appearances, and you always may. The force of character is cumulative. All the foregone days of virtue work their health into this. What makes the majesty of the heroes of the senate and the field, which so fills the imagination? The consciousness of a train of great days and victories behind. They shed a united light on the advancing actor. He is attended as by a visible escort of angels. That is it which throws thunder into Chatham's voice, and dignity into Washington's port, and America into Adams's eye. Honor is venerable to us because it is no ephemera. It is always ancient virtue. We worship it to-day because it is not of to-day. We love it and pay it homage, because it is not a trap for our love and homage, but is self-dependent, self-derived, and therefore of an old immaculate pedigree, even if shown in a young person.

I hope in these days we have heard the last of conformity and consistency. Let the words be gazetted and ridiculous henceforward. Instead of the gong for dinner, let us hear a whistle from the Spartan fife. Let us never bow and apologize more. A great man is coming to eat at my house. I do not wish to please him; I wish that he should wish to please me. I will stand here for humanity, and though I would make it kind, I would make it true. Let us affront and reprimand the smooth mediocrity and squalid contentment of the times, and hurl in the face of custom, and trade, and office, the fact which is the upshot of all history, that there is a great responsible Thinker and Actor working wherever a man works; that a true man belongs to no other time or place, but is the centre of things. Where he is, there is nature. He measures you, and all men, and all events. Ordinarily, every body in society reminds us of somewhat else, or of some other person. Character, reality, reminds you of nothing else; it takes place of the whole creation. The man must be so much, that he must make all circumstances indifferent. Every true man is a cause, a country, and an age; requires infinite spaces and numbers and time fully to accomplish his design;—and posterity seem to follow his steps as a train of clients. A man Caesar is born, and for ages after we have a Roman Empire. Christ is born, and millions of minds so grow and cleave to his genius, that he is confounded with virtue and the possible of man. An institution is the lengthened shadow of one man; as, Monachism, of the Hermit Antony; the Reformation, of Luther; Quakerism, of Fox; Methodism, of Wesley; Abolition, of Clarkson. Scipio, Milton called "the height of Rome"; and all history resolves itself very easily into the biography of a few stout and earnest persons.

Let a man then know his worth, and keep things under his feet. Let him not peep or steal, or skulk up and down with the air of a charity-boy, a bastard, or an interloper, in the world which exists for him. But the man in the street, finding no worth in himself which corresponds to the force which built a tower or sculptured a marble god, feels poor when he looks on these. To him a palace, a statue, or a costly book have an alien and forbidding air, much like a gay equipage, and seem to say like that, "Who are you, Sir?" Yet they all are his, suitors for his notice, petitioners to his faculties that they will come out and take possession. The picture waits for my verdict: it is not to command me, but I am to settle its claims to praise. That popular fable of the sot who was picked up dead drunk in the street, carried to the duke's house, washed and dressed and laid in the duke's bed, and, on his waking, treated with all obsequious ceremony like the duke, and assured that he had been insane, owes its popularity to the fact, that it symbolizes so well the state of man, who is in the world a sort of sot, but now and then wakes up, exercises his reason and finds himself a true prince.

Our reading is mendicant and sycophantic. In history, our imagination plays us false. Kingdom and lordship, power and estate, are a gaudier vocabulary than private John and Edward in a small house and common day's work; but the things of life are the same to both; the sum total of both is the same. Why all this deference to Alfred, and Scanderbeg, and Gustavus? Suppose they were virtuous; did they wear out virtue? As great a stake depends on your private act to-day, as followed their public and renowned steps. When private men shall act with original views, the lustre will be transferred from the actions of kings to those of gentlemen.

The world has been instructed by its kings, who have so magnetized the eyes of nations. It has been taught by this colossal symbol the mutual reverence that is due from man to man. The joyful loyalty with which men have everywhere suffered the king, the noble, or the great proprietor to walk among them by a law of his own, make his own scale of men and things, and reverse theirs, pay for benefits not with money but with honor, and represent the law in his person, was the hiero-glyphic by which they obscurely signified their consciousness of their own right and comeliness, the right of every man.

The magnetism which all original action exerts is explained when we inquire the reason of self-trust. Who is the Trustee? What is the aboriginal Self, on which a universal reliance may be grounded? What is the nature and power of that science-baffling star, without parallax, without calculable elements, which shoots a ray of beauty even into trivial and impure actions, if the least mark of independence appear? The inquiry leads us to that source, at once the essence of genius, of virtue, and of life, which we call Spontaneity or Instinct. We denote this primary wisdom as Intuition, whilst all later teachings are tuitions. In that deep force, the last fact behind which analysis cannot go, all things find their common origin. For the sense of being which in calm hours rises, we know not how, in the soul, is not diverse from things, from space, from light, from time, from man, but one with them, and proceeds obviously from the same source whence their life and being also proceed. We first share the life by which things exist, and afterwards see them as appearances in nature, and forget that we have shared their cause. Here is the fountain of action and of thought. Here are the lungs of that inspiration which giveth man wisdom, and which cannot be denied without impiety and atheism. We lie in the lap of immense intelligence, which makes us receivers of its truth and organs of its activity. When we discern justice, when we discern truth, we do nothing of ourselves, but allow a passage to its beams. If we ask whence this comes, if we seek to pry into the soul that causes, all philosophy is at fault. Its presence or its absence is all we can affirm. Every man discriminates between the voluntary acts of his mind, and his involuntary perceptions, and knows that to his involuntary perceptions a perfect faith is due. He may err in the expression of them, but he knows that these things are so, like day and night, not to be disputed. My wilful actions and acquisitions are but roving;— the idlest reverie, the faintest native emotion, command my curiosity and respect. Thoughtless people contradict as readily the statement of perceptions as of opinions, or rather much more readily; for they do not distinguish between perception and notion. They fancy that I choose to see this or that thing. But perception is not whimsical, but fatal. If I see a trait, my children will see it after me, and in course of time, all mankind,—although it may chance that no one has seen it before me. For my perception of it is as much a fact as the sun.

The relations of the soul to the divine spirit are so pure, that it is profane to seek to interpose helps. It must be that when God speaketh he should communicate, not one thing, but all things; should fill the world with his voice; should scatter forth light, nature, time, souls, from the centre of the present thought; and new date and new create the whole. Whenever a mind is simple, and receives a divine wisdom, old things pass away,—means, teachers, texts, temples fall; it lives now, and absorbs past and future into the present hour. All things are made sacred by relation to it,—one as much as another. All things are dissolved to their centre by their cause, and, in the universal miracle, petty and particular miracles disappear. If, therefore, a man claims to know and speak of God, and carries you backward to the phraseology of some old mouldered nation in another country, in another world, believe him not. Is the acorn better than the oak which is its fulness and completion? Is the parent better than the child into whom he has cast his ripened being? Whence, then, this worship of the past? The centuries are conspirators against the sanity and authority of the soul. Time and space are but physiological colors which the eye makes, but the soul is light; where it is, is day; where it was, is night; and history is an impertinence and an injury, if it be any thing more than a cheerful apologue or parable of my being and becoming.

Man is timid and apologetic; he is no longer upright; he dares not say "I think," "I am," but quotes some saint or sage. He is ashamed before the blade of grass or the blowing rose. These roses under my window make no reference to former roses or to better ones; they are for what they are; they exist with God to-day. There is no time to them. There is simply the rose; it is perfect in every moment of its existence. Before a leaf-bud has burst, its whole life acts; in the full-blown flower there is no more; in the leafless root there is no less. Its nature is satisfied, and it satisfies nature, in all moments alike. But man postpones or remembers; he does not live in the present, but with reverted eye laments the past, or, heedless of the riches that surround him, stands on tiptoe to foresee the future. He cannot be happy and strong until he too lives with nature in the present, above time.

This should be plain enough. Yet see what strong intellects dare not yet hear God himself, unless he speak the phraseology of I know not what David, or Jeremiah, or Paul. We shall not always set so great a price on a few texts, on a few lives. We are like children who repeat by rote the sentences of grandames and tutors, and, as they grow older, of the men of talents and character they chance to see,—painfully recollecting the exact words they spoke; afterwards, when they come into the point of view which those had who uttered these sayings, they understand them, and are willing to let the words go; for, at any time, they can use words as good when occasion comes. If we live truly, we shall see truly. It is as easy for the strong man to be strong, as it is for the weak to be weak. When we have new perception, we shall gladly disburden the memory of its hoarded treasures as old rubbish. When a man lives with God, his voice shall be as sweet as the murmur of the brook and the rustle of the corn.

And now at last the highest truth on this subject remains unsaid; probably cannot be said; for all that we say is the far-off remembering of the intuition. That thought, by what I can now nearest approach to say it, is this. When good is near you, when you have life in yourself, it is not by any known or accustomed way; you shall not discern the foot-prints of any other; you shall not see the face of man; you shall not hear any name;—the way, the thought, the good, shall be wholly strange and new. It shall exclude example and experience. You take the way from man, not to man. All persons that ever existed are its forgotten ministers. Fear and hope are alike beneath it. There is somewhat low even in hope. In the hour of vision, there is nothing that can be called gratitude, nor properly joy. The soul raised over passion beholds identity and eternal causation, perceives the self-existence of Truth and Right, and calms itself with knowing that all things go well. Vast spaces of nature, the Atlantic Ocean, the South Sea,—long intervals of time, years, centuries,—are of no account. This which I think and feel underlay every former state of life and circumstances, as it does underlie my present, and what is called life, and what is called death.

Life only avails, not the having lived. Power ceases in the instant of repose; it resides in the moment of transition from a past to a new state, in the shooting of the gulf, in the darting to an aim. This one fact the world hates, that the soul *becomes;* for that for ever degrades the past, turns all riches to poverty, all reputation to a shame, confounds the saint with the rogue, shoves Jesus and Judas equally aside. Why, then, do we prate of self-reliance? Inasmuch as the soul is present, there will be power not confident but agent. To talk of reliance is a poor external way of speaking. Speak rather of that which relies, because it works and is. Who has more obedience than I masters me, though he should not raise his finger. Round him I must revolve by the gravitation of spirits. We fancy it rhetoric, when we speak of eminent virtue. We do not yet see that virtue is Height, and that a man or a company of men, plastic and permeable to principles, by the law of nature must overpower and ride all cities, nations, kings, rich men, poets, who are not.

This is the ultimate fact which we so quickly reach on this, as on every topic, the resolution of all into the ever-blessed ONE. Self-existence is the attribute of the Supreme Cause, and it constitutes the measure of good by the degree in which it enters into all lower forms. All things real are so by so much virtue as they contain. Commerce, husbandry, hunting, whaling, war, eloquence, personal weight, are somewhat, and engage my respect as examples of its presence and impure action. I see the same law working in nature for conservation and growth. Power is in nature the essential measure of right. Nature suffers nothing to remain in her kingdoms which cannot help itself. The genesis and maturation of a planet, its poise and orbit, the bended tree recovering itself from the strong wind, the vital resources of every animal and vegetable, are demonstrations of the self-sufficing, and therefore self-relying soul.

Thus all concentrates: let us not rove; let us sit at home with the cause. Let us stun and astonish the intruding rabble of men and books and institutions, by a simple declaration of the divine fact. Bid the invaders take the shoes from off their feet, for God is here within. Let our simplicity judge them, and our docility to our own law demonstrate the poverty of nature and fortune beside our native riches.

But now we are a mob. Man does not stand in awe of man, nor is his genius admonished to stay at home, to put itself in communication with the internal ocean, but it goes abroad to beg a cup of water of the urns of other men. We must go alone. I like the silent church before the service begins, better than any preaching. How far off, how cool, how chaste the persons look, begirt each one with a precinct or sanctuary! So let us always sit. Why should we assume the faults of our friend, or wife, or father, or child, because they sit around our hearth, or are said to have the same blood? All men have my blood, and I have all men's. Not for that will I adopt their petulance or folly, even to the extent of being ashamed of it. But your isolation must not be mechanical, but spiritual, that is, must be elevation. At times the whole world seems to be in conspiracy to importune you with emphatic trifles. Friend, client, child, sickness, fear, want, charity, all knock at once at thy closet door, and say,—"Come out unto us." But keep thy state; come not into their confusion. The power men possess to annoy me, I give them by a weak curiosity. No man can come near me but through my act. "What we love that we have, but by desire we bereave ourselves of the love."

If we cannot at once rise to the sanctities of obedience and faith, let us at least resist our temptations; let us enter into the state of war, and wake Thor and Woden, courage and constancy, in our Saxon breasts. This is to be done in our smooth times by speaking the truth. Check this lying hospitality and lying affection. Live no longer to the expectation of these deceived and deceiving people with whom we converse. Say to them, O father, O mother, O wife, O brother, O friend, I have lived with you after appearances hitherto. Henceforward I am the truth's. Be it known unto you that henceforward I obey no law less than the eternal law. I will have no covenants but proximities. I shall endeavour to nourish my parents, to support my family, to be the chaste husband of one wife,—but these relations I must fill after a new and unprecedented way. I appeal from your customs. I must be myself. I cannot break myself any longer for you, or you. If you can love me for what I am, we shall be the happier. If you cannot, I will still seek to deserve that you should. I will not hide my tastes or aversions. I will so trust that what is deep is holy, that I will do strongly before the sun and moon whatever inly rejoices me, and the heart appoints. If you are noble, I will love you; if you are not, I will not hurt you and myself by hypocritical attentions. If you are true, but not in the same truth with me, cleave to your companions; I will seek my own. I do this not self-ishly, but humbly and truly. It is alike your interest, and mine, and all men's, however long we have dwelt in lies, to live in truth. Does this sound harsh to-day? You will soon love what is dictated by your nature as well as mine, and, if we follow the truth, it will bring us out safe at last.—But so you may give these friends pain. Yes, but I cannot sell my liberty and my power, to save their sensibility. Besides, all persons have their moments of reason, when they look out into the region of absolute truth; then will they justify me, and do the same thing.

The populace think that your rejection of popular standards is a rejection of all standard, and mere antinomianism; and the bold sensu-alist will use the name of philosophy to gild his crimes. But the law of consciousness abides. There are two confessionals, in one or the other of which we must be shriven. You may fulfil your round of duties by clearing yourself in the *direct,* or in the *reflex* way. Consider whether you have satisfied your relations to father, mother, cousin, neighbour, town, cat, and dog; whether any of these can upbraid you. But I may also neglect this reflex standard, and absolve me to myself. I have my own stern claims and perfect circle. It denies the name of duty to many offices that are called duties. But if I can discharge its debts, it enables me to dispense with the popular code. If any one imagines that this law is lax, let him keep its commandment one day.

And truly it demands something godlike in him who has cast off the common motives of humanity, and has ventured to trust himself for a taskmaster. High be his heart, faithful his will, clear his sight, that he may in good earnest be doctrine, society, law, to himself, that a simple purpose may be to him as strong as iron necessity is to others!

If any man consider the present aspects of what is called by distinc-tion *society,* he will see the need of these ethics. The sinew and heart of man seem to be drawn out, and we are become timorous, desponding whimperers. We are afraid of truth, afraid of fortune, afraid of death, and afraid of each other. Our age yields no great and perfect persons. We want men and women who shall renovate life and our social state, but we see that most natures are insolvent, cannot satisfy their own wants, have an ambition out of all proportion to their practical force, and do lean and beg day and night continually. Our housekeeping is mendicant, our arts, our occupations, our marriages, our religion, we have not chosen, but society has chosen for us. We are parlour soldiers. We shun the rugged battle of fate, where strength is born.

If our young men miscarry in their first enterprises, they lose all heart. If the young merchant fails, men say he is *ruined*. If the finest genius studies at one of our colleges, and is not installed in an office within one year afterwards in the cities or suburbs of Boston or New York, it seems to his friends and to himself that he is right in being disheartened, and in complaining the rest of his life. A sturdy lad from New Hampshire or Vermont, who in turn tries all the professions, who *teams it, farms it, peddles,* keeps a school, preaches, edits a newspaper, goes to Congress, buys a township, and so forth, in successive years, and always, like a cat, falls on his feet, is worth a hundred of these city dolls. He walks abreast with his days, and feels no shame in not "studying a profession," for he does not postpone his life, but lives already. He has not one chance, but a hundred chances. Let a Stoic open the resources of man, and tell men they are not leaning willows, but can and must detach themselves; that with the exercise of self-trust, new powers shall appear; that a man is the word made flesh, born to shed healing to the nations, that he should be ashamed of our compassion, and that the moment he acts from himself, tossing the laws, the books, idolatries, and customs out of the window, we pity him no more, but thank and revere him,—and that teacher shall restore the life of man to splendor, and make his name dear to all history.

It is easy to see that a greater self-reliance must work a revolution in all the offices and relations of men; in their religion; in their education; in their pursuits; their modes of living; their association; in their property; in their speculative views.

1. In what prayers do men allow themselves! That which they call a

holy office is not so much as brave and manly. Prayer looks abroad and asks for some foreign addition to come through some foreign virtue, and loses itself in endless mazes of natural and supernatural, and mediatorial and miraculous. Prayer that craves a particular commodity,—any thing less than all good,—is vicious. Prayer is the contemplation of the facts of life from the highest point of view. It is the soliloquy of a beholding and jubilant soul. It is the spirit of God pronouncing his works good. But prayer as a means to effect a private end is meanness and theft. It supposes dualism and not unity in nature and consciousness. As soon as the man is at one with God, he will not beg. He will then see prayer in all action. The prayer of the farmer kneeling in his field to weed it, the prayer of the rower kneeling with the stroke of his oar, are true prayers heard throughout nature, though for cheap ends. Caratach, in Fletcher's *Bonduca,* when admonished to inquire the mind of the god Audate, replies,—

> "His hidden meaning lies in our endeavours;
> Our valors are our best gods."

Another sort of false prayers are our regrets. Discontent is the want of self-reliance: it is infirmity of will. Regret calamities, if you can thereby help the sufferer; if not, attend your own work, and already the evil begins to be repaired. Our sympathy is just as base. We come to them who weep foolishly, and sit down and cry for company, instead of imparting to them truth and health in rough electric shocks, putting them once more in communication with their own reason. The secret of fortune is joy in our hands. Welcome evermore to gods and men is the self-helping man. For him all doors are flung wide: him all tongues greet, all honors crown, all eyes follow with desire. Our love goes out to him and embraces him, because he did not need it. We solicitously and apologetically caress and celebrate him, because he held on his way and scorned our disapprobation. The gods love him because men hated him. "To the persevering mortal," said Zoroaster, "the blessed Immortals are swift."

As men's prayers are a disease of the will, so are their creeds a disease of the intellect. They say with those foolish Israelites, 'Let not God speak to us, lest we die. Speak thou, speak any man with us, and we will obey.' Everywhere I am hindered of meeting God in my brother, because he has shut his own temple doors, and recites fables merely of his brother's, or his brother's brother's God. Every new mind is a new classification. If it prove a mind of uncommon activity and power, a Locke, a Lavoisier, a Hutton, a Bentham, a Fourier, it imposes its classification on other men, and lo! a new system. In proportion to the depth of the thought, and so to the number of the objects it touches and brings within reach of the pupil, is his complacency. But chiefly is this apparent in creeds and churches, which are also classifications of some powerful mind acting on the elemental thought of duty, and man's relation to the Highest. Such is Calvinism, Quakerism, Swedenborgism. The pupil takes the same delight in subordinating every thing to the new terminology, as a girl who has just learned botany in seeing a new earth and new seasons thereby. It will happen for a time, that the pupil will find his intellectual power has grown by the study of his master's mind. But in all unbalanced minds, the classification is idolized, passes for the end, and not for a speedily exhaustible means, so that the walls of the system blend to their eye in the remote horizon with the walls of the universe; the luminaries of heaven seem to them hung on the arch their master built. They cannot imagine how you aliens have any right to see,—how you can see; 'It must be somehow that you stole the light from us.' They do not yet perceive, that light, unsystematic, indomitable, will break into any cabin, even into theirs. Let them chirp awhile and call it their own. If they are honest and do well, presently their neat new pinfold will be too strait and low, will crack, will lean, will rot and vanish, and the immortal light, all young and joyful, million-orbed, million-colored, will beam over the universe as on the first morning.

2. It is for want of self-culture that the superstition of Travelling, whose idols are Italy, England, Egypt, retains its fascination for all educated Americans. They who made England, Italy, or Greece venerable in the imagination did so by sticking fast where they were, like an axis of the earth. In manly hours, we feel that duty is our place. The soul is no traveller; the wise man stays at home, and when his necessities, his duties, on any occasion call him from his house, or into foreign lands, he is at home still, and shall make men sensible by the expression of his

countenance, that he goes the missionary of wisdom and virtue, and visits cities and men like a sovereign, and not like an interloper or a valet.

I have no churlish objection to the circumnavigation of the globe, for the purposes of art, of study, and benevolence, so that the man is first domesticated, or does not go abroad with the hope of finding somewhat greater than he knows. He who travels to be amused, or to get somewhat which he does not carry, travels away from himself, and grows old even in youth among old things. In Thebes, in Palmyra, his will and mind have become old and dilapidated as they. He carries ruins to ruins.

Travelling is a fool's paradise. Our first journeys discover to us the indifference of places. At home I dream that at Naples, at Rome, I can be intoxicated with beauty, and lose my sadness. I pack my trunk, embrace my friends, embark on the sea, and at last wake up in Naples, and there beside me is the stern fact, the sad self, unrelenting, identical, that I fled from. I seek the Vatican, and the palaces. I affect to be intoxicated with sights and suggestions, but I am not intoxicated. My giant goes with me wherever I go.

3. But the rage of travelling is a symptom of a deeper unsoundness affecting the whole intellectual action. The intellect is vagabond, and our system of education fosters restlessness. Our minds travel when our bodies are forced to stay at home. We imitate; and what is imitation but the travelling of the mind? Our houses are built with foreign taste; our shelves are garnished with foreign ornaments; our opinions, our tastes, our faculties, lean, and follow the Past and the Distant. The soul created the arts wherever they have flourished. It was in his own mind that the artist sought his model. It was an application of his own thought to the thing to be done and the conditions to be observed. And why need we copy the Doric or the Gothic model? Beauty, convenience, grandeur of thought, and quaint expression are as near to us as to any, and if the American artist will study with hope and love the precise thing to be done by him, considering the climate, the soil, the length of the day, the wants of the people, the habit and form of the government, he will create a house in which all these will find themselves fitted, and taste and sentiment will be satisfied also.

Insist on yourself; never imitate. Your own gift you can present every moment with the cumulative force of a whole life's cultivation; but of the adopted talent of another, you have only an extemporaneous, half possession. That which each can do best, none but his Maker can teach him. No man yet knows what it is, nor can, till that person has exhibited it. Where is the master who could have taught Shakespeare? Where is the master who could have instructed Franklin, or Washington, or Bacon, or Newton? Every great man is a unique. The Scipionism of Scipio is precisely that part he could not borrow. Shakespeare will never be made by the study of Shakespeare. Do that which is assigned you, and you cannot hope too much or dare too much. There is at this moment for you an utterance brave and grand as that of the colossal chisel of Phidias, or trowel of the Egyptians, or the pen of Moses, or Dante, but different from all these. Not possibly will the soul all rich, all eloquent, with thousand-cloven tongue, deign to repeat itself; but if you can hear what these patriarchs say, surely you can reply to them in the same pitch of voice; for the ear and the tongue are two organs of one nature. Abide in the simple and noble regions of thy life, obey thy heart, and thou shalt reproduce the Foreworld again.

4. As our Religion, our Education, our Art look abroad, so does our spirit of society. All men plume themselves on the improvement of society, and no man improves.

Society never advances. It recedes as fast on one side as it gains on the other. It undergoes continual changes; it is barbarous, it is civilized, it is christianized, it is rich, it is scientific; but this change is not amelioration. For every thing that is given, something is taken. Society acquires new arts, and loses old instincts. What a contrast between the well-clad, reading, writing, thinking American, with a watch, a pencil, and a bill of exchange in his pocket, and the naked New Zealander, whose property is a club, a spear, a mat, and an undivided twentieth of a shed to sleep under! But compare the health of the two men, and you shall see that the white man has lost his aboriginal strength. If the traveller tell us truly, strike the savage with a broad axe, and in a day or two the flesh shall unite and heal as if you struck the blow into soft pitch, and the same blow shall send the white to his grave.

The civilized man has built a coach, but has lost the use of his feet.

He is supported on crutches, but lacks so much support of muscle. He has a fine Geneva watch, but he fails of the skill to tell the hour by the sun. A Greenwich nautical almanac he has, and so being sure of the information when he wants it, the man in the street does not know a star in the sky. The solstice he does not observe; the equinox he knows as little; and the whole bright calendar of the year is without a dial in his mind. His note-books impair his memory; his libraries overload his wit; the insurance-office increases the number of accidents; and it may be a question whether machinery does not encumber; whether we have not lost by refinement some energy, by a Christianity entrenched in establishments and forms, some vigor of wild virtue. For every Stoic was a Stoic; but in Christendom where is the Christian?

There is no more deviation in the moral standard than in the standard of height or bulk. No greater men are now than ever were. A singular equality may be observed between the great men of the first and of the last ages; nor can all the science, art, religion, and philosophy of the nineteenth century avail to educate greater men than Plutarch's heroes, three or four and twenty centuries ago. Not in time is the race progressive. Phocion, Socrates, Anaxagoras, Diogenes, are great men, but they leave no class. He who is really of their class will not be called by their name, but will be his own man, and, in his turn, the founder of a sect. The arts and inventions of each period are only its costume, and do not invigorate men. The harm of the improved machinery may compensate its good. Hudson and Behring accomplished so much in their fishing-boats, as to astonish Parry and Franklin, whose equipment exhausted the resources of science and art. Galileo, with an opera-glass, discovered a more splendid series of celestial phenomena than any one since. Columbus found the New World in an undecked boat. It is curious to see the periodical disuse and perishing of means and machinery, which were introduced with loud laudation a few years or centuries before. The great genius returns to essential man. We reckoned the improvements of the art of war among the triumphs of science, and yet Napoleon conquered Europe by the bivouac, which consisted of falling back on naked valor, and disencumbering it of all aids. The Emperor held it impossible to make a perfect army, says Las Casas, "without abolishing our arms, magazines, commissaries, and carriages, until, in imitation of the Roman custom, the soldier should receive his supply of corn, grind it in his hand-mill, and bake his bread himself."

Society is a wave. The wave moves onward, but the water of which it is composed does not. The same particle does not rise from the valley to the ridge. Its unity is only phenomenal. The persons who make up a nation to-day, next year die, and their experience dies with them.

And so the reliance on Property, including the reliance on governments which protect it, is the want of self-reliance. Men have looked away from themselves and at things so long, that they have come to esteem the religious, learned, and civil institutions as guards of property, and they deprecate assaults on these, because they feel them to be assaults on property. They measure their esteem of each other by what each has, and not by what each is. But a cultivated man becomes ashamed of his property, out of new respect for his nature. Especially he hates what he has, if he see that it is accidental,—came to him by inheritance, or gift, or crime; then he feels that it is not having; it does not belong to him, has no root in him, and merely lies there, because no revolution or no robber takes it away. But that which a man is does always by necessity acquire, and what the man acquires is living property, which does not wait the beck of rulers, or mobs, or revolutions, or fire, or storm, or bankruptcies, but perpetually renews itself wherever the man breathes. "Thy lot or portion of life," said the Caliph Ali, "is seeking after thee; therefore be at rest from seeking after it." Our dependence on these foreign goods leads us to our slavish respect for numbers. The political parties meet in numerous conventions; the greater the concourse, and with each new uproar of announcement, The delegation from Essex! The Democrats from New Hampshire! The Whigs of Maine! the young patriot feels himself stronger than before by a new thousand of eyes and arms. In like manner the reformers summon conventions, and vote and resolve in multitude. Not so, O friends! will the God deign to enter and inhabit you, but by a method precisely the reverse. It is only as a man puts off all foreign support, and stands alone, that I see him to be strong and to prevail. He is weaker by every recruit to his banner. Is not a man better than a town? Ask nothing of men, and in the endless mutation, thou only firm column must presently appear the upholder of all that surrounds thee. He who knows that power is inborn, that he is weak because he has looked for good out of him and elsewhere, and so perceiving, throws himself unhesitatingly on his thought, instantly rights himself, stands in the erect position, commands his limbs, works miracles; just as a man who stands on his feet is stronger than a man who stands on his head.

So use all that is called Fortune. Most men gamble with her, and gain all, and lose all, as her wheel rolls. But do thou leave as unlawful these winnings, and deal with Cause and Effect, the chancellors of God. In the Will work and acquire, and thou hast chained the wheel of Chance, and shalt sit hereafter out of fear from her rotations. A political victory, a rise of rents, the recovery of your sick, or the return of your absent friend, or some other favorable event, raises your spirits, and you think good days are preparing for you. Do not believe it. Nothing can bring you peace but yourself. Nothing can bring you peace but the triumph of principles.

COMPENSATION

Ralph Waldo Emerson

Ralph Waldo Emerson's essay "Compensation," published in 1841, discusses an idea that is familiar to Latter-day Saints: "It must needs be, that there is an opposition in all things." (2 Nephi 2:11.) It also discusses what many Church leaders have called "The Law of the Harvest," which the Lord explained as follows: "Fear not to do good, . . . for whatsoever ye sow, that shall ye also reap; therefore, if ye sow good ye shall also reap good for your reward." (D&C 6:33.) The same principle is taught from a negative perspective in the book of Job: "They that plow iniquity, and sow wickedness, reap the same." (Job 4:8.) And the book of Ecclesiastes admonishes, "Cast thy bread upon the waters: for thou shalt find it after many days." (Ecclesiastes 11:1.) Finally, the Prophet Joseph Smith declared, "There is a law, irrevocably decreed in heaven before the foundations of this world, upon which all blessings are predicated—and when we obtain any blessing from God, it is by obedience to that law upon which it is predicated." (D&C 130:20–21.)

COMPENSATION

I

The wings of Time are black and white,
Pied with morning and with night.
Mountain tall and ocean deep
Trembling balance duly keep.
In changing moon and in tidal wave
Glows the feud of Want and Have.
Gauge of more and less through space,
Electric star or pencil plays,
The lonely Earth amid the balls
That hurry through the eternal halls,
A makeweight flying to the void,
Supplemental asteroid,
Or compensatory spark,
Shoots across the neutral Dark.

II

Man's the elm, and Wealth the vine;
Stanch and strong the tendrils twine:
Though the frail ringlets thee deceive,
None from its stock that vine can reave.
Fear not, then, thou child infirm,
There's no god dare wrong a worm;
Laurel crowns cleave to deserts,
And power to him who power exerts.
Hast not thy share? On winged feet,
Lo! it rushes thee to meet;
And all that Nature made thy own,
Floating in air or pent in stone,
Will rive the hills and swim the sea,
And, like thy shadow, follow thee.

Ever since I was a boy, I have wished to write a discourse on Compensation: for, it seemed to me when very young, that, on this subject, life was ahead of theology, and the people knew more than the preachers taught. The documents too, from which the doctrine is to be drawn, charmed my fancy by their endless variety, and lay always before me, even in sleep; for they are the tools in our hands, the bread in our basket, the transactions of the street, the farm, and the dwelling-house, the greetings, the relations, the debts and credits, the influence of character, the nature and endowment of all men. It seemed to me also that in it might be shown men a ray of divinity, the present action of the Soul of this world, clean from all vestige of tradition, and so the heart of man might be bathed by an inundation of eternal love, conversing with that which he knows was always and always must be, because it really is now. It appeared, moreover, that if this doctrine could be stated in terms with any resemblance to those bright intuitions in which this truth is sometimes revealed to us, it would be a star in many dark hours and crooked passages in our journey that would not suffer us to lose our way.

I was lately confirmed in these desires by hearing a sermon at church. The preacher, a man esteemed for his orthodoxy, unfolded in the ordinary manner the doctrine of the Last Judgment. He assumed that judgment is not executed in this world; that the wicked are successful; that the good are miserable; and then urged from reason and from Scripture a compensation to be made to both parties in the next life. No offense appeared to be taken by the congregation at this doctrine. As far as I could observe, when the meeting broke up, they separated without remark on the sermon.

Yet what was the import of this teaching? What did the preacher mean by saying that the good are miserable in the present life? Was it that houses and lands, offices, wine, horses, dress, luxury, are had by unprincipled men, while the saints are poor and despised; and that a compensation is to be made to these last hereafter, by giving them the like gratifications another day, bank-stock and doubloons, venison and champagne? This must be the compensation intended; for, what else? Is it that they are to have leave to pray and praise, to love and serve men? Why, that they can do now. The legitimate inference the disciple would draw, was: "We are to have *such* a good time as the sinners have now;" or, to push it to its extreme import, "You sin now; we shall sin by-and-by; we would sin now, if we could; not being successful, we expect our revenge to-morrow."

The fallacy lay in the immense concession that the bad are successful; that justice is not done now. The blindness of the preacher consisted in deferring to the base estimate of the market of what constitutes a manly success, instead of confronting and convicting the world from the truth; announcing the presence of the Soul; the omnipotence of the Will: and so establishing the standard of good and ill, of success and falsehood, and summoning the dead to its present tribunal.

I find a similar base tone in the popular religious works of the day, and the same doctrines assumed by the literary men when occasionally they treat the related topics. I think that our popular theology has gained in decorum, and not in principle, over the superstitions it has displaced. But men are better than this theology. Their daily life gives it the lie. Every ingenuous and aspiring soul leaves the doctrine behind him in his own experience; and all men feel sometimes the falsehood which they cannot demonstrate. For men are wiser than they know. That which they hear in schools and pulpits without after/thought, if said in conversation, would probably be questioned in silence. If a man dogmatize in a mixed company on Providence and the divine laws, he is answered by a silence which conveys well enough to an observer the dissatisfaction of the hearer, but his incapacity to make his own statement.

I shall attempt in this and the following chapter to record some facts that indicate the path of the law of Compensation; happy beyond my expectation, if I shall truly draw the smallest arc of this circle.

POLARITY, or action and reaction, we meet in every part of nature; in darkness and light; in heat and cold; in the ebb and flow of waters; in male and female; in the inspiration and expiration of plants and animals; in the systole and diastole of the heart; in the undulations of fluids, and of sound; in the centrifugal and centripetal gravity; in electricity, galvanism and chemical affinity. Superinduce magnetism at one end of a needle; the opposite magnetism takes place at the other end. If the south attracts, the north repels. To empty here, you must condense there. An inevitable dualism bisects nature, so that each thing is a half, and suggests another thing to make it whole; as, spirit, matter; man, woman; subjective, objective; in, out; upper, under; motion, rest; yea, nay.

Whilst the world is thus dual, so is every one of its parts. The entire system of things gets represented in every particle. There is somewhat that resembles the ebb and flow of the sea, day and night, man and woman, in a single needle of the pine, in a kernel of corn, in each individual of every animal tribe. The reaction so grand in the elements, is repeated within these small boundaries. For example, in the animal kingdom, the physiologist has observed that no creatures are favorites, but a certain compensation balances every gift and every defect. A surplusage given to one part is paid out of a reduction from another part of the same creature. If the head and neck are enlarged, the trunk and extremities are cut short.

The theory of the mechanic forces is another example. What we gain in power is lost in time; and the converse. The periodic or compensating errors of the planets, is another instance. The influences of climate and soil in political history are another. The cold climate invigorates. The barren soil does not breed fevers, crocodiles, tigers or scorpions.

The same dualism underlies the nature and condition of man. Every excess causes a defect; every defect an excess. Every sweet hath its sour; every evil its good. Every faculty which is a receiver of pleasure has an equal penalty put on its abuse. It is to answer for its moderation with its life. For every grain of wit there is a grain of folly. For everything you have missed, you have gained something else; and for everything you gain, you lose something. If riches increase, they are increased that use them. If the gatherer gathers too much, nature takes out of the man what she puts into his chest; swells the estate, but kills the owner. Nature hates monopolies and exceptions. The waves of the sea do not more speedily seek a level from their loftiest tossing, than the varieties of condition tend to equalize themselves. There is always some leveling circumstance that puts down the overbearing, the strong, the rich, the fortunate, substantially on the same ground with all others. Is a man too strong and fierce for society, and by temper and position a bad citizen, a morose ruffian with a dash of the pirate in him; nature sends him a troop of pretty sons and daughters who are getting along in the dame's classes at the village school, and love and fear for them smooths his grim scowl to courtesy. Thus she contrives to intenerate the granite and felspar, takes the boar out and puts the lamb in, and keeps her balance true.

The farmer imagines power and place are fine things. But the President has paid dear for his White House. It has commonly cost him all his peace and the best of his manly attributes. To preserve for a short time so conspicuous an appearance before the world, he is content to eat dust before the real masters who stand erect behind the throne. Or, do men desire the more substantial and permanent grandeur of genius? Neither has this an immunity. He who by force of will or of thought is great, and overlooks thousands, has the responsibility of overlooking. With every influx of light, comes new danger. Has he light? he must bear witness to the light, and always outrun that sympathy which gives him such keen satisfaction, by his fidelity to new revelations of the incessant soul. He must hate father and mother, wife and child. Has he all that the world loves and admires and covets? he must cast behind him their admiration, and afflict them by faithfulness to his truth, and become a by-word and a hissing.

This Law writes the laws of cities and nations. It will not be balked of its end in the smallest iota. It is in vain to build or plot or combine against it. Things refuse to be mismanaged long. *Res nolunt diu male administrari.* Though no checks to a new evil appear, the checks exist, and will appear. If the government is cruel, the governor's life is not safe. If you tax too high, the revenue will yield nothing. If you make the criminal code sanguinary, juries will not convict. Nothing arbitrary, nothing artificial can endure. The true life and satisfactions of man seem to elude the utmost rigors or felicities of condition, and to establish themselves with great indifference under all varieties of circumstances. Under all governments the influence of character remains the same—in Turkey and in New England about alike. Under the primeval despots of

Egypt, history honestly confesses that man must have been as free as culture could make him.

These appearances indicate the fact that the universe is represented in every one of its particles. Everything in nature contains all the powers of nature. Everything is made of one hidden stuff; as the naturalist sees one type under every metamorphosis, and regards a horse as a running man, a fish as a swimming man, a bird as a flying man, a tree as a rooted man. Each new form repeats not only the main character of the type, but part for part all the details, all the aims, furtherances, hindrances, energies, and whole system of every other. Every occupation, trade, art, transaction, is a compend of the world, and a correlative of every other. Each one is an entire emblem of human life; of its good and ill, its trials, its enemies, its course and its end. And each one must somehow accommodate the whole man, and recite all his destiny.

The world globes itself in a drop of dew. The microscope cannot find the animalcule which is less perfect for being little. Eyes, ears, taste, smell, motion, resistance, appetite, and organs of reproduction that take hold on eternity, all find room to consist in the small creature. So do we put our life into every act. The true doctrine of omnipresence is, that God reappears with all his parts in every moss and cobweb. The value of the universe contrives to throw itself into every point. If the good is there, so is the evil; if the affinity, so the repulsion; if the force, so the limitation.

Thus is the universe alive. All things are moral. That soul which within us is a sentiment, outside of us is a law. We feel its inspirations; out there in history we can see its fatal strength. It is almighty. All nature feels its grasp. "It is in the world and the world was made by it." It is eternal, but it enacts itself in time and space. Justice is not postponed. A perfect equity adjusts its balance in all parts of life. *Oi chusoi Dios aei enpiptousi.* The dice of God are always loaded. The world looks like a multiplication-table or a mathematical equation, which, turn it how you will, balances itself. Take what figure you will, its exact value, no more nor less, still returns to you. Every secret is told, every crime is punished, every virtue rewarded, every wrong redressed, in silence and certainty. What we call retribution is the universal necessity by which the whole appears wherever a part appears. If you see smoke, there must be fire. If you see a hand or a limb, you know that the trunk to which it belongs, is there behind.

Every act rewards itself, or, in other words, integrates itself in a twofold manner; first, in the thing, or, in real nature; and secondly, in the circumstance, or, in apparent nature. Men call the circumstance the retribution. The causal retribution is in the thing, and is seen by the soul. The retribution in the circumstance, is seen by the understanding; it is inseparable from the thing, but is often spread over a long time, and so does not become distinct until after many years. The specific stripes may follow late after the offense, but they follow because they accompany it. Crime and punishment grow out of one stem. Punishment is a fruit that unsuspected ripens within the flower of the pleasure which concealed it. Cause and effect, means and ends, seed and fruit, cannot be severed; for the effect already blooms in the cause, the end pre-exists in the means, the fruit in the seed.

Whilst thus the world will be whole, and refuses to be disparted, we seek to act partially; to sunder; to appropriate; for example, to gratify the senses, we sever the pleasure of the senses from the needs of the character. The ingenuity of man has been dedicated always to the solution of one problem—how to detach the sensual sweet, the sensual strong, the sensual bright, etc., from the moral sweet, the moral deep, the moral fair; that is, again, to contrive to cut clean off this upper surface so thin as to leave it bottomless; to get a *one end,* without an *other end.* The soul says, Eat; the body would feast. The soul says, The man and woman shall be one flesh and one soul; the body would join the flesh only. The soul says, Have dominion over all things to the ends of virtue; the body would have the power over things to its own ends.

The soul strives amain to live and work through all things. It would be the only fact. All things shall be added unto it—power, pleasure, knowledge, beauty. The particular man aims to be somebody; to set up for himself; to truck and higgle for a private good; and, in particulars, to ride; that he may ride; to dress, that he may be dressed; to eat, that he may eat; and to govern that he may be seen. Men seek to be great; they would have offices, wealth, power and fame. They think that to be great is to possess one side of nature—the sweet, without the other side, the bitter.

Steadily this dividing and detaching is counteracted. Up to this day, it must be owned, no projector has had the smallest success. The parted water reunites behind our hand. Pleasure is taken out of pleasant things, profit out of profitable things, power out of strong things, as soon as we seek to separate them from the whole. We can no more halve things and get the sensual good, by itself, than we can get an inside that shall have no outside, or a light without a shadow. "Drive out nature with a fork, she comes running back."

Life invests itself with inevitable conditions, which the unwise seek to dodge, which one and another brags that he does not know; brags that they do not touch him—but the brag is on his lips, the conditions are in his soul. If he escapes them in one part; they attack him in another more vital part. If he has escaped them in form, and in the appearance, it is because he has resisted his life, and fled from himself, and the retribution is so much death. So signal is the failure of all attempts to make this separation of the good from the tax, that the experiment would not be tried—since to try is to be mad—but for the circumstance, that when the disease began in the will, of rebellion and separation, the intellect is at once infected, so that the man ceases to see God whole in each object, but is able to see the sensual allurement of an object, and not see the sensual hurt; he sees the mermaid's head, but not the dragon's tail; and thinks he can cut off that which he would have, from that which he would not have. "How secret art thou who dwellest in the highest heavens in silence, O thou only great God, sprinkling with an unwearied Providence certain penal blindnesses upon such as have unbridled desires!"

The human soul is true to these facts in the painting of fable, of history, of law, of proverbs, of conversation. It finds a tongue in literature unawares. Thus the Greeks called Jupiter, Supreme Mind; but having traditionally ascribed to him many base actions, they involuntarily made amends to Reason, by tying up the hands of so bad a god. He is made as helpless as a king of England. Prometheus knows one secret, which

Jove must bargain for; Minerva, another. He cannot get his own thunders; Minerva keeps the key of them.

> *"Of all the gods, I only know the keys*
> *That ope the solid doors within whose vaults*
> *His thunders sleep."*

A plain confession of the in-working of the All, and of its moral aim. The Indian mythology ends in the same ethics; and it would seem impossible for any fable to be invented and get any currency which was not moral. Aurora forgot to ask youth for her lover, and so though Tithonus is immortal, he is old. Achilles is not quite invulnerable; for Thetis held him by the heel when she dipped him in the Styx, and the sacred waters did not wash that part. Siegfried in the Nibelungen, is not quite immortal, for a leaf fell on his back while he was bathing in the Dragon's blood, and that spot which it covered is mortal. And so it always is. There is a crack in everything God has made. Always, it would seem, there is this vindictive circumstance stealing in at unawares, even into the wild poesy in which the human fancy attempted to make bold holiday, and to shake itself free of the old laws—this back-stroke, this kick of the gun, certifying that the law is fatal; that in Nature, nothing can be given, all things are sold.

This is that ancient doctrine of Nemesis, who keeps watch in the Universe, and lets no offense go unchastised. The Furies, they said, are attendants on Justice, and if the sun in heaven should transgress his path, they would punish him. The poets related that stone walls, and iron swords, and leathern thongs had an occult sympathy with the wrongs of their owners; that the belt which Ajax gave Hector, dragged the Trojan hero over the field at the wheels of the car of Achilles; and the sword which Hector gave Ajax, was that on whose point Ajax fell. They recorded that when the Thasians erected a statue to Theogenes, a victor in the games, one of his rivals went to it by night, and endeavored to throw it down by repeated blows, until at last he moved it from its pedestal and was crushed to death beneath its fall.

This voice of fable has in it somewhat divine. It came from thought above the will of the writer. That is the best part of each writer, which has nothing private in it. That is the best part of each, which he does not know; that which flowed out of his constitution, and not from his too active invention; that which in the study of a single artist you might not easily find, but in the study of many, you would abstract as the spirit of them all. Phidias it is not, but the work of man in that early Hellenic world, that I would know. The name and circumstance of Phidias, however convenient for history, embarrasses when we come to the highest criticism. We are to see that which man was tending to do in a given period, and was hindered, or, if you will, modified in doing, by the interfering volitions of Phidias, of Dante, of Shakespeare, the organ whereby man at the moment wrought.

Still more striking is the expression of this fact in the proverbs of all nations, which are always the literature of Reason, or the statements of an absolute truth, without qualification. Proverbs, like the sacred books of each nation, are the sanctuary of the Intuitions. That which the drowning world, chained to appearances, will not allow the realist to say in his own words, it will suffer him to say in proverbs without contradiction. And this law of laws which the pulpit, the senate and the college deny, is hourly preached in all markets and all languages by flights of proverbs, whose teaching is as true and as omnipresent as that of birds and flies.

All things are double, one against another. Tit for tat; an eye for an eye; a tooth for a tooth; blood for blood; measure for measure; love for love. Give and it shall be given you.—He that watereth shall be watered himself. What will you have? quoth God; pay for it and take it. Nothing venture, nothing have. Thou shalt be paid exactly for what thou hast done, no more, no less. Who doth not work shall not eat. Harm watch, harm catch. Curses always recoil on the head of him who imprecates them. If you put a chain around the neck of a slave, the other end fastens itself around your own. Bad counsel confounds the adviser. The devil is an ass.

It is thus written, because it is thus in life. Our action is overmastered and characterized above our will by the law of nature. We aim at a petty end quite aside from the public good, but our act arranges itself by irresistible magnetism in a line with the poles of the world.

A man cannot speak but he judges himself. With his will, or against his will, he draws his portrait to the eye of his companions by every word. Every opinion reacts on him who utters it. It is a thread-ball thrown at a mark, but the other end remains in the thrower's bag. Or, rather, it is a harpoon hurled at the whale, unwinding, as it flies, a coil of cord in the boat, and if the harpoon is not good, or not well thrown, it will go nigh to cut the steersman in twain, or to sink the boat.

You cannot do wrong without suffering wrong. "No man had ever a point of pride that was not injurious to him," said Burke. The exclusive in fashionable life does not see that he excludes himself from enjoyment, in the attempt to appropriate it. The exclusionist in religion does not see that he shuts the door of heaven on himself, in striving to shut out others. Treat men as pawns and ninepins, and you shall suffer as well as they. If you leave out their heart, you shall lose your own. The senses would make things of all persons; of women, of children, of the poor. The vulgar proverb, "I will get it from his purse or get it from his skin," is sound philosophy.

All infractions of love and equity in our social relations are speedily punished. They are punished by Fear. While I stand in simple relations to my fellow man, I have no displeasure in meeting him. We meet as water meets water, or a current of air meets another, with perfect diffusion and interpenetration of nature. But as soon as there is any departure from simplicity, and attempt at halfness, or good for me that is not good for him, my neighbor feels the wrong; he shrinks from me as far as I have shrunk from him; his eyes no longer seek mine; there is war between us; there is hate in him, and fear in me.

All these old abuses in society, the great and universal, and the petty and particular, all unjust accumulations of property and power, are avenged in the same manner. Fear is an instructor of great sagacity, and the herald of all revolutions. One thing he always teaches, that there is rottenness where he appears. He is a carrion crow, and though you see not well what he hovers for, there is death somewhere. Our property is timid, our laws are timid, our cultivated classes are timid. Fear for ages has boded, and mowed, and gibbered over our government and property. That obscene bird is not there for nothing. He indicates great wrongs which must be revised.

Of the like nature is that expectation of change which instantly follows the suspension of our voluntary activity. The terror of cloudless noon, the emerald of Polycrates, the awe of prosperity, the instinct which leads every generous soul to impose on itself tasks of a noble asceticism and vicarious virtue, are the tremblings of the balance of justice through the heart and mind of man.

Experienced men of the world know very well that it is best to pay scot and lot as they go along, and that a man often pays dear for a small frugality. The borrower runs in his own debt. Has a man gained anything who has received a hundred favors and rendered none? Has he gained by borrowing, through indolence or cunning, his neighbor's wares, or horses, or money? There arises on the deed the instant acknowledgment of benefit on the one part, and of debt on the other; that is, of superiority and inferiority. The transaction remains in the memory of himself and his neighbor; and every new transaction alters, according to its nature, their relation to each other. He may soon come to see that he had better have broken his own bones than to have ridden in his neighbor's coach, and that "the highest price he can pay for a thing is to ask for it."

A wise man will extend this lesson to all parts of life, and know that it is always the part of prudence to face every claimant, and pay every just demand on your time, your talents, or your heart. Always pay; for, first or last, you must pay your entire debt. Persons and events may stand for a time between you and justice, but it is only a postponement. You must pay at last your own debt. If you are wise you will dread a prosperity which only loads you with more. Benefit is the end of nature. But for every benefit which you receive, a tax is levied. He is great who confers the most benefits. He is base—and that is the one base thing in the universe—to receive favors and render none. In the order of nature we cannot render benefits to those from whom we receive them, or only seldom. But the benefit we receive must be rendered again, line for line, deed for deed, cent for cent, to somebody. Beware of too much good staying in your hand. It will fast corrupt and worm worms. Pay it away quickly in some sort.

Labor is watched over by the same pitiless laws. Cheapest, say the prudent, is the dearest labor. What we buy in a broom, a mat, a wagon, a knife, is some application of good sense to a common want. It is best to pay in your land a skilful gardener, or to buy good sense applied to gardening; in your sailor, good sense applied to navigation; in the house, good sense applied to cooking, sewing, serving; in your agent, good sense applied to accounts and affairs. So do you multiply your presence, or spread yourself throughout your estate. But because of the dual constitution of all things, in labor as in life there can be no cheating. The thief steals from himself. The swindler swindles himself. For the real price of labor is knowledge and virtue, whereof wealth and credit are signs. These signs, like paper-money, may be counterfeited or stolen, but that which they represent, namely, knowledge and virtue, cannot be counterfeited or stolen. These ends of labor cannot be answered but by real exertions of the mind, and in obedience to pure motives. The cheat, the defaulter, the gambler cannot extort the benefit, cannot extort the knowledge of material and moral nature which his honest care and pains yield to the operative. The law of nature is, Do the thing, and you shall have the power: but they who do not the thing have not the power.

Human labor, through all its forms, from the sharpening of a stake to the construction of a city or an epic, is one immense illustration of the perfect compensation of the universe. Everywhere and always this law is sublime. The absolute balance of Give and Take, the doctrine that every thing has its price; and if that price is not paid, not that thing but something else is obtained, and that it is impossible to get anything without its price, this doctrine is not less sublime in the columns of a ledger than in the budgets of states, in the laws of light and darkness, in all the action and reaction of nature. I cannot doubt that the high laws which each man sees ever implicated in those processes with which he is conversant, the stern ethics which sparkle on his chisel-edge, which are measured out by his plumb and foot-rule, which stand as manifest in the footing of the shop-bill as in the history of a state, do recommend to him his trade, and though seldom named, exalt his business to his imagination.

The league between virtue and nature engages all things to assume a hostile front to vice. The beautiful laws and substances of the world persecute and whip the traitor. He finds that things are arranged for truth and benefit, but there is no den in the wide world to hide a rogue. There is no such thing as concealment. Commit a crime, and the earth is made of glass. Commit a crime, and it seems as if a coat of snow fell on the ground, such as reveals in the woods the track of every partridge and fox and squirrel and mole. You cannot recall the spoken word, you cannot wipe out the foot-track, you cannot draw up the ladder, so as to leave no inlet or clew. Always some damning circumstance transpires. The laws and substances of nature, water, snow, wind, gravitation, become penalties to the thief.

On the other hand, the law holds with equal sureness for all right action. Love, and you shall be loved. All love is mathematically just, as much as the two sides of an algebraic equation. The good man has absolute good, which like fire turns every thing to its own nature, so that you cannot do him any harm; but as the royal armies sent against Napoleon, when he approached, cast down their colors and from enemies became friends, so do disasters of all kinds, as sickness, offense, poverty, prove benefactors.

> *"Winds blow and waters roll*
> *Strength to the brave, and power and deity.*
> *Yet in themselves are nothing."*

The good are befriended even by weakness and defect. As no man had ever a point of pride that was not injurious to him, so no man had ever a defect that was not somewhere made useful to him. The stag in the fable admired his horns and blamed his feet, but when the hunter came, his feet saved him, and afterwards, caught in the thicket, his horns destroyed him. Every man in his lifetime needs to thank his faults. As no man thoroughly understands a truth until at first he has contended against it, so no man has a thorough acquaintance with the hindrances or talents of men, until he has suffered from the one, and seen the triumph of the other over his own want of the same. Has he a defect of temper that unfits him to live in society? Thereby he is driven to entertain himself alone, and acquire habits of self-help; and thus, like the wounded oyster, he mends his shell with pearl.

Our strength grows out of our weakness. Not until we are pricked and stung and sorely shot at, awakens the indignation which arms itself with secret forces. A great man is always willing to be little. While he sits on the cushion of advantages, he goes to sleep. When he is pushed, tormented, defeated, he has a chance to learn something; he has been put on his wits, on his manhood; he has gained facts; learns his ignorance; is cured of the insanity of conceit; has got moderation and real skill. The wise man always throws himself on the side of his assailants. It is more his interest than it is theirs to find his weak point. The wound cicatrizes and falls off from him, like a dead skin, and when they would triumph, lo! he has passed on invulnerable. Blame is safer than praise. I hate to be defended in a newspaper. As long as all that is said, is said against me, I feel a certain assurance of success. But as soon as honeyed words of praise are spoken for me, I feel as one that lies unprotected before his enemies. In general, every evil to which we do not succumb, is a benefactor. As the Sandwich Islander believes that the strength and valor of the enemy he kills, passes into himself, so we gain the strength of the temptation we resist.

The same guards which protect us from disaster, defect, and enmity, defend us, if we will, from selfishness and fraud. Bolts and bars are not the best of our institutions, nor is shrewdness in trade a mark of wisdom. Men suffer all their life long, under the foolish superstition that they can be cheated. But it is as impossible for a man to be cheated by any one but himself, as for a thing to be, and not to be, at the same time. There is a third silent party to all our bargains. The nature and soul of things takes on itself the guarantee of the fulfilment of every contract, so that honest service cannot come to loss. If you serve an ungrateful master, serve him the more. Put God in your debt. Every stroke shall be repaid. The longer the payment is withholden, the better for you; for compound interest on compound interest is the rate and usage of this exchequer.

The history of persecution is a history of endeavors to cheat nature, to make water run up hill, to twist a rope of sand. It makes no difference whether the actors be many or one, a tyrant or a mob. A mob is a society of bodies voluntarily bereaving themselves of reason and traversing its work. The mob is man voluntarily descending to the nature of the beast. Its fit hour of activity is night. Its actions are insane like its whole constitution. It persecutes a principle; it would whip a right; it would tar and feather justice, by inflicting fire and outrage upon the houses and persons of those who have these. It resembles the prank of boys who run with fire-engines to put out the ruddy aurora streaming to the stars. The inviolate spirit turns their spite against the wrong doers. The martyr cannot be dishonored. Every lash inflicted is a tongue of fame; every prison a more illustrious abode; every burned book or house enlightens the world; every suppressed or expunged word reverberates through the earth from side to side. The minds of men are at last aroused; reason looks out and justifies her own, and malice finds all her work vain. It is the whipper who is whipped, and the tyrant who is undone.

Thus do all things preach the indifferency of circumstances. The man is all. Everything has two sides, a good and an evil. Every advantage has its tax. I learn to be content. But the doctrine of compensation is not the doctrine of indifferency. The thoughtless say, on hearing these representations—What boots it to do well? there is one event to good and evil; if I gain any good, I must pay for it; if I lose any good, I gain some other; all actions are indifferent.

There is a deeper fact in the soul than compensation, to-wit, its own nature. The soul is not a compensation, but a life. The soul *is*. Under all this running sea of circumstance, whose waters ebb and flow with perfect balance, lies the aboriginal abyss of real Being. Essence, or God, is not a relation, or a part, but the whole. Being is the vast affirmative, excluding negation, self-balanced, and swallowing up all relations, parts and times within itself. Nature, truth, virtue are the influx from thence. Vice is the absence or departure of the same. Nothing, Falsehood, may indeed stand as the great Night or shade, on which, as a background, the living universe paints itself forth; but no fact is begotten by it; it cannot work; for it is not. It cannot work any good; it cannot work any harm. It is harm inasmuch as it is worse not to be than to be.

We feel defrauded of the retribution due to evil acts, because the criminal adheres to his vice and contumacy, and does not come to a crisis or judgment anywhere in visible nature. There is no stunning confutation of his nonsense before men and angels. Has he therefore outwitted the law? Inasmuch as he carries the malignity and the lie with him, he so far deceases from nature. In some manner there will be a demonstration of the wrong to the understanding also; but should we not see it, this deadly deduction makes square the eternal account.

Neither can it be said, on the other hand, that the gain of rectitude must be bought by any loss. There is no penalty to virtue; no penalty to wisdom; they are proper additions of being. In a virtuous action, I properly *am;* in a virtuous act, I add to the world; I plant into deserts conquered from Chaos and Nothing, and see the darkness receding on the limits of the horizon. There can be no excess to love; none to knowledge; none to beauty, when these attributes are considered in the purest sense. The soul refuses all limits. It affirms in man always an Optimism, never a Pessimism.

His life is a progress, and not a station. His instinct is trust. Our instinct uses "more" and "less" in application to man, always of the *presence of the soul,* and not of its absence; the brave man is greater than the coward; the true, the benevolent, the wise, is more a man, and not less, than the fool and knave. There is, therefore, no tax on the good of virtue; for, that is the incoming of God himself, or absolute existence, without any comparative. Material good has its tax, and if it came without desert or sweat, has no root in me and the next wind will blow it away. But all the good of nature is the soul's and may be had, if paid for in nature's lawful coin, that is, by labor which the heart and the head allow. I no longer wish to meet a good I do not earn; for example, to find a pot of buried gold, knowing that it brings with it new responsibility. I do not wish more external goods—neither possessions, nor honors, nor powers, nor persons. The gain is apparent: the tax is certain. But there is no tax on the knowledge that the compensation exists, and that it is not desirable to dig up treasure. Herein I rejoice with a serene eternal peace. I contract the boundaries of possible mischief. I learn the wisdom of St. Bernard, "Nothing can work me damage except myself; the harm that I sustain, I carry about with me, and never am a real sufferer but by my own fault."

In the nature of the soul is the compensation for the inequalities of condition. The radical tragedy of nature seems to be the distinction of More and Less. How can Less not feel the pain; how not feel indignation or malevolence toward More? Look at those who have less faculty, and one feels sad, and knows not well what to make of it. Almost he shuns their eye; almost he fears they will upbraid God. What should they do? It seems a great injustice. But face the facts, and see them nearly, and these mountainous inequalities vanish. Love reduces them all, as the sun melts the iceberg in the sea. The heart and soul of all men being one, this bitterness of *His* and *Mine* ceases. His is mine. I am my brother, and my brother is me. If I feel overshadowed and outdone by great neighbors, I can yet love; I can still receive; and he that loveth, maketh his own the grandeur he loves. Thereby I make the discovery that my brother is my guardian, acting for me with the friendliest designs, and the estate I so admired and envied, is my own. It is the nature of the soul to appropriate and make all things its own. Jesus and Shakespeare are fragments of the soul, and by love I conquer and incorporate them in my own conscious domain. His virtue—is not that mine? His wit—if it cannot be made mine, it is not wit.

Such, also, is the natural history of calamity. The changes which break up at short intervals the prosperity of men, are advertisements of a nature whose law is growth. Evermore it is the order of nature to grow, and every soul is by this intrinsic necessity quitting its whole system of things, its friends, and home, and laws, and faith, as the shell-fish crawls out of its beautiful but stony case, because it no longer admits of its growth, and slowly forms a new house. In proportion to the vigor of the individual, these revolutions are frequent, until in some happier mind they are incessant, and all worldly relations hang very loosely about him, becoming, as it were, a transparent fluid membrane through which the living form is always seen, and not as in most men an indurated heterogeneous fabric of many dates, and of no settled character, in which the man is imprisoned. Then there can be enlargement, and the man of to-day scarcely recognizes the man of yesterday. And such should be the outward biography of man in time, a putting off of dead circumstances day by day. But to us, in our lapsed estate, resting not advancing, resisting, not cooperating with the divine expansion, this growth comes by shocks.

We cannot part with our friends. We cannot let our angels go. We do not see that they only go out, that archangels may come in. We are idolaters of the old. We do not believe in the riches of the soul, in its proper eternity and omnipresence. We do not believe there is any force in to-day to rival or recreate that beautiful yesterday. We linger in the ruins of the old tent, where once we had bread and shelter and organs, nor believe that the spirit can feed, cover and nerve us again. We cannot again find aught so dear, so sweet, so graceful. But we sit and weep in vain. The voice of the Almighty saith, 'Up and onward for evermore!' We cannot stay amid the ruins. Neither will we rely on the New; and so we walk ever with reverted eyes, like those monsters who look backwards.

And yet the compensations of calamity are made apparent to the understanding also, after long intervals of time. A fever, a mutilation, a cruel disappointment, a loss of wealth, a loss of friends seems at the moment unpaid loss, and unpayable. But the sure years reveal the deep remedial force that underlies all facts. The death of a dear friend, wife, brother, lover, which seemed nothing but privation, somewhat later assumes the aspect of a guide or genius; for it commonly operates revolutions in our way of life, terminates an epoch of infancy or of youth which was waiting to be closed, breaks up a wonted occupation, or a household, or style of living, and allows the formation of new ones more friendly to the growth of character. It permits or constrains the formation of new acquaintances, and the reception of new influences that prove of the first importance to the next years; and the man or woman who would have remained a sunny garden flower, with no room for its roots and too much sunshine for its head, by the falling of the walls and the neglect of the gardener, is made the banyan of the forest, yielding shade and fruit to wide neighborhoods of men.

THE GREATEST THING IN THE WORLD

Henry Drummond

Henry Drummond was born at Stirling, near Edinburgh, Scotland, in 1851. Even as a child he had a spiritual disposition, which was nourished by his family's strong religious influence. His uncle, Peter Drummond, founded the Stirling Tract Company, which published millions of copies of religious pamphlets.

Drummond later studied at the University of Edinburgh and became a lecturer on natural science in the Free Church College at Glasgow. Concerned about the influence of Darwin's theory of evolution on religious life, he gave a series of addresses that were published in 1883 in his book *Natural Law in the Spiritual World,* which sold hundreds of thousands of copies. Drummond stressed the idea that, if studied deeply, natural laws would reveal the spiritual truths on which they were based, and that ultimately natural and spiritual laws were the same. For Latter-day Saints, this recalls the Lord's words in Doctrine and Covenants 29:34: "All things unto me are spiritual, and not at any time have I given unto you a law which was temporal."

On several occasions Drummond delivered addresses in London to social and political leaders of the time. The substance of these addresses appeared in his famous booklets, beginning with the *Greatest Thing in the World* (published in 1880), which is based on the teachings of the Apostle Paul on charity, or love: "Now abideth faith, hope, charity, these three; but the greatest of these is charity." (1 Corinthians 13:13.)

The prophet Mormon added further insight in these words: "If ye have not charity, ye are nothing, for charity never faileth. Wherefore, cleave unto charity, which is the greatest of all, for all things must fail—but charity is the pure love of Christ, and it endureth forever; and whoso is found possessed of it at the last day, it shall be well with him. Wherefore, . . . pray unto the Father with all the energy of heart, that ye may be filled with this love, which he hath bestowed upon all who are true followers of his Son, Jesus Christ; that ye may become the sons of God; that when he shall appear we shall be like him, for we shall see him as he is; that we may have this hope; that we may be purified even as he is pure." (Moroni 7:46–48.)

THE GREATEST THING IN THE WORLD

Though I speak with the tongues of men and of angels, and have not love, I am become as a sounding brass, or a tinkling cymbal. And though I have the gift of prophecy, and understand all mysteries, and all knowledge; and though I have all faith, so that I could remove mountains, and have not LOVE *I am nothing. And though I bestow all my goods to feed the poor, and though I give my body to be burned, and have not Love, it profiteth me nothing.*

> *Love suffereth long, and is kind;*
> *Love envieth not;*
> *Love vaunteth not itself is not puffed up,*
> *Doth not behave itself unseemly,*
> *Seeketh not her own,*
> *Is not easily provoked,*
> *Thinketh no evil;*
> *Rejoiceth not in iniquity, but rejoiceth in the truth;*
> *Beareth all things, believeth all things, hopeth all things, endureth all things.*

Love never faileth: but whether there be prophecies, they shall fail; whether there be tongues, they shall cease; whether there be knowledge, it shall vanish away. For we know in part, and we prophesy in part. But when that which is perfect is come, then that which is in part shall be done away. When I was a child, I spake as a child, I understood as a child, I thought as a child: but when I became a man, I put away childish things. For now we see through a glass, darkly; but then face to face: now I know in part; but then shall I know even as also I am known. And now abideth faith, hope, Love, these three; but the greatest of these is Love.—I COR xiii.

Every one has asked himself the great question of antiquity as of the modern world: What is the *summum bonum*—the supreme good? You have life before you. Once only you can live it. What is the noblest object of desire, the supreme gift to covet?

We have been accustomed to be told that the greatest thing in the religious world is Faith. That great word has been the key-note for centuries of the popular religion; and we have easily learned to look upon it as the greatest thing in the world. Well, we are wrong. If we have been told that, we may miss the mark. I have taken you, in the chapter which I have just read, to Christianity at its source; and there we have seen, "The greatest of these is love." It is not an oversight. Paul was speaking of faith just a moment before. He says, "If I have all faith, so that I can remove mountains, and have not love, I am nothing. "So far from forgetting, he deliberately contrasts them, "Now abideth Faith, Hope, Love," and without a moment's hesitation, the decision falls, "The greatest of these is Love."

And it is not prejudice. A man is apt to recommend to others his own strong point. Love was not Paul's strong point. The observing student can detect a beautiful tenderness growing and ripening all through his character as Paul gets old; but the hand that wrote, "The greatest of these is love," when we meet it first, is stained with blood.

Nor is this letter to the Corinthians peculiar in singling out love as the *summum bonum*. The masterpieces of Christianity are agreed about it. Peter says, "Above all things have fervent love among yourselves." *Above all things*. And John goes farther, "God is love." And you remember the profound remark which Paul makes elsewhere, "Love is the fulfilling of the law." Did you ever think what he meant by that? In those days men were working their passage to Heaven by keeping the Ten Commandments, and the hundred and ten other commandments which they had manufactured out of them. Christ said, I will show you a more simple way. If you do one thing, you will do these hundred and ten things, without ever thinking about them. If you love, you will unconsciously fulfil the whole law. And you can readily see for yourselves how that must be so. Take any of the commandments. "Thou shalt have no other gods before Me." If a man love God, you will not require to tell him that. Love is the fulfilling of that law. "Take not His name in vain." Would he ever dream of taking His name in vain if he loved Him? "Remember the Sabbath day to keep it holy." Would he not be too glad to have one day in seven to dedicate more exclusively to the object of his affection? Love would fulfil all these laws regarding God. And so, if he loved Man, you would never think of telling him to honour his father and mother. He could not do anything else. It would be preposterous to tell him not to kill. You could only insult him if you suggested that he should not steal. How could he steal from those he loved? It would be superfluous to beg him not to bear false witness against his neighbour. If he loved him it would be the last thing he would do. And you would never dream of urging him not to covet what his neighbours had. He would rather they possessed it than himself. In this way "Love is the fulfilling of the law." It is the rule for fulfilling all rules, the new commandment for keeping all the old commandments, Christ's one secret of the Christian life.

Now Paul had learned that; and in this noble eulogy he has given us the most wonderful and original account extant of the *summum bonum*. We may divide it into three parts. In the beginning of the short chapter, we have Love *contrasted*; in the heart of it, we have Love *analysed*; towards the end we have Love *defended* as the supreme gift.

The Contrast

Paul begins by contrasting Love with other things that men in those days thought much of. I shall not attempt to go over those things in detail. Their inferiority is already obvious.

He contrasts it with eloquence. And what a noble gift it is, the power of playing upon the souls and wills of men, and rousing them to lofty purposes and holy deeds. Paul says, "If I speak with the tongues of men and of angels, and have not love, I am become as sounding brass, or a tinkling cymbal." And we all know why. We have all felt the brazenness of words without emotion, the hollowness, the unaccountable unpersuasiveness, of eloquence behind which lies no Love.

He contrasts it with prophecy. He contrasts it with mysteries. He contrasts it with faith. He contrasts it with charity. Why is Love greater than faith? Because the end is greater than the means. And why is it greater than charity? Because the whole is greater than the part. Love is greater than faith, because the end is greater than the means. What is the use of having faith? It is to connect the soul with God. And what is the object of connecting man with God? That he may become like God. But God is Love. Hence Faith, the means, is in order to Love, the end. Love, therefore, obviously is greater than faith.

It is greater than charity, again, because the whole is greater than a part. Charity is only a little bit of Love, one of the innumerable avenues of Love, and there may even be, and there is, a great deal of charity without Love. It is a very easy thing to toss a copper to a beggar on the street; it is generally an easier thing than not to do it. Yet Love is just as often in the withholding. We purchase relief from the sympathetic feelings roused by the spectacle of misery, at the copper's cost. It is too cheap—too cheap for us, and often too dear for the beggar. If we really loved him we would either do more for him, or less.

Then Paul contrasts it with sacrifice and martyrdom. And I beg the little band of would-be missionaries and I have the honour to call some of you by this name for the first time—to remember that though you give your bodies to be burned, and have not Love, it profits nothing— nothing! You can take nothing greater to the heathen world than the impress and reflection of the Love of God upon your own character. That is the universal language. It will take you years to speak in Chinese, or in the dialects of India. From the day you land, that language of Love, understood by all, will be pouring forth its unconscious eloquence. It is the man who is the missionary, it is not his words. His character is his message. In the heart of Africa, among the great Lakes, I have come across black men and women who remembered the only white man they ever saw before—David Livingstone; and as you cross his footsteps in that dark continent, men's faces light up as they speak of the kind Doctor who passed there years ago. They could not understand him; but they felt the Love that beat in his heart. Take into your new sphere of labour, where you also mean to lay down your life, that simple charm, and your lifework must succeed. You can take nothing greater, you need take nothing less. It is-not worth while going if you take anything less. You may take every accomplishment; you may be braced for every sacrifice; but if you give your body to be burned, and have not Love, it will profit you and the cause of Christ nothing.

The Analysis

After contrasting Love with these things, Paul, in three verses, very short, gives us an amazing analysis of what this supreme thing is. I ask you to look at it. It is a compound thing, he tells us. It is like light. As you have seen a man of science take a beam of light and pass it through a crystal prism, as you have seen it come out on the other side of the prism broken up into its component colours—red, and blue, and yellow, and violet, and orange, and all the colours of the rainbow—so Paul passes this thing, Love, through the magnificent prism of his inspired intellect, and it comes out on the other side broken up into its elements. And in these few words we have what one might call the Spectrum of Love, the analysis of Love. Will you observe what its elements are? Will you notice that they have common names; that they are virtues which we hear about every day; that they are things which can be practised by every man in every place in life; and how, by a multitude of small things and ordinary virtues, the supreme thing, the *summum bonum*, is made up?

The Spectrum of Love has nine ingredients:—

Patience . . . ."Love suffereth long."
Kindness . . . ."And is kind."
Generosity . . . . . ."Love envieth not."
Humility . . . ."Love vaunteth not itself, is not puffed up."
Courtesy . . . ."Doth not behave itself unseemly."
Unselfishness . . . . ."Seeketh not her own."
Good Temper . . . ."Is not easily provoked."
Guilelessness . . . . ."Thinketh no evil."
Sincerity . . . ."Rejoiceth not in iniquity, but rejoiceth in the truth."

Patience; kindness; generosity; humility; courtesy; unselfishness; good temper; guilelessness; sincerity—these make up the supreme gift, the stature of the perfect man. You will observe that all are in relation to men, in relation to life, in relation to the known to-day and the near to-morrow, and not to the unknown eternity. We hear much of love to God; Christ spoke much of love to man. We make a great deal of peace with heaven; Christ made much of peace on earth. Religion is not a strange or added thing, but the inspiration of the secular life, the breathing of an eternal spirit through this temporal world. The supreme thing, in short, is not a thing at all, but the giving of a further finish to the multitudinous words and acts which make up the sum of every common day.

There is no time to do more than make a passing note upon each of these ingredients. Love is *Patience*. This is the normal attitude of Love; Love passive, Love waiting to begin; not in a hurry; calm; ready to do its work when the summons comes, but meantime wearing the ornament of a meek and quiet spirit. Love suffers long; beareth all things; believeth all things; hopeth all things. For Love understands, and therefore waits.

Kindness. Love active. Have you ever noticed how much of Christ's life was spent in doing kind things—in *merely* doing kind things? Run over it with that in view and you will find that He spent a great proportion of His time simply in making people happy, in doing good turns to people. There is only one thing greater than happiness in the world, and that is holiness; and it is not in our keeping; but what God *has* put in our power is the happiness of those about us, and that is largely to be secured by our being kind to them.

"The greatest thing," says some one, "a man can do for his Heavenly Father is to be kind to some of His other children." I wonder why it is that we are not all kinder than we are? How much the world needs it. How easily it is done. How instantaneously it acts. How infallibly it is remembered. How superabundantly it pays itself back—for there is no debtor in the world so honourable, so superbly honourable, as Love. "Love never faileth." Love is success, Love is happiness, Love is life. "Love, I say," with Browning, "is energy of Life."

> *"For life, with all it yields of joy and woe*
> *And hope and fear,*
> *Is just our chance o' the prize of learning love—*
> *How love might be, hath been indeed, and is."*

Where Love is, God is. He that dwelleth in Love dwelleth in God. God is love. Therefore *love*. Without distinction, without calculation, without procrastination, love. Lavish it upon the poor, where it is very easy; especially upon the rich, who often need it most; most of all upon our equals, where it is very difficult, and for whom perhaps we each do least of all. There is a difference between *trying to please* and *giving pleasure* Give pleasure. Lose no chance of giving pleasure. For that is the ceaseless and anonymous triumph of a truly loving spirit.

"I shall pass through this world but once. Any good thing therefore that I can do, or any kindness that I can show to any human being, let me do it now. Let me not defer it or neglect it, for I shall not pass this way again."

Generosity. "Love envieth not" This is Love in competition with others. Whenever you attempt a good work you will find other men doing the same kind of work, and probably doing it better. Envy them not. Envy is a feeling of ill-will to those who are in the same line as ourselves, a spirit of covetousness and detraction. How little Christian work even is a protection against un-Christian feeling. That most despicable of all the unworthy moods which cloud a Christian's soul assuredly waits for us on the threshold of every work, unless we are fortified with this grace of magnanimity. Only one thing truly need the Christian envy, the large, rich, generous soul which "envieth not."

And then, after having learned all that, you have to learn this further thing, *Humility*—to put a seal upon your lips and forget what you have done. After you have been kind, after Love has stolen forth into the world and done its beautiful work, go back into the shade again and say nothing about it Love hides even from itself. Love waives even self-satisfaction. "Love vaunteth not itself, is not puffed up."

The fifth ingredient is a somewhat strange one to find in this *summum bonum*: *Courtesy*. This is Love in society, Love in relation to etiquette. "Love doth not behave itself unseemly." Politeness has been defined as love in trifles. Courtesy is said to be love in little things. And the one secret of politeness is to love. Love cannot behave itself unseemly. You can put the most untutored person into the highest society, and if they have a reservoir of love in their heart, they will not behave themselves unseemly. They simply cannot do it. Carlyle said of Robert Burns that there was no truer gentleman in Europe than the ploughman-poet. It was because he loved everything—the mouse, and the daisy, and all the things, great and small, that God had made. So with this simple passport he could mingle with any society, and enter courts and palaces from his little cottage on the banks of the Ayr. You know the meaning of the word "gentleman." It means a gentle man—a man who does things gently, with love. And that is the whole art and mystery of it. The gentleman cannot in the nature of things do an ungentle, an ungentlemanly thing. The un-gentle soul, the inconsiderate, unsympathetic nature cannot do anything else. "Love doth not behave itself unseemly."

Unselfishness. "Love seeketh not her own." Observe: Seeketh not even that which is her own. In Britain the Englishman is devoted, and rightly, to his rights. But there come times when a man may exercise even the higher right of giving up his rights. Yet Paul does not summon us to give up our rights. Love strikes much deeper. It would have us not seek them at all, ignore them, eliminate the personal element altogether from our calculations. It is not hard to give up our rights. They are often external. The difficult thing is to give up ourselves. The more difficult thing still is not to seek things for ourselves at all. After we have sought them, bought them, won them, deserved them, we have taken the cream off them for ourselves already. Little cross then, perhaps, to give them up. But not to seek them, to look every man not on his own things, but on the things of others—*id opus est.* "Seekest thou great things for thyself? "said the prophet; "*seek them not.*" Why? Because there is no greatness in things. Things cannot be great. The only greatness is unselfish love. Even self-denial in itself is nothing, is almost a mistake. Only a great purpose or a mightier love can justify the waste. It is more difficult, I have said, not to seek our own at all, than, having sought it, to give it up. I must take that back. It is only true of a partly selfish heart. Nothing is a hardship to Love, and nothing is hard. I believe that Christ's yoke is easy. Christ's "yoke" is just His way of taking life. And I believe it is an easier way than any other. I believe it is a happier way than any other. The most obvious lesson in Christ's teaching is that there is no happiness in having and getting anything, but only in giving. I repeat, *there is no happiness in having or in getting, but only in giving.* And half the world is on the wrong scent in the pursuit of happiness. They think it consists in having and getting, and in being served by others. It consists in giving, and in serving others. He that would be great among you, said Christ, let him serve. He that would be happy, let him remember that there is but one way—it is more blessed, it is more happy, to give than to receive.

The next ingredient is a very remarkable one: *Good Temper.* "Love is not easily provoked." Nothing could be more striking than to find this here. We are inclined to look upon bad temper as a very harmless weakness. We speak of it as a mere infirmity of nature, a family failing, a matter of temperament, not a thing to take into very serious account in estimating a man's character. And yet here, right in the heart of this analysis of love, it finds a place; and the Bible again and again returns to condemn it as one of the most destructive elements in human nature.

The peculiarity of ill temper is that it is the vice of the virtuous. It is often the one blot on an otherwise noble character. You know men who are all but perfect, and women who would be entirely perfect, but for an easily ruffled, quick-tempered, or "touchy" disposition. This compatibility of ill temper with high moral character is one of the strangest and saddest problems of ethics. The truth is there are two great classes of sins—sins of the *Body*, and sins of the *Disposition*. The Prodigal Son may be taken as a type of the first, the Elder Brother of the second. Now society has no doubt whatever as to which of these is the worse. Its brand falls, without a challenge, upon the Prodigal. But are we right? We have no balance to weigh one another's sins, and coarser and finer are but human words; but faults in the higher nature may be less venial than those in the lower, and to the eye of Him who is Love, a sin against Love may seem a hundred times more base. No form of vice, not worldliness, not greed of gold, not drunkenness itself, does more to unChristianise society than evil temper. For embittering life, for breaking up communities, for destroying the most sacred relationships, for devastating homes, for withering up men and women, for taking the bloom off childhood; in short, for sheer gratuitous misery-producing power, this influence stands alone. Look at the Elder Brother, moral, hardworking, patient, dutiful—let him get all credit for his virtues—look at this man, this baby, sulking outside his own father's door. "He was angry," we read, "and would not go in." Look at the effect upon the father, upon the servants, upon the happiness of the guests. Judge of the effect upon the Prodigal—and how many prodigals are kept out of the

Kingdom of God by the unlovely characters of those who profess to be inside? Analyse, as a study in Temper, the thunder-cloud itself as it gathers upon the Elder Brother's brow. What is it made of? Jealousy, anger, pride, uncharity, cruelty, self-righteousness, touchiness, doggedness, sullenness—these are the ingredients of this dark and loveless soul. In varying proportions, also, these are the ingredients of all ill temper. Judge if such sins of the disposition are not worse to live in, and for others to live with, than sins of the body. Did Christ indeed not answer the question Himself when He said, "I say unto you, that the publicans and the harlots go into the Kingdom of Heaven before you." There is really no place in Heaven for a disposition like this. A man with such a mood could only make Heaven miserable for all the people in it. Except, therefore, such a man be born again, he cannot, he simply cannot, enter the Kingdom of Heaven. For it is perfectly certain— and you will not misunderstand me—that to enter Heaven a man must take it with him.

You will see then why Temper is significant. It is not in what it is alone, but in what it reveals. This is why I take the liberty now of speaking of it with such unusual plainness. It is a test for love, a symptom, a revelation of an unloving nature at bottom. It is the intermittent fever which bespeaks unintermittent disease within; the occasional bubble escaping to the surface which betrays some rottenness underneath; a sample of the most hidden products of the soul dropped involuntarily when off one's guard; in a word, the lightning form of a hundred hideous and un-Christian sins. For a want of patience, a want of kindness, a want of generosity, a want of courtesy, a want of unselfishness, are all instantaneously symbolised in one flash of Temper.

Hence it is not enough to deal with the temper. We must go to the source, and change the inmost nature, and the angry humours will die away of themselves. Souls are made sweet not by taking the acid fluids out, but by putting something in—a great Love, a new Spirit, the Spirit of Christ. Christ, the Spirit of Christ, interpenetrating ours, sweetens, purifies, transforms all. This only can eradicate what is wrong, work a chemical change, renovate and regenerate, and rehabilitate the inner man. Will-power does not change men. Time does not change men. Christ does. Therefore "Let that mind be in you which was also in

Christ Jesus." Some of us have not much time to lose. Remember, once more, that this is a matter of life or death. I cannot help speaking urgently, for myself, for yourselves. "Whoso shall offend one of these little ones, which believe in me, it were better for him that a millstone were hanged about his neck, and that he were drowned in the depth of the sea." That is to say, it is the deliberate verdict of the Lord Jesus that it is better not to live than not to love. *It is better not to live than not to love.*

Guilelessness and *Sincerity* may be dismissed almost with a word. Guilelessness is the grace for suspicious people. And the possession of it is the great secret of personal influence. You will find, if you think for a moment, that the people who influence you are people who believe in you. In an atmosphere of suspicion men shrivel up; but in that atmosphere they expand, and find encouragement and educative fellowship. It is a wonderful thing that here and there in this hard, uncharitable world there should still be left a few rare souls who think no evil. This is the great unworldliness. Love "thinketh no evil," imputes no motive, sees the bright side, puts the best construction on every action. What a delightful state of mind to live in! What a stimulus and benediction even to meet with it for a day! To be trusted is to be saved. And if we try to influence or elevate others, we shall soon see that success is in proportion to their belief of our belief in them. For the respect of another is the first restoration of the self-respect a man has lost; our ideal of what he is becomes to him the hope and pattern of what he may become.

"Love rejoiceth not in iniquity, but rejoiceth in the truth." I have called this *Sincerity* from the words rendered in the Authorised Version by "rejoiceth in the truth." And, certainly, were this the real translation, nothing could be more just. For he who loves will love Truth not less than men. He will rejoice in the Truth—rejoice not in what he has been taught to believe; not in this Church's doctrine or in that; not in this ism or in that ism; but "in *the Truth.*" He will accept only what is real; he will strive to get at facts; he will search for Truth with a humble and unbiased mind, and cherish whatever he finds at any sacrifice. But the more literal translation of the Revised Version calls for just such a sacrifice for truth's sake here. For what Paul really meant is, as we there read,

"Rejoiceth not in unrighteousness, but rejoiceth with the truth," a quality which probably no one English word—and certainly not *Sincerity*—adequately defines. It includes, perhaps more strictly, the self-restraint which refuses to make capital out of others' faults; the charity which delights not in exposing the weakness of others, but "covereth all things"; the sincerity of purpose which endeavours to see things as they are, and rejoices to find them better than suspicion feared or calumny denounced.

So much for the analysis of Love. Now the business of our lives is to have these things fitted into our characters. That is the supreme work to which we need to address ourselves in this world, to learn Love. Is life not full of opportunities for learning Love? Every man and woman every day has a thousand of them. The world is not a play-ground; it is a schoolroom. Life is not a holiday, but an education. And the one eternal lesson for us all is *how better we can love* What makes a man a good cricketer? Practice. What makes a man a good artist, a good sculptor, a good musician? Practice. What makes a man a good linguist, a good stenographer? Practice. What makes a man a good man? Practice. Nothing else. There is nothing capricious about religion. We do not get the soul in different ways, under different laws, from those in which we get the body and the mind. If a man does not exercise his arm he develops no biceps muscle; and if a man does not exercise his soul, he acquires no muscle in his soul, no strength of character, no vigour of moral fibre, nor beauty of spiritual growth. Love is not a thing of enthusiastic emotion. It is a rich, strong, manly, vigorous expression of the whole round Christian character—the Christlike nature in its fullest development. And the constituents of this great character are only to be built up by ceaseless practice.

What was Christ doing in the carpenter's shop? Practising. Though perfect, we read that He *learned* obedience, He *increased* in wisdom and in favour with God and man. Do not quarrel therefore with your lot in life. Do not complain of its never-ceasing cares, its petty environment, the vexations you have to stand, the small and sordid souls you have to live and work with. Above all, do not resent temptation; do not be perplexed because it seems to thicken round you more and more, and ceases neither for effort nor for agony nor prayer. That is the practice which God appoints you; and it is having its work in making you patient, and humble, and generous, and unselfish, and kind, and courteous. Do not grudge the hand that is moulding the still too shapeless image within you. It is growing more beautiful though you see it not, and every touch of temptation may add to its perfection. Therefore keep in the midst of life. Do not isolate yourself. Be among men, and among things, and among troubles, and difficulties, and obstacles. You remember Goethe's words: *Es bildet ein Talent sich in der Stille, Doch ein Character in dem Strom der Welt.* "Talent develops itself in solitude; character in the stream of life." Talent develops itself in solitude—the talent of prayer, of faith, of meditation, of seeing the unseen; Character grows in the stream of the world's life. That chiefly is where men are to learn love.

How? Now, how? To make it easier, I have named a few of the elements of love. But these are only elements. Love itself can never be defined. Light is a something more than the sum of its ingredients—a glowing, dazzling, tremulous ether. And love is something more than all its elements— a palpitating, quivering, sensitive, living thing. By synthesis of all the colours, men can make whiteness, they cannot make light. By synthesis of all the virtues, men can make virtue, they cannot make love. How then are we to have this transcendent living whole conveyed into our souls? We brace our wills to secure it. We try to copy those who have it. We lay down rules about it. We watch. We pray. But these things alone will not bring Love into our nature. Love is an *effect*. And only as we fulfil the right condition can we have the effect produced. Shall I tell you what the *cause* is?

If you turn to the Revised Version of the First Epistle of John you will find these words: "We love, because He first loved us." "We love," not "We love *Him*" That is the way the old Version has it, and it is quite wrong. "We *love*—because He first loved us." Look at that word "because." It is the cause of which I have spoken. "Because He first loved us," the effect follows that we love, we love Him, we love all men. We cannot help it. Because He loved us, we love, we love everybody. Our heart is slowly changed. Contemplate the love of Christ, and you will love. Stand before that mirror, reflect Christ's character, and you will be changed into the same image from tenderness to tenderness. There is no other way. You cannot love to order. You can only look at the lovely object, and fall in love with it, and grow into likeness to it. And so look at this Perfect Character, this Perfect Life. Look at the great Sacrifice as He laid down Himself, all through life, and upon the Cross of Calvary; and you must love Him. And loving Him, you must become like Him. Love begets love. It is a process of induction. Put a piece of iron in the presence of a magnetised body, and that piece of iron for a time becomes magnetised. It is charged with an attractive force in the mere presence of the original force, and as long as you leave the two side by side, they are both magnets alike. Remain side by side with Him who loved us, and gave Himself for us, and you too will become a centre of power, a permanently attractive force; and like Him you will draw all men unto you, like Him you will be drawn unto all men. That is the inevitable effect of Love. Any man who fulfils that cause must have that effect produced in him. Try to give up the idea that religion comes to us by chance, or by mystery, or by caprice. It comes to us by natural law, or by supernatural law, for all law is Divine. Edward Irving went to see a dying boy once, and when he entered the room he just put his hand on the sufferer's head, and said, "My boy, God loves you," and went away. And the boy started from his bed, and called out to the people in the house, "God loves me! God loves me!" It changed that boy. The sense that God loved him overpowered him, melted him down, and began the creating of a new heart in him. And that is how the love of God melts down the unlovely heart in man, and begets in him the new creature, who is patient and humble and gentle and unselfish. And there is no other way to get it. There is no mystery about it We love others, we love everybody, we love our enemies, because He first loved us.

The Defence

Now I have a closing sentence or two to add about Paul's reason for singling out love as the supreme possession. It is a very remarkable reason. In a single word it is this: *it lasts.* "Love," urges Paul, "never faileth." Then he begins again one of his marvellous lists of the great things of the day, and exposes them one by one. He runs over the things that men thought were going to last, and shows that they are all fleeting, temporary, passing away.

"Whether there be prophecies, they shall fail." It was the mother's ambition for her boy in those days that he should become a prophet. For hundreds of years God had never spoken by means of any prophet, and at that time the prophet was greater than the king. Men waited wistfully for another messenger to come, and hung upon his lips when he appeared as upon the very voice of God. Paul says, "Whether there be prophecies, they shall fail." This Book is full of prophecies. One by one they have "failed"; that is, having been fulfilled their work is finished; they have nothing more to do now in the world except to feed a devout man's faith.

Then Paul talks about tongues. That was another thing that was greatly coveted. "Whether there be tongues, they shall cease." As we all know, many, many centuries have passed since tongues have been known in this world. They have ceased. Take it in any sense you like. Take it, for illustration merely, as languages in general—a sense which was not in Paul's mind at all, and which though it cannot give us the specific lesson will point the general truth. Consider the words in which these chapters were written—Greek. It has gone. Take the Latin—the other great tongue of those days. It ceased long ago. Look at the Indian language. It is ceasing. The language of Wales, of Ireland, of the Scottish Highlands is dying before our eyes. The most popular book in the English tongue at the present time, except the Bible, is one of Dickens's works, his *Pickwick Papers*. It is largely written in the language of London streetlife; and experts assure us that in fifty years it will be unintelligible to the average English reader.

Then Paul goes farther, and with even greater boldness adds, "Whether there be knowledge, it shall vanish away." The wisdom of the ancients, where is it? It is wholly gone. A schoolboy to-day knows more than Sir Isaac Newton knew. His knowledge has vanished away. You put yesterday's newspaper in the fire. Its knowledge has vanished away. You buy the old editions of the great encyclopaedias for a few pence. Their knowledge has vanished away. Look how the coach has been superseded by the use of steam. Look how electricity has superseded that, and swept a hundred almost new inventions into oblivion. One of the greatest living authorities, Sir William Thomson, said the other day, "The steam-engine is passing away." "Whether there be knowledge, it shall vanish away." At every workshop you will see, in the back yard, a heap of old iron, a few wheels, a few levers, a few cranks, broken and eaten with rust. Twenty years ago that was the pride of the city. Men flocked in from the country to see the great invention; now it is superseded, its day is done. And all the boasted science and philosophy of this day will soon be old. But yesterday, in the University of Edinburgh, the greatest figure in the faculty was Sir James Simpson, the discoverer of chloroform. The other day his successor and nephew, Professor Simpson, was asked by the librarian of the University to go to the library and pick out the books on his subject that were no longer needed. And his reply to the librarian was this: "Take every text-book that is more than ten years old, and put it down in the cellar." Sir James Simpson was a great authority only a few years ago: men came from all parts of the earth to consult him; and almost the whole teaching of that time is consigned by the science of to-day to oblivion. And in every branch of science it is the same. "Now we know in part. We see through a glass darkly."

Can you tell me anything that is going to last? Many things Paul did not condescend to name. He did not mention money, fortune, fame; but he picked out the great things of his time, the things the best men thought had something in them, and brushed them peremptorily aside. Paul had no charge against these things in themselves. All he said about them was that they would not last. They were great things, but not supreme things. There were things beyond them. What we are stretches past what we do, beyond what we possess. Many things that men denounce as sins are not sins; but they are temporary. And that is a favourite argument of the New Testament. John says of the world, not that it is wrong, but simply that it "passeth away." There is a great deal in the world that is delightful and beautiful; there is a great deal in it that is great and engrossing; but it will not last. All that is in the world, the lust of the eye, the lust of the flesh, and the pride of life, are but for a little while. Love not the world therefore. Nothing that it contains is worth the life and consecration of an immortal soul. The immortal soul must give itself to something that is immortal. And the only immortal things are these: "Now abideth faith, hope, love, but the greatest of these is love."

Some think the time may come when two of these three things will also pass away —faith into sight, hope into fruition. Paul does not say so. We know but little now about the conditions of the life that is to come. But what is certain is that Love must last. God, the Eternal God, is Love. Covet therefore that everlasting gift, that one thing which it is certain is going to stand, that one coinage which will be current in the Universe when all the other coinages of all the nations of the world shall be useless and unhonoured. You will give yourselves to many things, give yourselves first to Love. Hold things in their proportion. *Hold things in their proportion.* Let at least the first great object of our lives be to achieve the character defended in these words, the character,—and it is the character of Christ—which is built around Love.

I have said this thing is eternal. Did you ever notice how continually John associates love and faith with eternal life? I was not told when I was a boy that "God so loved the world that He gave His only begotten Son, that whosoever believeth in Him should have everlasting life." What I was told, I remember, was, that God so loved the world that, if I trusted in Him, I was to have a thing called peace, or I was to have rest, or I was to have joy, or I was to have safety. But I had to find out for myself that whosoever trusteth in Him—that is, whosoever loveth Him, for trust is only the avenue to Love—hath everlasting *life*. The Gospel offers a man life. Never offer men a thimbleful of Gospel. Do not offer them merely joy, or merely peace, or merely rest, or merely safety; tell them how Christ came to give men a more abundant life than they have, a life abundant in love, and therefore abundant in salvation for themselves, and large in enterprise for the alleviation and redemption of the world. Then only can the Gospel take hold of the whole of a man, body, soul, and spirit, and give to each part of his nature its exercise and reward. Many of the current Gospels are addressed only to a part of man's nature. They offer peace, not life; faith, not Love; justification, not regeneration. And men slip back again from such religion because it has never really held them. Their nature was not all in it. It offered no deeper and gladder life-current than the life that was lived before. Surely it stands to reason that only a fuller love can compete with the love of the world.

To love abundantly is to live abundantly, and to love for ever is to live for ever. Hence, eternal life is inextricably bound up with love We want to live for ever for the same reason that we want to live tomorrow. Why do you want to live tomorrow? It is because there is some one who loves you, and whom you want to see tomorrow, and be with, and love back. There is no other reason why we should live on than that we love and are beloved. It is when a man has no one to love him that he commits suicide. So long as he has friends, those who love him and whom he loves, he will live; because to live is to love. Be it but the love of a dog, it will keep him in life; but let that go and he has no contact with life, no reason to live. The "energy of life" has failed. Eternal life also is to know God, and God is love. This is Christ's own definition. Ponder it. "This is life eternal, that they might know Thee the only true God, and Jesus Christ whom Thou hast sent." Love must be eternal. It is what God is. On the last analysis, then, love is life. Love never faileth, and life never faileth, so long as there is love. That is the philosophy of what Paul is showing us; the reason why in the nature of things Love should be the supreme thing—because it is going to last; because in the nature of things it is an Eternal Life. That Life is a thing that we are living now, not that we get when we die; that we shall have a poor chance of getting when we die unless we are living now. No worse fate can befall a man in this world than to live and grow old alone, unloving, and unloved. To be lost is to live in an unregenerate condition, loveless and unloved; and to be saved is to love; and he that dwelleth in love dwelleth already in God. For God is love.

Now I have all but finished. How many of you will join me in reading this chapter once a week for the next three months? A man did that once and it changed his whole life. Will you do it? It is for the greatest thing in the world. You might begin by reading it every day, especially the verses which describe the perfect character. "Love suffereth long, and is kind; love envieth not; love vaunteth not itself." Get these ingredients into your life. Then everything that you do is eternal. It is worth doing. It is worth giving time to. No man can become a saint in his sleep; and to fulfil the condition required demands a certain amount of prayer and meditation and time, just as improvement in any direction, bodily or mental, requires preparation and care. Address yourselves to that one thing; at any cost have this transcendent character exchanged for yours. You will find as you look back upon your life that the moments that stand out, the moments when you have really lived, are the moments when you have done things in a spirit of love. As memory scans the past, above and beyond all the transitory pleasures of life, there leap forward those supreme hours when you have been enabled to do unnoticed kindnesses to those round about you, things too trifling to speak about, but which you feel have entered into your eternal life. I have seen almost all the beautiful things God has made; I have enjoyed almost every pleasure that He has planned for man; and yet as I look back I see standing out above all the life that has gone four or five short experiences when the love of God reflected itself in some poor imitation, some small act of love of mine, and these seem to be the things which alone of all one's life abide. Everything else in all our lives is transitory. Every other good is visionary. But the acts of love which no man knows about, or can ever know about—they never fail.

In the Book of Matthew, where the Judgment Day is depicted for us in the imagery of One seated upon a throne and dividing the sheep from the goats, the test of a man then is not, "How have I believed?" but "How have I loved?" The test of religion, the final test of religion, is not religiousness, but Love. I say the final test of religion at that great Day is not religiousness, but Love; not what I have done, not what I have believed, not what I have achieved, but how I have discharged the common charities of life. Sins of commission in that awful indictment are not even referred to. By what we have not done, *by sins of omission*, we are judged. It could not be otherwise. For the withholding of love is the negation of the spirit of Christ, the proof that we never knew Him, that for us He lived in vain. It means that He suggested nothing in all our thoughts, that He inspired nothing in all our lives, that we were not once near enough to Him to be seized with the spell of His compassion for the world. It means that—

> *"I lived for myself, I thought for myself,*
> *For myself, and none beside—*
> *Just as if Jesus had never lived,*
> *As if He had never died."*

It is the Son of *Man* before whom the nations of the world shall be gathered. It is in the presence of *Humanity* that we shall be charged. And the spectacle itself, the mere sight of it, will silently judge each one. Those will be there whom we have met and helped: or there, the unpitied multitude whom we neglected or despised. No other Witness need be summoned. No other charge than lovelessness shall be preferred. Be not deceived. The words which all of us shall one Day hear, sound not of theology but of life, not of churches and saints but of the hungry and the poor, not of creeds and doctrines but of shelter and clothing, not of Bibles and prayer-books but of cups of cold water in the name of Christ. Thank God the Christianity of to-day is coming nearer the world's need. Live to help that on. Thank God men know better, by a hairsbreadth, what religion is, what God is, who Christ is, where Christ is. Who is Christ? He who fed the hungry, clothed the naked, visited the sick. And where is Christ? Where?—whoso shall receive a little child in My name receiveth Me. And who are Christ's? Every one that loveth is born of God.

THE STRENGTH OF BEING CLEAN

David Starr Jordan

David Starr Jordan was born January 19, 1851, near Gainesville, New York. He studied biology at Cornell University and was inspired to specialize in ichthyology—the branch of zoology that deals with fish—by famous naturalist Louis Agassiz. In 1885 Jordan became president of Indiana University in Bloomington, Indiana, and in 1891 he was named the first president of the newly opened Leland Stanford Junior University (now Stanford University) in Stanford, California, where he served until 1913. He devoted his later years to international peace, acting as chief director of the World Peace Foundation. He died in 1931.

A prolific writer and speaker, Jordan turned out dozens of essays on a variety of inspirational topics. In "The Strength of Being Clean," published in 1900 and subtitled "A Study of the Quest for Unearned Happiness," he spoke of several kinds of cleanliness, and he warned readers about the dangers of alcohol, tobacco, and other drugs: "One and all these various drugs tend to give the impression of a power or a pleasure, or an activity, which we do not possess. . . . One and all their supposed pleasures are followed by a reaction of subjective pains as spurious and as unreal as the pleasures which they follow. Each of them, if used to excess, brings in time insanity, incapacity, and death."

His message reminds us of the words of the Lord to the Saints in Joseph Smith's day: "Go ye out from among the wicked. Save yourselves. Be ye clean that bear the vessels of the Lord." (D&C 38:42.)

THE STRENGTH OF BEING CLEAN

I wish in this address to make a plea for sound and sober life. I base this plea on two facts: to be clean is to be strong; no one can secure happiness without earning it.

Among the inalienable rights of man—as our fathers have taught us—are these three: "life, liberty, and the pursuit of happiness." So long as man is alive and free, he will, in one way or another, seek that which gives him pleasure, hence life, liberty, and the pursuit of happiness are in essence the same. But the pursuit of happiness is an art in itself. To seek it is not necessarily to find it, and failure may destroy both liberty and life. Of some phases of this pursuit I wish to speak to-day. My message is an old one. If by good chance some part of it is true, this truth is as old as life itself. And if it be true, it is a message that needs to be repeated many times to each generation of men.

It is one of the laws of life that each acquisition has its cost. No organism can exercise power without yielding up part of its substance. The physiological law of transfer of energy is the basis of human success and happiness. There is no action without expenditure of energy, and if energy be not expended, the power to generate it is lost.

This law shows itself in a thousand ways in the life of man. The arm which is not used becomes palsied. The wealth which comes by chance weakens and destroys. The good which is unused turns to evil. The charity which asks no effort "cannot relieve the misery she creates." The religion which another man would give us we cannot take as a gift. There is no Christliness without endeavour. The truth which another man has won from nature or from life is not our truth until we have lived it. Only that becomes real or helpful to any man which has cost the sweat of his brow, the effort of his brain, or the anguish of his soul. He who would be wise must daily earn his wisdom. The parable of the talents is the expression of this law, for he who adds not effort to power soon loses the power he had. The responsibility for effort rests with the individual. This need is the meaning of individuality, and by it each must work out his own salvation, with fear and trembling it may be sometimes, and all times with perseverance and patience.

The greatest source of failure in life comes from this. It is easier to be almost right than to be right; to wish, than to gain. In default of gold, there is always something almost as good, and which glitters equally. In default of possession, illusion can be had, and more cheaply. It is possession only which costs. Illusion can be had on easy terms, though the final end of deception is failure and misery. Happiness must be earned, like other good things, else it cannot be held. It can be deserved only where its price has been somehow paid. Nothing worth having is given away in this world,—nor in any other that we know of. No one rides dead-head on the road to happiness. He who tries to do so, never reaches his destination. He is left in the dumps.

It is probably too much to say that all of human misery can be traced to the dead-head habit. Misery has as many phases as humanity. But if we make this statement negatively, it will not be far from the truth. No one is ever miserable who would truly pay the price of happiness. No one is really miserable who has not tried to cheapen life.

The price which every good and perfect gift demands, we would somehow or other get out of paying. But we can never cheat the gods. Their choicest gifts lie not on the bargain counters. Our reward comes with our effort. It is part of the same process. In this matter, man gets what he deserves, meted out with the justice of eternity.

In the sense in which I shall use these terms, sorrow and misery are not the same thing. They are not on speaking terms with each other. True sorrow, the pain of loss, is a hallowed suffering. "For ever the other left," is a necessity in a world which each one must leave as he entered it,—alone. And we would not have it otherwise, for there is in the nature of things no other possibility. So long as we live we must take chances. Sorrow is sacred. Misery is accursed. Sorrow springs from our relations to others. Misery we have all to ourselves. As real happiness is the glow which accompanies normal action, the reflex of the abundance of life, so is misery the shadow of dullness, the reflex of failing or morbid life. Misery is nature's protest against degeneration.

Human misery may be a symptom, a cause, or an effect. It is an expression of degeneration, and therefore a symptom of mental and spiritual decay. It is a cause of weakness and discouragement, and therefore of further degeneration and deeper misery. It is an effect of degeneration, and behind personal degeneration lies a multitude of causes. None of its causes are simple. Some are subjective, the visible signs of weak mind or mean spirit. Some are objective, the product of evil social conditions, to which the weak mind or mean spirit responds to its further injury. None of these can be removed by any single social panacea. "The poor we have always with us," and there will always be those who shall show that "the way of the transgressor is hard." "The soul that sinneth it shall die," will not become a forgotten axiom so long as instability of will is a part of human nature.

When I was a boy I once had a primer which gave the names of many things which were good and many which were bad. Good things were faith, hope, charity, piety, and integrity, while anger, selfishness and trickery were rightly put down as bad. But among the good things, the primer placed "adversity." This I could not understand, and to this day I remember how I was puzzled by it. The name "adversity" had a pretty sound, but I found that its meaning was the same as "bad luck." How can bad luck be a good thing?

Now that I have grown older and have watched men's lives and actions for many years, I can see how bad luck is really good. Good or bad is not in the thing itself, but in how we take it. If we yield and break down under it, it is not good; but neither are we good. It is not in the luck, but in ourselves, that the badness is. But if we take hold of bad luck bravely, manfully, we may change it into good luck, and when we do so we make ourselves stronger for the next struggle. It was a fable of the Norsemen, that when a man won a victory over another, the strength of the conquered went over into his veins. This old fancy has its foundation in fact. Whoever has conquered fortune has luck on his side for the rest of his life.

So adversity is good, if only we know how to take it. Shall we shrink under it, or shall we react against it? Shall we yield or shall we conquer? To react against adversity is to make fortune our servant. Its strength goes over to us. To yield is to make us fortune's slave. Our strength is turned against us in the pressure of circumstances. A familiar illustration of what I mean by reaction is this: Why do men stand upright? It is because the earth pulls them down. If a man yields to its attraction he soon finds himself prone on the ground. In this attitude he is helpless. He can do nothing there, so he reacts against the force of gravitation. He stands upon his feet, and the more powerful the force may be, the more necessary it is that the active man should resist it. When the need for activity ceases, man no longer stands erect. He yields to the force he has resisted. When he is asleep the force of gravitation has its own way so far as his posture is concerned. But activity and life demand reaction, and it is only through resistance that man can conquer adversity.

In like fashion temptation has its part to play in the development of character. The strength of life is increased by the conquest of temptation. We may call no man virtuous till he has won such a victory. It is not the absence of temptation, but the reaction from it, that ensures the persistence of virtue. If sin entice thee, consent thou not, and after awhile its allurements will cease to attract.

In every walk in life, strength comes from effort. It is the habit of self-denial which gives the advantage to men we call self-made. A self-made man, if he is made at all, has already won the battle of life. He is often very poorly put together. His education is incomplete; his manners may be uncouth. His prejudices are often strong. He may worship himself and his own oddities. But if he is successful in any way in life, he has learned to resist. He has learned the value of money, and he has learned how to refuse to spend it. He has learned the value of time, and how to convert it into money, and he has learned to resist all temptations to throw either money or time away. He has learned to say *no*. To say *no* at the right time, and then to stand by it, is the first element of success.

I heard once of a university (it may be in Tartary, or it may be in Dreamland) where the students were placed in a row, and each one knocked down every morning, to teach him self-control. By this means he was made slow to anger. To resist wrath helps one to resist other impulses. There is a great value in the habit of self-restraint, even when self-gratification is harmless in itself. Some day self-denial will be systematically taught to children. It ought to be part of the training of men, not through statutes and regulations, but through the growth of severer habits. Whenever we say *no* to ourselves, we gain strength to say *no,* if need be, to others.

The Puritans were strong in their day, and their strength has been the backbone of our republic. Their power lay not in the narrowness of their creed, but in the severity of their practices. Much that they condemned was innocent in itself. Some things which they permitted were injurious. But they were ready to resist whatever they thought was wrong. In this resistance they found strength; and they found happiness, too, and somewhat of this strength and this happiness has fallen to our inheritance.

We may wander far from the creeds of our fathers; we may adopt far different clothing, and far other customs and practices. But if we would have the Puritan's strength, we must hold the Puritan's hatred of evil. Our course of life must be as narrow as his; for the way that leads to power in life must ever be strait and stony. It is still true, and will be true for ever, that the broad roads and flowery paths lead to weakness and misery, not to happiness and strength. There is no real happiness that does not involve self-denial.

So there never was unearned happiness, yet thousands there be in quest of it, and some have thought for the moment that they held it in their grasp. The failure of this quest is the source of the great problems of society,—the labour problem, the temperance problem, the social evil, and the thousand others which vex civilised society; problems which can never be solved until each man shall solve his own for himself. Each pleasure that comes to us free from effort and free from responsibility turns into misery in our hands. Happiness comes from the normal exercise of life's functions in any grade, doing, thinking, fighting, overcoming, planning, loving. It is active, positive, strengthening. It does not burn out as it glows. Happiness leaves room for more happiness. Even war and strife make room for love. Love, too, is a positive word. Not love, —but loving. And loving brings happiness only as it works itself out into living action. The love that would end in no helping act and no purpose or responsibility is a mere torture of the mind.

The brain is the organ of consciousness, and therefore the seat of conscious happiness. Happiness is the signal, "All is well," that is passed from one nerve-cell to another. To choose among different possible courses of action is the primary function of the intellect. To choose at all, implies the choice of the best. In the long run, only those who choose the best survive. The *best* each one must find out for himself. To choose the best is the art of existence. Of all the fine arts, this is the finest and noblest. By the *best* we mean that which makes for abundance of life,— for ourselves and for others. The best for to-day may not be the real best, as the best for self may not be the best for others, and if it is not best in the long run, it is not the best at all. The conciliation of duties to self with duties to others, of altruism with egoism, is again the art of life. To learn this art is to develop the greatest effectiveness, the most perfect self-realisation, and therefore the greatest possibility for happiness.

In the quest for happiness, effectiveness rather than pleasure must be the real object of pursuit. For effectiveness in a high sense will bring happiness, while many of the apparent pleasures of life are only the masks of misery. To the tendency to forsake normal effort to follow these, we give the name of temptation. Temptation resisted strengthens the mind and the soul. Not to escape temptation, but to master it, is the way to righteousness. Innocence is not necessarily virtue, and may be farther from it than vice itself. We may call no man virtuous till he has passed from innocence to the conquest of temptation. Any fool may be innocent. It takes a wise man to be virtuous.

In a recent journal, Mr. William C. Morrow tells a story of a clergyman and a vagabond. They met by chance on the street, where the very incongruity of their lives drew them together. Each was tempted by the other. The young student of divinity, fresh from the seminary, in black broadcloth and unspotted necktie, seemed to the vagabond so pure, so clean, so innocent, that suddenly his soul arose in revolt against his past life, his vulgar surroundings, his squalid future. The inspiration of the unspoiled example gave him strength to resist. For a moment, at least, he threw off the chains which years of weakness had fastened upon him. The clergyman, on the other hand, found a fascination in sin. It seemed to come to him as an illumination of the realities of life, a contrast to a life of empty words and dry asceticism. All the yearning curiosity of his suppressed impulses called out for the freedom of the vagabond. His mouth watered for the untasted fruits of life. These unknown joys seemed to him the only joys there were. He had never known temptation, and hence had never resisted it. To his innocence, the cheap meanness of sin was not revealed.

As it chanced, so the story goes, when next the pair met, the vagabond and the minister, they had exchanged places. From the curb-stone pulpit, the vagabond spoke to his fellow sinners in words that burned, for they came from the fulness of his experience. He had met the Devil face to face, and could speak as one who knew him, and who would, if he could, cast off his horrid chains. As he went on with his harangue, the other came up, dishevelled of garment and unsteady of step, his speech reeking with foulness and profanity. The pleasures of sin were his for the season, and the policeman led him on to the city jail to sober up. There he would have leisure to cast up the account in the bitterness which follows unresisted temptation.

Perhaps this is not a true story, but its like is true every day. It is only the strength of past resistance that saves us from sin. If we know it and fight it, it will not take us unawares.

In the barber shop of a hotel in Washington, this inscription is written on the mirror: "There is no pleasure in life equal to that of the conquest of a vicious habit." This the barber keeps before him every day. It is no idle word, but the lesson of his life; a life of struggle against the temptation of self-indulgence.

In general, the sinner is not the man who sets out in life to be wicked. There are some such, fiends by blood and birth, but you and I do not meet them very often. The sinner is the man who cannot say *no*. For sin to become wickedness is a matter of slow transition. One virtue after another is yielded up as vice calls for the sacrifice. In Kipling's fable of Parrenness, the slave of vice is asked to surrender one after another his trust in man, his faith in woman, and the hopes and conscience of his childhood. In exchange for all these, the demon left him just a little crust of dry bread.

It is because decay goes on step by step that bad men are not all bad, as good men are not wholly good. In the stories of Bret Harte, the gamblers and sots are capable of pure impulses and of noble self-devotion. The pathos of Dickens rests largely on the same kindly fact.

It is indeed a fact, and those who would save such people should keep it constantly in mind.

I number among my friends, if he be living yet, which I doubt, an old miner, who has had a hard, wild life. He was a victim of drink, and the savage Keeley cure did not save him from delirium tremens. He walked from Los Gatos to Palo Alto for such help as might be found there. As he sat waiting in my house, a little child, who had never known sin, came into the room and fearlessly offered him his hand. This a grown man would not do without shrinking, but the child had not learned to be a respecter of persons. The scarred face lightened; the visions of demons vanished for a moment, and the poor man repeated almost to himself these words of Dickens: "I know now how Jesus could liken the kingdom of God to a child."

The primal motive of most forms of sin is the desire to make a short cut to happiness. We yield to temptation because it promises pleasure without the effort of earning it. This promise is one which has never been fulfilled in all the history of all the ages, and it is time that men were coming to realise that fact. The happiness that is earned lasts to make way for more happiness. The unearned pleasures are mere illusions, and as they pass away, their final legacy is weakness and pain. They leave "a dark brown taste in the mouth;" their recollection is "different in the morning." Such pleasures, as Robert Burns, who had tried many of them, truthfully says, "are like poppies spread," or "like the snowfalls on the river."

But true happiness leaves no reaction. The mind is at rest within itself, and the consciousness is filled with the joy of living.

The short cuts to happiness which temptation commonly offers to you and to me, I may roughly divide into five classes:

1. *Indolence.* This is the attempt to secure the pleasures of rest without the effort that justifies rest and makes it welcome. When a man shuns effort, he is in no position to resist temptation. So, through all the ages, idleness has been known as the parent of all the vices. "Life drives him hard" who has nothing in the world to do. The dry-rot of ennui, the vague self-disgust of those who cannot "deal with time," is the natural result of idleness. It is said that "the very fiends weave ropes of sand,

rather than face pure hell in idleness." It is only where even such poor effort is impossible that absolute misery can be found. The indolent ennui of the hopelessly rich and the indolent misery of the helplessly poor have this much in common. The quest for happiness is become a passive one, waiting for the joy that never comes. But life can never remain passive. That only is passive which is dead, and all the many evils of life come through the open door of unresisted temptation.

2. *Gambling.* In all its forms gambling is the desire to get something for nothing. Burglary and larceny have the same motive. Along this line, the difference between gambling and stealing is one fixed by social customs and prejudices. The thief may be a welcome member of society if he is the right kind of a thief, and successful in keeping within the rules we have adopted for our game of social advancement. In society, money is power. It is the visible representation of stored up power, whether of ourselves or of others. It is said that the "love of money is the root of all evil." The love of money is the love of power. But it is not true that the love of power is the root of all evil. To love power is natural to the strong. To wish for money is natural to him who knows how to use it. The desire to get money without earning it is the root of all evil. Only evil comes through the search for unearned happiness through unearned power. To get something for nothing, in whatever way, demoralises effort. The man who gets a windfall spends his days watching the wind. The man who wins in a lottery spends his gains in more lottery tickets. The man who loses in a lottery does the same thing. In all forms of gambling, to win is to lose, for the winner's integrity is placed in jeopardy. To lose is to lose, for the loser throws good money after bad, and that, too, is demoralising.

The appeal to chance, the spirit of speculation, whatever form it may take, is adverse to individual prosperity. It makes for personal degeneration and therefore for social decay.

3. *Licentiousness.* More wide-spread and more insidious than the quest for unearned power is the search for the unearned pleasures of love, without love's duties or love's responsibilities. The way to unearned love lies through the valley of the shadow of death. The path is white with dead men's bones.

Just as honest love is the most powerful influence for good that can enter into a man's life, so is love's counterfeit the most disintegrating. Love is a sturdy plant of vigorous growth, with wondrous promise of flower and fruitage, but it will not spring from the ashes of lust.

In the economy of human life, love looks forward to the future. Its glory is in its altruism. The mother gives her life and strength to the care of the child, and to the building of the home. The father stands guard over the life and welfare of mother and child alike. To shirk responsibility is to destroy the home. The equal marriage demands equal purity of heart, and equal chastity of intention. Without this, "Sweet love were slain," and "Love is the greatest thing in the world," because it is the greatest source of happiness.

Not strife nor war nor hatred is love's greatest enemy. Love's arch foe is lust. To shirk the bonds of love for the irresponsible joys of lust is the Devil's choicest temptation. Open vice brings with a certainty disease and degradation. To associate with the vile is to assume their vileness, and this in no occult or metaphorical sense, either. Secret vice comes to the same end, but all the more surely, because the folly of lying is added to the other agencies of decay. The man who tries to lead a double life is either a neurotic freak, or else the prince of fools. Generally he is something of both at first, and at the last an irreclaimable scoundrel. That society is so severe in its condemnation of the double life is an expression of the bitterness of its own experience. There is real meaning behind each of society's conventionalities. Its condemnation is never unreasoning, though it may lack in sense of proportion. "Even the angels," Emerson says, "must respect the proprieties." The basis of the proprieties of social life is that no man should shrink from the cost of that which he desires. It is not only the gross temptations which the wise man must resist. There is much that passes under other names which is only veiled licentiousness. The word flirtation covers a multitude of sin. To breathe the aroma of love, in pure selfishness, without an atom of altruistic responsibility, is the motive of flirtation. To touch a woman's hand in wantonness may be to poison her life and yours. The strongest forces of human life are not subjects for idle play. The real heart and soul of a man are measured by the truth he shows to woman. A man's ideal of womanhood is fixed by the woman he seeks. By a man's ideal of womanhood we may know the degree of his manhood.

4. *Precocity.* In the hotbed of modern society there is a tendency to precocious growth. Precocious virtue, as the Sunday-school books used to describe it, is bad enough; but precocious vice is most monstrous. Precocious fruit is not good fruit. The first ripened apples have always a worm at the core. What is worth having must bide its time. To seize it before its time is to pluck it prematurely.

It may be that "boys will be boys," as people say, but if boys will be boys in a bad sense, they will never be men. The wild oats they sow sprout early and grow fast, and "send their roots into the spinal column, till by and by, to our horror, we find ourselves grown through and through." Our duties to our after selves are more vital than our duties to our present selves, or our duties to society. To guard his own future is the greatest duty the young man owes to society. If all men lived in such fashion that remorse was unknown, the ills of society would mostly vanish. It is our own past deeds which are our real masters.

In the life of the lower animals nature guards against precocity. Among the beasts no one takes to himself the pleasures of life till he can carry its responsibilities. The precocious fish dies in the act of spawning. The old males among polygamous animals—cattle, deer, fur-seals—bar out the young. Their place they must take before they can enjoy it. The female scorns the male who is immature. He must bide his time, and develop his strength in patience.

But the immature child is brought at once among temptations he cannot resist, because he cannot understand them. The gauntlet of obscene suggestions in our cities is one of the most terrible our children have to face. We judge of the wickedness of Pompeii by evil signs and paintings, which the baptism of fire and eighteen centuries of burial have failed to purify. They are still mute witnesses of a personal degeneration toward which they once served to entice. If San Francisco were to be buried to-day, some future generation would judge us thus severely. The bill-boards of the vulgar theatres, with their suggestions of vice and crime, might be mute witnesses to the social decay of our republic. They do not tell the whole story of American life, but their testimony is honest so far as it goes. It is the call to unearned pleasures, the call to degradation, and our children, as they pass, cannot choose but listen.

The children on our streets grow old before their time, and there is no fate more horrible because there is none more hopeless. Were it not for the influx of new life from the farms, our cities would be depopulated. Strive as we may, we cannot save our children from the corrosion of vulgarity and obscene suggestion. The subtle incitement to vice comes to every home. Its effect is shown in precocious knowledge, the loss of the bloom of youth, the quest for pleasures unearned, because sought for out of time.

Vulgarity has in some measure its foundation in precocity. It is an expression of arrested development in matters of good taste or good character. To be vulgar is to do that which is not the best of its kind. It is to do poor things in poor ways, and to be satisfied with that. Vulgarity weakens the mind, and thus brings all other weakness in its train. It is vulgar to wear dirty linen when one is not engaged in dirty work. It is vulgar to like poor music, to read weak books, to feed on sensational newspapers, to trust to patent medicines, to find amusement in trashy novels, to enjoy vulgar theatres, to find pleasure in cheap jokes, to tolerate coarseness and looseness in any of its myriad forms. We find the corrosion of vulgarity everywhere, and its poison enters every home. The bill-boards of our cities are covered with its evidences, our newspapers are redolent with it, our story-books reek with it, our schools are tainted by it, and we cannot keep it out of our homes, or our churches, or our colleges.

It is the hope of civilisation that our republic may outgrow the toleration of vulgarity, but that is still a long way in the future. It is said that "vulgarity is the besetting sin of democracy." This one might believe, were it not that the most vulgar city in the world, the one from which vulgarity rises like an exhalation, is one of the least democratic. It is in democracy, the training of the common man, that we can find the only permanent antidote to vulgarity.

The second power of vulgarity is obscenity, and this vice is like the pestilence. Wherever it finds lodgment it kills. It fills the mind with vile pictures, which will come up again and again, standing in the way of all healthful effort. Those who have studied the life history of the homeless poor tell us that obscenity, and not drink, is the primal cause of the ineffectiveness of most of them. In the ranks of the unemployed, besides the infirm and the unfortunate, is the vast residue of the unemployable. The most of these are rendered so by the utter decay of force which comes from the habit of obscenity. The forces which make for vulgarity tend also toward obscenity, for all inane vulgarity tends to grow obscene. The open door of the saloon makes it a centre of corrosion, and the miserable habit of treating, which we call American, but which exists wherever the tippling-house exists, spreads and intensifies it. There is no great virtue in statutes to keep men sober. I would as soon "see the whole world drunk through choice as sober through compulsion," because compulsion cannot give strength to the individual man. The resistance to temptation must come from within. So far as the drink of drunkards is concerned, prohibition does not prohibit. But to clean up a town, to free it from corrosion, saves men, and boys and girls too, from vice, and who shall say that moral sanitation is not as much the duty of the community as physical sanitation? The city of the future will not permit the existence of slums and dives and tippling-houses. It will prohibit their existence for the same reason that it now prohibits pig-pens and dung-heaps and cesspools. For where all these things are, slums and cesspools, saloons and pig-pens, there the people grow weak and die.

A form of vulgarity is profanity. This is the sign of a dull, coarse, unrefined nature. There are times, perhaps, when profanity is picturesque and effective. In Arizona sometimes it is so, and I have seen it so in Wyoming. But not indoors nor in the streets nor under normal conditions. It is then simply an insult to the atmosphere which is vulgarised for the purpose. It is not that profanity is offensive to God. He may deal with it in his own way. It is offensive to man and destructive to him. It hurts the man who uses it. "What cometh out of a man defileth him," and the man thus defiled extends his corrosion to others.

5. *Intemperance.* The basis of intemperance is the effort to secure through drugs the feeling of happiness when happiness does not exist. Men destroy their nervous system for the tingling pleasures they feel as its structures are torn apart. There are many drugs which cause this

pleasure, and in proportion to the delight they seem to give is the real mischief they work.

Pain is the warning to the brain that something is wrong in the organ in which the pain is felt. Sometimes that which should be felt as pain is interpreted as pleasure. If a man lay his fingers upon an anvil and strike them one by one with a hammer, the brain will feel the shock as pain. It will give orders to have the blows checked.

But if, through some abnormal condition, some twist of the nerves, or clot on the brain, the injury were felt as exquisite delight, there would arise the impulse to repeat it. This would be a temptation. The knowledge of the injury which the eye would tell to the brain would lead the will to stop the blows. The impulse of delight would plead for their repetition, and in this fashion the hand might be sacrificed for a feeling of pleasure, which is no pleasure at all, but a form of mania. Of this character is the effect of all nerve-exciting drugs. As a drop of water is of the nature of the sea, so in its degree is the effect of alcohol, opium, tobacco, cocaine, kola, tea or coffee, of the nature of mania. They give a feeling of pleasure or rest, when rest or pleasure does not exist. This feeling arises from injury to the nerves which the brain does not truthfully interpret.

There have been men in abnormal conditions who felt mutilation as pleasure in the way I have just described. Men have paid others to pinch their bodies, to tear their flesh, to bruise their bones, for the exquisite delight in self-mutilation. This feeling is the basis for the extraordinary mania which shows itself from time to time among those sects who call themselves Flagellantes and Penitentes. Such extravagance is not religion; it was never translated into sane and helpful life; it is madness, and drunkenness is madness also. Differing in degree and somewhat in kind, it has yet the same original motive, self-destruction, because of the temptation of imaginary pleasure.

To make clear what I have to say, we must consider for a moment the nature of the mind. It is the brain's business to know, to think, to will, and to act. All these functions taken together we call the mind. The brain is hidden in darkness, sheltered within a bony box, and from all the nerves of sense it receives impressions of the outside world and of the conditions of the parts of the body. These impressions are the basis of knowledge. All that we know comes to us in one way or another through the nerves of sense. It is all drawn from our experience of the world through the brain.

These impressions are compared one with another, and brought into relations with past experiences, that the mind may deduce the real truth from them. This is the process of thought, which has many forms and many variations.

The purpose of knowledge is action. When we see or feel or hear anything, what are we going to do about it? The function of sensation is to enable the body to act safely and wisely. Hence the brain controls the muscles. Hence thought always tends to go over into action. The sense organs are the brain's only teacher. The muscles are its only servants. But there are many orders which can be issued to these servants. There are many sensations and many thoughts, each calling for action, and these actions may be incongruous one with another. How shall the brain choose? This is the function of the will. It is the duty of the will to choose the best action and to suppress all the others. The power of attention enables us to fix the mind on the sensations or impressions of most worth, and to push the others into the background. These competing sensations are not alone those of the present; the memory pictures of all past impressions linger in the brain, and these arise, bidden or unbidden, to mingle with the others. To know the relation of these, to distinguish present impressions from memories, to distinguish recollections from realities, is the condition of sanity. This is mental health, when the machinery of the brain and nerves performs each its appointed task; when the mind is clear, the will strong, the attention persistent, and all is well with the world.

But there are many conditions in which the machinery of the brain fails. The mind grows confused. It cannot tell memories from realities. Its power of attention flags. A fixed idea, not related to external things, may take possession of the mind, or the will may fail, and the mind may be controlled by a thousand vagrant impressions (really forgotten memory pictures) in as many seconds. In any case, the response of the muscles in action becomes uncertain. The action does not respond to external conditions, but to internal whims. The deeds which result from these whims may be dangerous to the subject himself, or to others. This is a condition of mania, or of mental irresponsibility.

Some phase of mental unsoundness is the natural effect of any of those drugs called stimulants or narcotics. Alcohol gives a feeling of warmth or vigour or exhilaration, when the real warmth or vigour or exhilaration does not exist. Tobacco gives a feeling of rest which is not restfulness. The use of opium seems to intensify the imagination, giving its clumsy wings a wondrous power of flight. It destroys the sense of time and space, but it is in time and space alone that man has his being. Cocaine gives a strength which is not strength. Strychnine quickens the motor response which follows sensation. Coffee and tea, like alcohol, enable one to borrow from his future store of force for present purposes, and none of these make any provision for paying back the loan. One and all these various drugs tend to give the impression of a power or a pleasure, or an activity, which we do not possess. One and all their function is to force the nervous system to lie. One and all the result of their habitual use is to render the nervous system incapable of ever telling the truth. One and all their supposed pleasures are followed by a reaction of subjective pains as spurious and as unreal as the pleasures which they follow. Each of them, if used to excess, brings in time insanity, incapacity, and death. With each of them, the first use makes the second easier. To yield to temptation, makes it easier to yield again. The weakening effect on the will is greater than the injury to the body. In fact, the harm alcoholic and similar excesses do to the body is wholly secondary. It is the visible reflex of the harm already done to the nervous system. . . .

There is nothing more hopeless than the ineffective remorse of a man who drinks and wishes that he did not. If you don't want to do a thing, then don't do it. The only way to reform is to stop, stop! stop! and go at once to doing something else.

The really "good fellow" can be convivial when he is sober. It is a poor kind of good fellowship which cannot be found till it is saturated with drink.

But whatever you may think or do as to table drinking, the use of beer, coffee, and the like, there is no question as to the evil of perpendicular drinking, or drinking for drink's sake. Men who drink in saloons do so for the most part for the wrench on the nervous system. They drink to forget. They drink to be happy. They drink to be drunk. Sometimes it is a periodical attack of madness. Sometimes it is a chronic thirst. Whichever it is, its indulgence destroys the soundness of life; it destroys accuracy of thought and action; it destroys wisdom and virtue; it destroys faith and hope and love. It brings a train of subjective horrors, which the terrified brain cannot interpret, and which we call delirium tremens. This is mania, indeed, but every act which injures the faithfulness of the nervous system is a step long or short in this direction.

Some six years ago, in the San Francisco *Examiner,* Mr. Arthur McEwen records the words of an old sailor, called "Longshore Pots," who gave a striking account of what he calls "The Shock." A young man with money and ambition starts out to enjoy life. He is "Hail fellow well met," "afraid of no man," and "nobody's enemy but his own." He frequents the clubs; he plays the races, and he is with the gayest in all gay company. He thinks well of himself; he has a good time, and he knows no reason why others should not think well of him. This goes on for a year or two, when the pace begins to prove too rapid. The "difference in the morning" becomes disagreeable. It interferes with business, it spoils pleasure. The only thing to do is to go still faster. The race down the cocktail route helps to forget. Suddenly the man gets sight of himself. He catches his face in the glass. He sees himself as others see him. Instead of "the jolly good fellow, which nobody can deny," he gets the glimpse of a useless, helpless sot. He sees a man who has spent his substance, has disgraced his name, has ruined his home, has broken the heart of his wife, has beggared his children, has lost the respect of others, and the respect of himself. This is the Shock! When it has come, he is henceforth good for nothing, for there is no virtue in maudlin remorse; no hope in alcoholic repentance. There is nothing that can save him but to stop, and it takes something of manhood to do this.

Such tears of remorse are not "tears from the depths of some divine despair." They are rather due to the fact that alcohol irritates the lachrymal glands. Harold Frederic's story of Theron Ware is a characteristic study of the deterioration of the good young man who is only "accidentally good," and who has within him neither manliness nor strength when temptation comes in unexpected forms.

With most men sin comes not as a result of strong passion, ungovernable impulses, and revolt against conventions. As with Theron Ware, it is an outcome of weak will, scanty brains, and unchecked selfishness, brought in contact with petty or nasty temptation of corrosion.

It is true that there are cases of another kind. There are some men whose untamable independence leads them into paths of danger simply as a revolt from tiresome conventionalities. They sin because they will not be tied to the apron strings of society. For these lawless, turbulent, self-defiant spirits, there is always great hope; for when they find themselves entangled in the conventionalities of evil, tied to the apron strings of the devil, they are likely to break away again, and lead lives all the more worthy, because they have found the path of wisdom and strength for themselves. To this class belong the subjects of the great conversions, the real brands who have snatched themselves from the real burnings.

"What a world this would be without coffee," said one old pessimist to another, as they sat and growled together at an evening reception. "What a world it is with coffee," said the other, for he knew that the only solace coffee could give was, that it seemed for the moment to repair the injury its own excessive use had brought. No stimulant or narcotic can ever do more than this. They help us to forget time and space and ourselves,—all we have worth remembering. "With health and a day" man "can put the pomp of emperors to shame." Without time and space he can do nothing. He is nothing.

"There is joy in life," says Sullivan, the pugilist, "but it is known only to the man who has a few jolts of liquor under his belt." To know this kind of joy is to put oneself beyond the reach of all others.

The joy of the blue sky, the bright sunshine, the rushing torrent, the songs of birds, "sweet as children's prattle is," the breath of the meadows, the glow of effort, the beauty of poetry, the achievement of thought, the thousand and thousand real pleasures of life, are inaccessible to him "who has a few jolts of liquor under his belt," while the sorrows he feels, or thinks he feels, are as unreal as his joys, and as unworthy of a life worth living.

There was once, I am told, a man who came into his office smacking his lips, and said to his clerk, "The world looks very different to the man who has had a good glass of brandy and soda in the morning." "Yes," said the clerk, "and the man looks different to the world."

And this is natural and inevitable, for the pleasure which exists only in imagination leads to action which has likewise nothing to do with the demands of life. The mind is confused, and may be delighted with the confusion, but the confused muscles tremble and halt. The tongue is loosened and utters unfinished sentences; the hand is loosened, and the handwriting is shaky; the muscles of the eyes are unharnessed, and the two eyes move independently and see double; the legs are loosened, and the confusion of the brain shows itself in the confused walk. And if this confusion is long continued, the mental deterioration shows itself in external things, the shabby hat and seedy clothing, and the gradual drop of the man from stratum to stratum of society, till he brings up some night in the ditch. As the world looks more and more different to him, so does he look more and more different to the world.

A prominent lawyer of Boston once told me that the great impulse to total abstinence came to him when a young man, from hearing his fellow lawyers talking over their cups. The most vital secrets of their clients' business were made public property when their tongues were loosened by wine; and this led my friend to the firm resolution that nothing should go into his mouth which would prevent him from keeping it closed unless he wanted to open it. The time will come when the only opening for the ambitious man of intemperate habits will be in politics. It is rapidly becoming so now. Private employers dare not trust their business to the man who drinks. The great corporations dare not. He is not wanted on the railroads. The steamship lines have long since cast him off. The banks dare not use him. He cannot keep accounts. Only the people, long-suffering and generous, remain as his resource. For this reason, municipal government is his specialty; and while this patience of the people lasts, our cities will breed scandals as naturally as our swamps breed malaria.

Akin to intemperance is the drug habit. I have no desire to indulge in sweeping condemnations. The development of corrective and preventive surgery is one of the glories of modern science. The use of medicines for corrective and preventive purposes is often most wise and necessary; but the constant recourse to drugs for every conceivable purpose is one of the most discouraging features of our civilisation. The vast array of nerve foods, tonics and appetizers have some poisonous stimulant as the basis of their effects. The cures they perform are, for the most part, cheats and impositions, and the final evil results invite fresh attacks from frauds and impostors. There is no agent in the degradation of the American press more potent than the advertisement of the quack doctor. The desire to secure this advertisement leads the paper to pander to the tastes of the fools on whose life blood the medical frauds will feed.

All that a drug can do, for the most part, is to change the stress in the process of life. It can create nothing. It cannot bring health. Health is to the physical body what happiness is to the mind. It is the glow that accompanies normal effort; and this glow must be preceded by effort. No drug can take the place of exercise, and no hysteria of the imagination is substitute for the sanity of health. The drug habit, and its second stage, patent medicine habit, and its third stage called mental healing, arise from the desire to make a short cut to health, and thus to happiness. Its continuance is the mark as well as the cause of personal degeneration. It has been said that "civilisation is a disease of the nerves." This is nonsense, as the wisdom, effort, continuity, and virtue on which civilisation depends are matters demanding the most perfect mental health. But a "disease of the nerves" is among civilisation's by-products. The conquests of civilisation, in the hands of incompetents, are as "edged tools in the hands of fools." They furnish effectual means of enforcing the penalties of folly. Whether, in medical matters, one places his faith in the touch of a king or a lunatic, in blessed handkerchiefs or old bones, in a figment of the imagination or in a bottle of cocaine or the oil of celery, the mental attitude is much the same. It is the attitude of skepticism toward knowledge. The philosophy of ignorance is the doubt of the existence of knowledge or skill. Its hope is that of finding without effort the short cut to results which only knowledge and skill give.

A wise teacher of women, Anne Payson Call, has said that "always and ever sham emotions torture, whether they be of love, religion, or liquor." A sham emotion, in this sense, is an impulse or sensation, cultivated for its own sake, with no purpose that it shall ever be translated into action. This is the "rose pink sentimentalism" so abhorred by Carlyle as "the second power of a lie, the tissue of deceit that has never been and never can be woven into action."

And in the lives of women, in particular, the short cut to happiness through emotionalism is one too often traversed. "Emotional excess," continues Miss Call, "is a woman's form of drunkenness. Nervous prostration is her delirium tremens."

For emotion or sensation to go over into action is to follow the normal law of the mind. To cultivate sensation for sensation's sake, with no purpose beyond it, whether of art, music, love, or religion, is to live a sensuous life, and this is ultimately a life of weakness and decadence. To cultivate emotion without effort at action is to keep the nervous system in a state of excitement as ineffective as the exhilaration of alcohol. The influence of intense sentimentalism and emotional gush, whether religious or secular, is as evil as the influence of liquor, and works in much the same way, a fact to which the wise John Wesley long ago called the attention of his followers.

If religious excitement is used as a source of pleasurable thrills, it is as destructive to the nervous system as any other form of lying that may be forced upon it. The religion which shows itself in trances, catalepsy, and hysteria is not religion at all, but mania. It is a sign of the softening of the brain, not of the salvation to the soul.

Of like nature is the disposition to live in dreams, to give oneself up to reverie. To live in two worlds at once is to unfit oneself for life in any world. It is to make a short cut to unreal happiness by turning oneself away from the only way to the happiness that now is. There are many other ways in which the evils of short cuts to happiness show themselves. The habit of envy is one of these, the jealousy of the weak for the fortunate, the belief that in some way or another our misery is the work of some one whose patience seems rewarded with prosperity. Many a vagabond looks upon a man with a clean collar as a man who has robbed him, and to make the most of this jealousy is the stock in trade of many of our agitators and politicians. The motive force of much that calls itself social reform is the hope that those who deserve nothing will get something at the next social deal. A social condition which shall not demand personal responsibility is the Utopia of thousands of dreamers.

But the point of all I have to say is this: What is worth having comes at the cost which corresponds to its worth. If the end of life is to enjoy life, we must so live that enjoyment is possible to the end. If the end of life is to help our neighbours, the conditions remain exactly the same. This is the lesson of human experience as to the search for happiness.

All forms of subjective enjoyment are pleasures that begin and end with self, and are unrelated to external things, are insane and unwholesome, destructive to effectiveness in life and of rational enjoyment. And this is true of spurious emotions alike, whether the pious, ecstasies of a half-starved monk, the neurotic excesses of the sentimentalist, or the riots of a debauchee.

It is not for you, taking Kipling's words, "with all your life's work to be done, that you must needs go dancing down the devil's swept and garnished causeway, because forsooth there is a light woman's smile at the end of it." It is not for you to seek strength by hazard or chance. Power has its price, and its price is straight effort.

It is not for you to seek pleasure and strength in drugs, whose only function is to deceive you, whose gifts of life are not so real as your own face in the glass.

It is not for you to believe that idleness brings rest, or that unearned rest brings pleasure. You are young men and strong, and it is for you to resist corrosion, and to help stamp it out of civilised society.

A man ought to be stronger than anything that can happen to him. He is the strong man who can say *no.* He is the wise man who, for all his life, can keep mind and soul and body clean.

"I know of no more encouraging fact," says Thoreau, "than the ability of a man to elevate his life by conscious endeavour. It is something to paint a particular picture, or to carve a statue, and so make a few objects beautiful. It is far more glorious to carve and paint the very atmosphere and medium through which we look. This morally we can do."

THE POWER OF TRUTH

William George Jordan

William George Jordan, born in 1864, was editor of the *Saturday Evening Post* and, later, secretary to the U.S. House of Governors. He wrote numerous motivational essays that were widely published. Jordan's essays were so popular among members of the Church that several of them were serialized in the *Improvement Era.* In 1908, the magazine's managing editor wrote, "We are pleased to announce to our readers that arrangements have been made for the right to print in the *Improvement Era,* beginning in June, sixteen chapters under the above caption ["Self-Control, Its Kingship and Majesty"], by William George Jordan, the author of *Great Truths* [British edition of *The Power of Truth;* the American edition was published in 1902]. . . . We are confident our readers will be delighted with these essays which contain in epigrammatic form such counsel on the right attitude toward life as is universally needed." (*Improvement Era,* May 1908, 553.) The magazine later serialized other works by Jordan, including *The Crown of Individuality, Little Problems of Married Life,* and, as late as 1934, *The Power of Truth.*

President Heber J. Grant noted in a general conference address in October 1913 that he had received a letter from William George Jordan:

"I sent him a number of tracts, a Book of Mormon and some pamphlets, and in acknowledging their receipt he thanked me for them and expressed the hope that some day he might visit Utah and learn by personal contact regarding our people. 'From what I know of your people,' he said, 'your religion more than that of other creeds yields dividends of finer individual lives; no faith is of any value unless it does yield dividends of better lives.' I feel that compliments or praise of this kind, coming from those who are not of us, are precious, and should be appreciated by every Latter-day Saint." (Conference Report, October 1913, 89–90.)

In 1937 President Grant printed a private edition of *The Power of Truth*, which he distributed to the elders serving in the European Mission. In the front of the volume he noted, "It gives me much pleasure indeed, before leaving for home, to give to each of the missionaries a copy of this excellent book. The first, second and last paragraphs in the first article, 'The Power of Truth,' have made a very profound impression on my mind. I am sure you will enjoy reading these three paragraphs and also the entire contents of the book."

In the title essay, William George Jordan attempts, in part, to answer the question of Pontius Pilate to Jesus: "Art thou a king then? Jesus answered, Thou sayest that I am a king. To this end was I born, and for this cause came I into the world, that I should bear witness unto the truth. Every one that is of the truth heareth my voice. Pilate saith unto him, What is truth?" (John 18:37–38.) Had Pilate but known that the Savior had already answered that question: "*I* am the way, *the truth,* and the life: no man cometh unto the Father, but by me." (John 14:6; italics added.)

To Latter-day Saints, Jordan's essay also brings to mind the final verse of John Jaques's powerful hymn:

> *Then say, what is truth? 'Tis the last and the first,*
> *For the limits of time it steps o'er.*
> *Though the heavens depart, and the earth's fountains burst,*
> *Truth, the sum of existence, will weather the worst,*
> *Eternal, unchanged, evermore.*

THE POWER OF TRUTH

Truth is the rock foundation of every great character. It is loyalty to the right as we see it; it is courageous living of our lives in harmony with our ideals; it is always—power.

Truth ever defies full definition. Like electricity, it can only be explained by noting its manifestation. It is the compass of the soul, the guardian of conscience, the final touchstone of right. Truth is the revelation of the ideal; but it is also an inspiration to realize that ideal, a constant impulse to live it.

Lying is one of the oldest vices in the world—it made its début in the first recorded conversation in history, in a famous interview in the Garden of Eden. Lying is the sacrifice of honour to create a wrong impression. It is masquerading in misfit virtues. Truth can stand alone, for it needs no chaperone or escort. Lies are cowardly, fearsome things that must travel in battalions. They are like a lot of drunken men, one vainly seeking to support another. Lying is the partner and accomplice of all the other vices. It is the cancer of moral degeneracy in an individual life.

Truth is the oldest of all virtues; it antedated man, it lived before there was man to perceive it or to accept it. It is the unchangeable, the constant. Law is the eternal truth of Nature—the unity that always produces identical results under identical conditions. When a man discovers a great truth in Nature he has the key to the understanding of a million phenomena; when he grasps a great truth in morals he has in it the key to his spiritual re-creation. For the individual, there is no such thing as theoretic truth; a great truth that is not absorbed by our whole mind and life, and has not become an inseparable part of our living, is not a real truth to us. If we know the truth and do not live it, our life is—a lie.

In speech, the man who makes Truth his watchword is careful in his words; he seeks to be accurate, neither under-stating nor over-coloring. He never states as a fact that of which he is not sure. What he says has the ring of sincerity, the hallmark of pure gold. If he praises you, you accept his statement as "net"; you do not have to work out a problem in mental arithmetic on the side to see what discount you ought to make before you accept his judgment. His promise counts for something, you accept it as being as good as his bond, you know that no matter how much it may cost him to verify and fulfil his word by his deed, he will do it. His honesty is not policy. The man who is honest merely because it is "the best policy" is not really honest, he is only politic. Usually such a man would forsake his seeming loyalty to truth and would work overtime for the devil—if he could get better terms.

Truth means "that which one troweth or believes." It is living simply and squarely by our belief; it is the externalising of a faith in a series of actions. Truth is ever strong, courageous, virile, though kindly, gentle, calm, and restful. There is a vital difference between error and untruthfulness. A man may be in error and yet live bravely by it; he who is untruthful in his life knows the truth but denies it. The one is loyal to what he believes; the other is traitor to what he knows.

"What is truth?" Pilate's great question, asked of Christ near two thousand years ago, has echoed unanswered through the ages. We get constant revelations of parts of it, glimpses of constantly new phrases, but never complete, final definition. If we but live up to the truth that we know, and seek ever to know more, we have put ourselves into the spiritual attitude of receptiveness to know Truth in the fulness of its power. Truth is the sun of morality, and, like that lesser sun in the heavens, we can walk by its light, live in its warmth and life, even if we see but a small part of it, and receive but a microscopic fraction of its rays.

Which of the great religions of the world is the real, the final, the absolute truth? We must make our individual choice, and live by it as best we can. Every new sect, every new cult, has in it a grain of truth at least; it is this that attracts attention and wins adherents. This mustard-seed of truth is often overestimated, darkening the eyes of man to the untrue parts or phases of the varying religious faiths. But in exact proportion to the basic truth they contain do religions last, become permanent and growing, and satisfy and inspire the hearts of men. Mushrooms of error have a quick growth, but they exhaust their vitality and die, while Truth still lives.

The man who makes the acquisition of wealth the goal and

ultimatum of his life, seeing it as an end rather than a means to an end, is not true. Why does the world usually make wealth the criterion of success, and riches the synonym of attainment? Real success in life means the individual's conquest of himself; it means "how he has bettered himself," not "how has he bettered his fortune?" The great question of life is not "What have I?" but "What am I?"

Man is usually loyal to what he most desires. The man who lies to save a penny merely proclaims that he esteems a penny more than he does his honor. He who sacrifices his ideals, truth and character, for mere money or position is weighing his conscience in one pan of a scale against a bag of gold in the other. He is loyal to what he finds the heavier, that which he desires the more—the money. But this is not truth. Truth is the heart's loyalty to abstract right, made manifest in concrete instances.

The tradesman who lies, cheats, misleads, and overcharges, and then seeks to square himself with his anaemic conscience by saying, "Lying is absolutely necessary to business," is as untrue in his statement as he is in his acts. He justifies himself with the same petty defence as the thief who says it is necessary to steal in order to live. The permanent business prosperity of an individual, a city, or a nation rests finally on commercial integrity alone, despite all that the cynics may say, or all the exceptions whose temporary success may mislead them. It is truth alone that lasts.

The politician who is vacillating, temporising, shifting, constantly trimming his sails to catch every puff of wind of popularity, is a trickster who succeeds only until he is found out. A lie may live for a time, truth for all time. A lie never lives by its own vitality, merely continues to exist because it simulates truth. When it is unmasked, it dies.

When each of four newspapers in one city puts forth the claim that its circulation is larger than all the others combined, there must be an error somewhere. Where there is untruth there is always conflict, discrepancy, impossibility. If all the truths of life and experience from the first second of time, or for any section of eternity, were brought together, there would be perfect harmony, perfect accord, union, and unity, but if two lies come together, they quarrel and seek to destroy each other.

It is in the trifles of daily life that truth should be our constant guide and inspiration. Truth is not a dress-suit, consecrated to special occasions; it is the strong, well-woven, durable homespun for daily living.

The man who forgets his promises is untrue. We rarely lose sight of those promises made to us for our individual benefit; these we regard as cheques we always seek to cash at the earliest moment. "The miser never forgets where he hides his treasure," says one of the old philosophers. Let us cultivate that sterling honour that holds our word so supreme, so sacred, that to forget it would seem a crime, to deny it would be impossible.

The man who says pleasant things and makes promises which to him are light as air, but to someone else seem the rock upon which a life's hope is built, is cruelly untrue. He who does not regard his appointments, carelessly breaking them or ignoring them, is the thoughtless thief of another's time. It reveals selfishness, carelessness, and lax business morals. It is untrue to the simplest justice of life.

Men who split hairs with their conscience, who mislead others by deft, shrewd phrasing, which may be true in letter yet lying in spirit, and designedly uttered to produce a false impression, are untruthful in the most cowardly way. Such men would cheat even in the game of solitaire. Like murderers, they forgive themselves their crime in congratulating themselves on the cleverness of their alibi.

The parent who preaches honor to his child and gives false statistics about the child's age to the inspector, to save paying the full fare, is not true.

The man who keeps his religion in camphor all the week, and takes it out only on Sunday, is not true. He who seeks to get the highest wages for the least possible amount of service is not true. The man who has to sing lullabies to his conscience before he himself can sleep is not true.

Truth is the straight line in morals. It is the shortest distance between a fact and the expression of it. The foundations of truth should ever be laid in childhood. It is then that parents should instil into the young mind the instant, automatic turning to truth, making it the constant atmosphere of the mind and life. Let the child know that "Truth above all things" should be the motto of its life. Parents make a great mistake when they look upon a lie as a disease in morals; it is not always a disease in itself, it is but a symptom. Behind every untruth is some reason, some cause, and it is this cause that should be removed. The lie may be the result of fear, the attempt to cover a fault and to escape punishment; it may be merely the evidence of an over-active imagination; it may reveal maliciousness or obstinacy; it may be the hunger for praise that leads the child to win attention and to startle others by wonderful stories; it may be merely carelessness in speech, the reckless use of words; it may be acquisitiveness that makes lying the handmaid of theft. But if, in the life of the child or the adult, the symptom be made to reveal the disease, and that be then treated, truth reasserts itself and the moral health is restored.

Constantly telling a child not to lie is giving life and intensity to "the lie." The true method is to quicken the moral muscles from the positive side, urge the child to be honest, to be faithful, to be loyal, to be fearless to the truth. Tell him ever of the nobility of courage to speak the true, to live the right, to hold fast to principles of honor in every trifle—then he need never fear to face any of life's crises.

The parents must live truth, or the child will not live it. The child will startle you with its quickness in puncturing the bubble of your pretended knowledge; in instinctively piercing the heart of a sophistry without being conscious of process; in relentlessly enumerating your unfulfilled promises; in detecting with the justice of a court of equity a technicality of speech that is virtually a lie. He will justify his own lapses from truth by appeal to some white lie told to a visitor, and unknown to be overheard by the little one, whose mental powers we ever underestimate in theory though we may over-praise in words.

Teach the child in a thousand ways, directly and indirectly, the power of truth, the beauty of truth, and the sweetness and rest of companionship with truth.

And if truth be the rock-foundation of the child's character, as a fact, not as a theory, the future of that child is as fully assured as it is possible for human prevision to guarantee.

The power of Truth, in its highest, purest, and most exalted phases, stands squarely on four basic lines of relation—the love of truth, the search for truth, faith in truth, and work for truth.

The love of Truth is the cultivated hunger for it in itself and for itself, without any thought of what it may cost, what sacrifices it may entail, what theories or beliefs of a lifetime may be laid desolate. In its supreme phase, this attitude of life is rare, but unless one can *begin* to put himself into harmony with this view, the individual will only creep in truth, when he might walk bravely. With the love of truth the individual scorns to do a mean thing, no matter what be the gain, even if the whole world would approve. He would not sacrifice the sanction of his own high standard for any gain; he would not willingly deflect the needle of his thought and act from the true North, as he knows it, by the slightest possible variation. He himself would know of the deflection—that would be enough. What matters it what the world thinks if he have his own disapproval?

The man who has a certain religious belief and fears to discuss it, lest it may be proved wrong, is not loyal to his belief; he has but a coward's faithfulness to his prejudices. If he were a lover of truth, he would be willing at any moment to surrender his belief for a higher, better, and truer faith.

The man who votes the same ticket in politics, year after year, without caring for issues, men, or problems, merely voting in a certain way because he always has voted so, is sacrificing loyalty to truth, to a weak, mistaken, stubborn attachment to a worn-out precedent. Such a man should stay in his cradle all his life—because he spent his early years there.

The search for Truth means that the individual must not merely follow truth as he sees it, but he must, so far as he can, search to see that he is right. When the *Kearsarge* was wrecked on the Roncador Reef, the captain was sailing correctly by his chart. But his map was an old one; the sunken reef was not marked down. Loyalty to back-number standards means stagnation. In China they plough to-day, but they plough with the instrument of four thousand years ago. The search for truth is the angel of progress—in civilization and in morals. While it makes us bold and aggressive in our own life, it teaches us to be tender and sympathetic with others. Their life may represent a station we have passed in our progress, or one we must seek to reach. We can then congratulate ourselves without condemning them. All the truths of the world are not concentrated in our creed. All the sunshine of the world is not focussed on our doorstep. We should ever speak the truth—but only in love and kindness. Truth should ever extend the hand of love; never the hand clenching a bludgeon.

Faith in Truth is an essential to perfect companionship with truth. The individual must have perfect confidence and assurance of the final triumph of right and order and justice, and believe that all things are evolving toward that divine consummation, no matter how dark and dreary life may seem from day to day. No real success, no lasting happiness, can exist except it be founded on the rock of truth. The prosperity that is based on lying, deception, and intrigue is only temporary—it cannot last, any more than a mushroom can outlive an oak. Like the blind Samson, struggling in the temple, the individual whose life is based on trickery always pulls down the supporting columns of his own edifice, and perishes in the ruins. No matter what price a man may pay for truth, he is getting it at a bargain. The lying of others can never hurt us long; it always carries with it our exoneration in the end. During the siege of Sebastopol, the Russian shells that threatened to destroy a fort opened a hidden spring of water in the hillside, and saved the thirsting people they sought to kill.

Work for the interests and advancement of Truth is a necessary part of real companionship. If a man has a love of truth, if he searches to find it, and has faith in it, even when he cannot find it, will he not work to spread it? The strongest way for man to strengthen the power of truth in the world is to live it himself in every detail of thought, word, and deed—to make himself a sun of personal radiation of truth, and to let his silent influence speak for it, and his direct acts glorify it, so far as he can in his sphere of life and action. Let him first seek to *be,* before he seeks to teach or to do, in any line of moral growth.

Let man realize that Truth is essentially an *intrinsic* virtue, in his relation to himself even if there were no other human being living; it becomes *extrinsic* as he radiates it in his daily life. Truth is, first, intellectual honesty, the craving to know the right; second, it is moral honesty, the hunger to live the right.

Truth is not a mere absence of the vices. This is only a moral vacuum. Truth is the living, pulsing, breathing, of the virtues of life. Mere refraining from wrong-doing is but keeping the weeds out of the garden of one's life. But this must be followed by positive planting of the seeds of right to secure the flowers of true living. To the negatives of the Ten Commandments must be added the positives of the Beatitudes. The one condemns, the other commends! the one forbids, the other inspires; the one emphasises the act, the other the spirit behind the act. The whole truth rests not in either, but in both.

A man cannot truly believe in God without believing in the final inevitable triumph of Truth. If you have Truth on your side, you can pass through the dark valley of slander, misrepresentation, and abuse, undaunted, as though you wore a magic suit of mail that no bullet could enter, no arrow could pierce. You can hold your head high, toss it fearlessly and defiantly, look every man calmly and unflinchingly in the eye, as though you rode, a victorious king, returning at the head of your legions with banners waving and lances glistening, and bugles filling the air with music. You can feel the great expansive wave of moral health singing through you as the quickened blood courses through the body of him who is gladly, gloriously proud of physical health. You will know that all will come right in the end, that it *must* come, that error must flee before the great white light of truth, as darkness slinks away into nothingness in the presence of the sunburst. Then, with Truth as your guide, your companion, your ally and inspiration, you tingle with the consciousness of your kinship with the Infinite, and all the petty trials, sorrows, and sufferings of life fade away like temporary, harmless visions seen in a dream.

The Courage to Face Ingratitude

Ingratitude, the most popular sin of humanity, is forgetfulness of the heart. It is the revelation of the emptiness of pretended loyalty. The individual who possesses it finds it the shortest cut to all the other vices.

Ingratitude is a crime more despicable than revenge, which is only returning evil for evil, while ingratitude returns evil for good. People who are ungrateful rarely forgive you if you do them a good turn. Their microscopic hearts resent the humiliation of having been helped by a superior, and this rankling feeling filtering through their petty natures often ends in hate and treachery.

Gratitude is thankfulness expressed in action. It is the instinctive radiation of justice, giving new life and energy to the individual from whom it emanates. It is the heart's recognition of kindness that the lips cannot repay. Gratitude never counts its payments. It realises that no debt of kindness can ever be outlawed, ever be cancelled, ever paid in full. Gratitude ever feels the insignificance of its instalments; ingratitude the nothingness of the debt. Gratitude is the flowering of a seed of kindness; ingratitude is the dead inactivity of a seed dropped on a stone.

The expectation of gratitude is human; the rising superior to ingratitude is almost divine. To desire recognition of our acts of kindness, and to hunger for appreciation and the simple justice of a return of good for good, is natural. But man never rises to the dignity of true living until he has the courage that dares to face ingratitude calmly, and to pursue his course unchanged when his good works meet with thanklessness or disdain.

Man should have only one court of appeal as to his actions, not "what will be the result?" "how will it be received?" but "is it right?" Then he should live his life in harmony with this standard alone, serenely, bravely, loyally, and unfalteringly, making "right for right's sake" both his ideal and his inspiration.

Man should not be an automatic gas machine, cleverly contrived to release a given quantity of illumination under the stimulus of a nickel. He should be like the great sun itself, which ever radiates light, warmth, life, and power, because it cannot help doing so, because these qualities fill the heart of the sun, and for it to have them means that it must give them constantly. Let the sunlight of our sympathy, tenderness, love, appreciation, influence, and kindness ever go out from us as a glow to brighten and hearten others. But do not let us ever spoil it all by going through life constantly collecting receipts, as vouchers, to stick on the file of our self-approval.

It is hard to see those who have sat at our board in the days of our prosperity flee as from a pestilence when misfortune darkens our doorway; to see the loyalty upon which we would have staked our life, that seemed firm as a rock, crack and splinter like thin glass at the first real test; to know that the fire of friendship at which we could ever warm our hands in our hour of need, has turned to cold, dead, grey ashes, where warmth is but a haunting memory.

To realize that he who once lived in the sanctuary of our affection, in the frank confidence where conversation seemed but our soliloquy and to whom our aims and aspirations have been thrown open with no Bluebeard chamber of reserve, has been secretly poisoning the waters of our reputation and undermining us by his lies and treachery, is hard indeed. But no matter how the ingratitude stings us, we should just swallow the sob, stifle the tear, smile serenely and bravely, and seek to forget.

In justice to ourselves we should not permit the ingratitude of a few to make us condemn the whole world. We pay too much tribute to a few human insects when we let their wrong-doing paralyze our faith in humanity. It is a lie of the cynics that says "*all* men are ungrateful," a companion lie to "*all* men have their price." We must trust humanity if we would get good from humanity. He who thinks all mankind is vile is a pessimist who mistakes his introspection for observation; he looks into his own heart and thinks he sees the world. He is like a cross-eyed man, who never sees what he seems to be looking at.

Confidence and credit are the corner-stones of business, as they are of society. Withdraw them from business and the activities and enterprises of the world would stop in an instant, topple and fall into chaos. Withdraw confidence in humanity from the individual, and he becomes but a breathing, selfish egotist, the one good man left, working overtime in nursing his petty grudge against the world because a few whom he has favored have been ungrateful.

If a man receives a counterfeit dollar he does not straightway lose his faith in all money—at least, there are no such instances on record in this country. If he has a run of three or four days of dull weather he does not say, "the sun ceases to exist, there are surely no bright days to come in the whole calendar of time."

If a man's breakfast is rendered an unpleasant memory by some item of food that has outlived its usefulness, he does not forswear eating. If a man finds under a tree an apple with a suspicious-looking hole on one side, he does not condemn the whole orchard; he simply confines his criticism to that apple. But he who has helped someone who, later, did not pass a good examination on gratitude, says in a voice plaintive with the consciousness of injury, and with a nod of his head that implies the wisdom of Solomon, "I have had my experience, I have learned my lesson. This is the last time I will have faith in any man. I did this for him, and that for him, and now look at the result!"

Then he unrolls a long schedule of favors, carefully itemized and added up, till it seems the pay-roll of a great city. He complains of the injustice of one man, yet he is willing to be unjust to the whole world, making it bear the punishment of the wrong of an individual. There is too much vicarious suffering already in this earth of ours, without this lilliputian attempt to extend it by syndicating one man's ingratitude. If one man drinks to excess, it is not absolute justice to send the whole world to jail.

The farmer does not expect every seed that he sows in hope and faith to fall on good ground and bring forth its harvest; he is perfectly certain that this will not be so, cannot be. He is counting on the final outcome of many seeds, on the harvest of all rather than on the harvest of one. If you really want gratitude, and must have it, be willing to make many men your debtors.

The more unselfish, charitable, and exalted the life and mission of the individual, the larger will be the number of instances of ingratitude that must be met and vanquished. The thirty years of Christ's life was a tragedy of ingratitudes. Ingratitude is manifest in three degrees of intensity in the world—He knew them all in numberless bitter instances.

The first phase, the simplest and most common, is that of thoughtless thanklessness, as was shown in the case of the ten lepers healed in one day—nine departed without a word, only *one* gave thanks.

The second phase of ingratitude is denial, a positive sin, not the mere negation of thanklessness. This was exemplified in Peter, whose selfish desire to stand well with two maids and some bystanders, in the hour when he had the opportunity to be loyal to Christ, forgot his friendship, lost all thought of his indebtedness to his Master, and denied Him, not once or twice, but three times.

The third phase of ingratitude is treachery, where selfishness grows vindictive, as shown by Judas, the honoured treasurer of the little band of thirteen, whose jealousy, ingratitude, and thirty pieces of silver made possible the tragedy of Calvary.

These three—thanklessness, denial, and treachery—run the gamut of ingratitude, and the first leads to the second, and the second prepares the way for the third.

We must ever tower high above dependence on human gratitude, or we can do nothing really great, nothing truly noble. The expectation of gratitude is the alloy of an otherwise virtuous act. It ever dulls the edge of even our best actions. Most persons look at gratitude as a prospective tariff on virtues. The man who is weakened in well-doing by the ingratitude of others is serving God on a salary basis. He is a hired soldier, not a volunteer. He should be honest enough to see that he is working for a reward; like a child, he is being good for a bonus. He is really regarding his kindness and his other expressions of goodness as moral stock he is willing to hold only so long as they pay dividends.

There is in such living always a touch of the pose; it is waiting for the applause of the gallery. We must let the consciousness of doing right, of living up to our ideals, be our reward and stimulus, or life will become to us but a series of failures, sorrows, and disappointments.

Much of the seeming ingratitude in life comes from our magnifying of our own acts, our minifying of the acts of others. We may have over-estimated the importance of something that we have done; it may have been most trivial, purely incidental, yet the marvellous working of the loom of time brought out great and unexpected results to the recipient of our favour. We often feel that wondrous gratitude is due to us, though we were in no wise the inspiration of the success we survey with such a feeling of pride. A chance introduction given by us in the street may, through an infinity of circumstances, make our friend a millionaire. Thanks may be due to us for the introduction, and perhaps not even that, for it might have been unavoidable, but surely we err when we expect him to be meekly grateful to us for his subsequent millions.

The essence of truest kindness lies in the grace with which it is performed. Some men seem to discount all gratitude, almost make it impossible, by the way in which they grant favours. They make you feel so small, so mean, so inferior; your cheeks burn with indignation in the acceptance of the boon you seek at their hands. You feel it is like a bone thrown at a dog, instead of the quick, sympathetic graciousness that forestalls your explanations and waives your thanks with a smile, the pleasure of one friend who has been favoured with the opportunity to be of service to another. The man who makes another feel like an insect reclining on a red-hot stove while he is receiving a favor, has no right to expect future gratitude—he should feel satisfied if he receives forgiveness.

Let us forget the good deeds we have done by making them seem small in comparison with the greater things we are doing, and the still greater acts we hope to do. This is true generosity, and will develop gratitude in the soul of him who has been helped, unless he is so petrified in selfishness as to make it impossible. But constantly reminding a man of the favors he has received from you almost cancels the debt. The care of the statistics should be his privilege; you are usurping his prerogative when you recall them. Merely because it has been our good fortune to be able to serve someone, we should not act as if we held a mortgage on his immortality, and expect him to swing the censor of adulation for ever in our presence.

That which often seems to us to be ingratitude may be merely our own ignorance of the subtle phases of human nature. Sometimes a man's heart is so full of thankfulness that he cannot speak, and in the very intensity of his appreciation mere words seem to him paltry, petty, and inadequate, and the depth of the eloquence of his silence is misunderstood. Sometimes the consciousness of his inability to repay develops a strange pride—genuine gratitude it may be, though unwise in its lack of expression—a determination to say nothing until the opportunity for which he is waiting to enable him to make his gratitude an actuality. There are countless instances in which true gratitude has all the semblance of the basest ingratitude, as certain harmless plants are made by Nature to resemble poison-ivy.

Ingratitude is someone's protest that you are no longer necessary to him; it is often the expression of rebellion at the discontinuance of favors. People are rarely ungrateful until they have exhausted their assessments. Profuse expressions of gratitude do not cancel an indebtedness any more than a promissory note settles an account. It is a beginning, not a finality. Gratitude that is extravagant in words is usually economical in all other expressions.

No good act performed in the world ever dies. Science tells us that no atom of matter can ever be destroyed, that no force, once started, ever ends; it merely passes through a multiplicity of ever-changing phases. Every good deed done to others is a great force that starts an unending pulsation through time and eternity. We may not know it, we may never hear a word of gratitude or of recognition, but it will all come back to us in some form as naturally, as perfectly, as inevitably, as echo answers to sound. Perhaps not as we expect it, how we expect it, nor where; but sometime, somehow, somewhere, it comes back, as the dove that Noah sent from the Ark returned with its green leaf of revelation.

Let us conceive of gratitude in its largest, most beautiful sense, that if we receive any kindness we are debtor, not merely to one man, but to the whole world. As we are each day indebted to thousands for the comforts, joys, consolations, and blessings of life, let us realize that it is only by kindness to all that we can begin to repay the debt to one, begin to make gratitude the atmosphere of all our living, and a constant expression in outward acts, rather than in mere thoughts. Let us see the awful cowardice and the injustice of ingratitude, not to take it too seriously in others, not to condemn it too severely, but merely to banish it for ever from our own lives, and to make every hour of our living the radiation of the sweetness of gratitude.

People Who Live in Air-Castles

Living in an air-castle is about as profitable as owning a half-interest in a rainbow. It is no more nourishing than a dinner of twelve courses—

eaten in a dream. Air-castles are built of golden moments of time, and their only value is in the raw material thus rendered valueless.

The atmosphere of air-castles is heavy and stupefying with the incense of vague hopes and phantom ideals. In them man lulls himself into dreaming inactivity with the songs of the mighty deeds he is going to do, the great influence he some day will have, the vast wealth that will be his, sometime, somehow, somewhere, in the rosy, sunlit days of the future. The architectural error about air-castles is that the owner builds them *downward* from their gilded turrets in the clouds, instead of *upward* from a solid, firm foundation of purpose and energy. This diet of mental lotus-leaves is a mental narcotic, not a stimulant.

Ambition, when wedded to tireless energy, is a great thing and a good thing, but in itself it amounts to little. Man cannot raise himself to higher things by what he would like to accomplish, but only by what he endeavours to accomplish. To be of value, ambition must ever be made manifest in zeal, in determination, in energy consecrated to an ideal. If it be thus reinforced, thus combined, the thin airy castle melts into nothingness, and the individual stands on a new strong foundation of solid rock, whereon, day by day and stone by stone, he can rear a mighty material structure of life-work to last through time and eternity. The air-castle ever represents the work of an architect without a builder; it means plans never put into execution. They tell us that man is the architect of his own fortunes. But if he be merely architect he will make only an air-castle of his life; he should be architect and builder too.

Living in the future is living in an air-castle. To-morrow is the grave where the dreams of the dreamer, the toiler who toils not, are buried. The man who says he will lead a newer and better life to-morrow, who promises great things for the future, and yet does nothing in the present to make that future possible, is living in an air-castle. In his arrogance he is attempting to perform a miracle; he is seeking to turn water into wine, to have harvest without seed-time, to have an end without a beginning.

If we would make our lives worthy of us, grand and noble, solid and impregnable, we must forsake air-castles of dreaming for strong-holds of doing. Every man with an ideal has a right to live in the glow and inspiration of it, and to picture the joy of attainment, as the tired traveller fills his mind with the thought of the brightness of home, to quicken his steps and to make the weary miles seem shorter; but the worker should never really worry about the future, think little of it except for inspiration, to determine his course, as mariners study the stars, to make his plans wisely, and to prepare for that future by making each separate day the best and truest that he can.

Let us live up to the fulness of our possibilities each day. Man has only one day of life—to-day. He *did* live yesterday, he *may* live to-morrow, but he *has* only to-day.

The secret of true living—mental, physical and moral, material and spiritual—may be expressed in five words: *Live up to your portion.* This is the magic formula that transforms air-castles into fortresses.

Men sometimes grow mellow and generous in the thought of what they would do if great wealth came to them. "If I were a millionaire," they say—and they let the phrase melt sweetly in their mouths as though it were a caramel—"I would subsidize genius; I would found a college; I would build a great hospital; I would erect model tenements; I would show the world what real charity is." Oh, it is all so easy, so easy, this vicarious benevolence, this spending of other people's fortunes! Few of us, according to the latest statistics, have a million, but we all have something, some part of it. Are we living up to our portion? Are we generous with what we have?

The man who is selfish with one thousand pounds will not develop angelic wings of generosity when his million comes. If the generous spirit be a reality with the individual, instead of an empty boast, he will, every hour, find opportunity to make it manifest. The radiation of kindness need not be expressed in money at all. It may be shown in a smile of human interest, a glow of sympathy, a word of fellowship with the sorrowing and the struggling, an instinctive outstretching of a helping hand to one in need.

No man living is so poor that he cannot evidence his spirit of benevolence toward his fellowman. It may assume that rare and wondrously beautiful phase of divine charity, in realizing how often a motive is misrepresented in the act, how sin, sorrow, and suffering have warped and disguised latent good, in substituting a word of gentle tolerance for some cheap tinsel of shabby cynicism that pretends to be wit. If we are not rich enough to give "cold, hard" cash, let us at least be too rich to give "cold, hard" words. Let us leave our air-castles of vague self-adulation for so wisely spending millions we have never seen, and rise to the dignity of living up to the full proportion of our possessions, no matter how slight they may be. Let us fill the world around us with love, brightness, sweetness, gentleness, helpfulness, courage, and sympathy, as if they were the only legal tender and we were Monte Cristos with untold treasures of such gold ever at our call.

Let us cease saying: "If I were," and say ever: "I am." Let us stop living in the subjunctive mood, and begin to live in the indicative.

The one great defence of humanity against the charge of unfulfilled duties is "lack of time." The constant clamoring for time would be pathetic were it not for the fact that most individuals throw away more of it than they use. Time is the only really valuable possession of man, for without it every power within him would cease to exist. Yet he recklessly squanders his great treasure as if it were valueless. The wealth of the whole world could not buy one second of time. Yet Society assassins dare to say in public that they have been "killing time." The time fallacy has put more people into air-castles than all other causes combined. Life is only time; eternity is only more time; immortality is merely man's right to live through unending time.

"If I had a library I would read," is the weak plaint of some other tenant of an air-castle. If a man does not read the two or three good books in his possession or accessible to him, he would not read if he had the British Museum brought to his bedside, and the British Army delegated to continual service in handing him books from the shelves. The time sacrificed to reading sensational newspapers might be consecrated to good reading, if the individual were willing merely to live up to his portion of opportunity.

The man who longs for some crisis in life wherein he may show mighty courage, while he is expending no portion of that courage in bearing bravely the petty trials, sorrows, and disappointments of daily life, is living in an air-castle. He is just a sparrow looking enviously at the mountain crags where the hardy eagle builds her nest, and dreaming of being a great bird like that, perhaps even daring in a patronizing way to criticise her method of flight, and to plume himself with the medals he could win for flying if he only would. It is the day-by-day heroism that vitalizes all of a man's power in an emergency, that gives him confidence that when need comes he will and *must* be ready.

The air-castle typifies any delusion or folly that makes man forsake real living for an idle, vague existence. Living in air-castles means that a man sees life in a wrong perspective. He permits his lower self to dominate his higher self; he who should tower as a mighty conqueror over the human weakness, sin, and folly that threaten to destroy his better nature, binds upon his own wrists the manacles of habit that hold him a slave. He loses the crown of his kingship because he sells his royal birthright for temporary ease and comfort and the showy things of the world, sacrificing so much that is best in him for mere wealth, success, positions, or the plaudits of the world. He forsakes the throne of individuality for the air-castle of delusion.

The man who wraps himself in the Napoleonic cloak of his egotism, hypnotizing himself into believing that he is superior to all other men, that the opera-glasses of the universe are focused upon him, and that he treads the stage alone, had better wake up. He is living in an air-castle. He who, like Narcissus, falls in love with his own reflection, and thinks he has a monopoly of the great work of the world, whose conceit rises from him like the smoke from the magic bottle of the genii, and spreads till it shuts out and conceals the universe, is living in an air-castle.

The man who believes that all humanity is united in conspiracy against him, who feels that his life is the hardest in all the world, and lets the cares, sorrows, and trials that come to us all eclipse the glorious sun of his happiness, darkening his eyes to his privileges and his blessings, is living in an air-castle.

The woman who thinks the most beautiful creature in the world is seen in her mirror, and who exchanges her queenly heritage of noble living for the shams, jealousies, follies, frivolities, and pretences of society is living in an air-castle.

The man who makes wealth his god instead of his servant, who is determined to get rich, rich at any cost, and who is willing to sacrifice honesty, honour, loyalty, character, family—everything he should hold dear—for the sake of a mere stack of money-bags, is, despite his robes of ermine, only a rich pauper living in an air-castle.

The man of ultra-conservatism, the victim of false content, who has no plans, no ideals, no aspirations beyond the dull round of daily duties in which he moves like a gold-fish in a globe, is often vain enough to boast of his lack of progressiveness, in cheap shopworn phrases from those whom he permits to do his thinking for him. He does not realize that faithfulness to duties, in its highest sense, means the constant aiming at the performance of higher duties, living up, so far as can be, to the maximum of one's possibilities, not resignedly plodding along at the minimum. A piece of machinery will do this, but real men ever seek to rise to higher uses. Such a man is living in an air-castle.

With patronizing contempt he scorns the man of earnest, thoughtful purpose, who sees his goal far before him but is willing to pay any honest price to attain it; content to work day by day unceasingly, through storm and stress, and sunshine and shadow, with sublime confidence that Nature is storing up every stroke of his effort, that, though times often seem dark and progress but slight, results *must* come if he have but courage to fight bravely to the end. This man does not live in an air-castle; he is but battling with destiny for the possession of his heritage, and is strengthened in character by his struggle, even though all that he desires may not be fully awarded him.

The man who permits regret for past misdeeds, or sorrow for lost opportunities, to keep him from recreating a proud future from the new days committed to his care, is losing much of the glory of living. He is repudiating the manna of new life given each new day, merely because he misused the manna of years ago. He is doubly unwise, because he has the wisdom of his past experiences and does not profit by it, merely because of a technicality of useless, morbid regret. He is living in an air-castle.

The man who spends his time lamenting the fortune he once had, or the fame that has taken its winged flight into oblivion, frittering away his golden hours erecting new monuments in the cemetery of his past achievements and his former greatness, making what he ever *was* ever plead apology for what he *is,* lives in an air-castle. To the world and to the individual a single egg of new hope and determination, with its wondrous potency of new life, is greater than a thousand nests full of the eggs of dead dreams or unrealized ambitions.

Whatever keeps a man from living his best, truest, and highest life now, in the indicative present, if it be something that he himself places as an obstacle in his own path of progress and development, is to him an air-castle.

Some men live in the air-castle of indolence; others in the air-castle of dissipation, of pride, of avarice, of deception, of bigotry, of worry, of intemperance, of injustice, of intolerance, of procrastination, of lying, of selfishness, or of some other mental or moral characteristic that withdraws them from the real duties and privileges of living.

Let us find out what is the air-castle in which we, individually, spend most of our time, and we can then begin a re-creation of ourselves. The bondage of the air-castle must be fought nobly and untiringly.

As man spends his hours and his days and his weeks in an air-castle, he finds that the delicate gossamer-like strands and lines of the phantom structure gradually become less and less airy; they begin to grow firm and firmer, strengthening with the years, until, at last, solid walls hem him in. Then he is startled by the awful realization that habit and habitancy have transformed his air-castle into a prison from which escape is difficult.

And then he learns that the most deceptive and dangerous of all things is—the air-castle.

Swords and Scabbards

It is the custom of grateful states and nations to present swords as tokens of highest honor to the victorious leaders of their armies and navies. The sword presented to Admiral Schley by the people of Philadelphia, at the close of America's war with Spain, cost over $3,500, the greater part of which was spent on the jewels and decorations on the scabbard. A little more than half a century ago, when General Winfield Scott, for whom Admiral Schley was named, received a beautiful sword from the state of Louisiana, he was asked how it pleased him.

"It is a very fine sword, indeed," he said, "but there is one thing about it I would have preferred different. The inscription should be on the blade, not on the scabbard. The scabbard may be taken from us; the sword, never."

The world spends too much time, money, and energy on the scabbard of life; too little on the sword. The scabbard represents outside show, vanity, and display; the sword, intrinsic worth. The scabbard is ever the semblance; the sword the reality. The scabbard is the temporal; the sword is the eternal. The scabbard is the body; the sword is the soul. The scabbard typifies the material side of life; the sword the true, the spiritual, the ideal.

The man who does not dare follow his own convictions, but who lives in terror of what society will say, falling prostrate before the golden calf of public opinion, is living an empty life of mere show. He is sacrificing his individuality, his divine right to live his life in harmony with his own high ideals, to a cowardly, toadying fear of the world. He is not a voice, with the strong note of individual purpose; he is but the thin echo of the voice of thousands. He is not brightening, sharpening, and using the sword of his life in true warfare; he is lazily ornamenting a useless scabbard with the hieroglyphics of his folly.

The man who lives beyond his means, who mortgages his future for his present, who is generous before he is just, who is sacrificing everything to keep up with the procession of his superiors, is really losing much of life. He, too, is decorating the scabbard, and letting the sword rust in its sheath.

Life is not a competition with others. In its truest sense it is a rivalry with ourselves. We should each day seek to break the record of our yesterday. We should seek each day to live stronger, better, truer lives; each day to master some weakness of yesterday; each day to repair past follies; each day to surpass ourselves. And this is but progress. And individual, conscious progress, progress unending and unlimited, is the one great thing that differentiates man from all the other animals. Then we will care naught for the petty, useless decorations of society's approval on the scabbard. For us it will be enough to know that the blade of our purpose is kept ever keen and sharp for the defence of right and truth, never to wrong the rights of others, but ever to right the wrongs of ourselves and those around us.

Reputation is what the world thinks a man is; character is what he really is. Anyone can play shuttlecock with a man's reputation; his character is his alone. No one can injure his character but he himself. Character is the sword; reputation is the scabbard. Many men acquire insomnia in standing guard over their reputations, while their character gives them no concern. Often they make new dents in their character in their attempt to cut a deep, deceptive filigree on the scabbard of their reputation. Reputation is the shell a man discards when he leaves life for immortality. His character he takes with him.

The woman who spends thousands in charitable donations, and is hard and uncharitable in her judgments, sentimentally sympathetic with human sin and weakness in the abstract, while she arrogates to herself omniscience in her harsh condemnation of individual lapses, is charitable only on the outside. She is letting her tongue undo the good work of her hand. She is too enthusiastic in decorating the scabbard of publicity to think of the sword of real love of humanity.

He who carries avarice to the point of becoming a miser, hoarding gold that is made useless to him because it does not fulfil its one function, circulation, and regarding the necessities of life as luxuries, is one of Nature's jests, that would be humorous were it not so serious. He is the most difficult animal to classify in the whole natural history of humanity—he has so many of the virtues. He is a striking example of ambition, economy, frugality, persistence, will-power, self-denial, loyalty to purpose, and generosity to his heirs. These noble qualities he spoils in the application. His speciality is the scabbard of life. He spends his days in making a solid gold scabbard for the tin sword of a wasted existence.

The shoddy airs and ostentations, extravagance, and prodigality of some who have suddenly become rich, is gold-plating the scabbard without improving the blade. The superficial veneer of refinement really accentuates the native vulgarity. The more you polish woodwork, the more you reveal the grain. Some of the sudden legatees of fortune have the wisdom to acquire the reality of refinement through careful training. This is the true method of putting the sword itself in order instead of begemming the scabbard.

The girl who marries merely for money or for a title, is a feminine Esau of the beginning of the century. She is selling her birthright of love for the pottage of an empty name, forfeiting the possibility of a life of love, all that true womanhood should hold most dear, for a mere bag of gold or a crown. She is decorating the scabbard with a crest and heraldic designs, and with ornaments of pure gold set with jewels. She feels that this will be enough for life, and that she does not need love—real love, that has made this world a paradise, despite all the other people present. She does not realize that there is but one real reason, but one justification for marriage, and that is—love; all the other motives are not reasons, they are only excuses. The phrase, "marrying a man for his money," as the world bluntly puts it, is incorrect—the woman merely marries the money, and takes the man as an incumbrance or mortgage on the property.

The man who procrastinates, filling his ears with the lovely song of "to-morrow," is following the easiest and most restful method of shortening the possibilities of life. Procrastination is stifling action by delay, it is killing decision by inactivity, it is drifting on the river of time, instead of rowing bravely towards a desired harbor. It is watching the sands in the hourglass run down before beginning any new work, then reversing the glass and repeating the observation. The folly of man in thus delaying is apparent, when any second his life may stop, and the sands of that single hour may run their course—and he will not be there to see.

Delay is the narcotic that paralyzes energy. When Alexander was asked how he conquered the world, he said, "By not delaying." Let us not put off till tomorrow the duty of to-day; that which our mind tells us should be done to-day, our mind and body should execute. To-day is the sword we should hold and use; to-morrow is but the scabbard from which each new to-day is withdrawn.

The man who wears an oppressive, pompous air of dignity, because he has accomplished some little work of importance, because he is vested with a brief mantle of authority, loses sight of the true perspective of life. He is destitute of humor; he takes himself seriously. It is a thousand dollar scabbard on a two-dollar sword.

The man who is guilty of envy is the victim of the oldest vice in the history of the world, the meanest and most despicable of human traits. It began in the Garden of Eden, when Satan envied Adam and Eve. It caused the downfall of man and the first murder—Cain's unbrotherly act to Abel. Envy is a paradoxical vice. It cannot suffer bravely the prosperity of another, it has mental dyspepsia because someone else is feasting, it makes its owner's clothes turn into rags at sight of another's velvet. Envy is the malicious contemplation of the beauty, honors, success, happiness, or triumph of another. It is the mud that inferiority throws at success. Envy is the gangrene of unsatisfied ambition, it eats away purpose and kills energy. It is egotism gone to seed; it always finds the secret of its non-success in something outside itself.

Envy is the scabbard, but emulation is the sword. Emulation regards the success of another as an object-lesson; it seeks in the triumph of another the why, the reason, the inspiration of method. It seeks to attain the same heights by the path it thus discovers, not to hurl down from his eminence him who points out the way of attainment. Let us keep the sword of emulation ever brightened and sharpened in the battle of honest effort, not idly dulling and rusting in the scabbard of envy.

The supreme folly of the world, the saddest depths to which the human mind can sink, is atheism. He surely is to be pitied who permits the illogical philosophy of petty infidels, or his misinterpretations of the revelations of science, to cheat him of his God. He pins his faith to some ingenious sophistry in the reasoning of those whose books he has read to sum up for him the whole problem, and in hopeless egotism shuts his eyes to the million proofs in nature and life, because the full plans of Omnipotence are not made clear to him.

On the technicality of his failure to understand some one point—perhaps it is why sin, sorrow, suffering, and injustice exist in the world—he declares he will not believe. He might as well disbelieve in the sky above him because he cannot see it all; discredit the air he breathes because it is invisible; doubt the reality of the ocean because his feeble vision can take in but a few miles of the great sea; deny even life itself because he cannot see it, and no anatomist has found the subtle essence to hold it up to view on the end of his scalpel.

He dares to disbelieve in God despite His countless manifestations, because he is not taken into the full confidence of the Creator and permitted to look over and check off the ground-plans of the universe. He sheathes the sword of belief in the dingy scabbard of infidelity. He does not see the proof of God in the daily miracle of the rising and setting of the sun, in the seasons, in the birds, in the flowers, in the countless stars, moving in their majestic regularity at the command of eternal law, in the presence of love, justice, truth in the hearts of men, in that supreme confidence that is inborn in humanity, making even the lowest savage worship the Infinite in some form. It is the petty vanity of cheap reasoning that makes man permit the misfit scabbard of infidelity to hide from him the glory of the sword of belief.

The philosophy of swords and scabbards is as true of nations as of individuals. When France committed the great crime of the nineteenth century, by condemning Dreyfus to infamy and isolation, deafening her ears to the cries of justice, and seeking to cover her shame with greater shame, she sheathed the sword of a nation's honor in the scabbard of a nation's crime. The breaking of the sword of Dreyfus when he was cruelly degraded before the army typified the degradation of the French nation in breaking the sword of justice and preserving carefully the empty scabbard with its ironic inscription "Vive la justice."

The scabbard is ever useless in the hour of emergency; *then* it is upon the sword itself that we must rely. Then the worthlessness of show, sham, pretence, gilded weakness is revealed to us. Then the trivialities of life are seen in their true form. The nothingness of everything but the real, the tried, the true, is made luminant in an instant. Then we know whether our living has been one of true preparation, of keeping the sword clean, pure, sharp, and ready, or one of mere idle, meaningless, day-by-day markings of folly on the empty scabbard of a wasted life.

The Conquest of the Preventable

This world would be a delightful place to live in—if it were not for the people. They really cause all the trouble. Man's worst enemy is always man. He began to throw the responsibility of his transgressions on someone else in the Garden of Eden, and he has been doing so ever since.

The greater part of the pain, sorrow, and misery in life is purely a human invention; yet man, with a cowardly irreverence, dares to throw the responsibility on God. It comes through breaking laws—laws natural, physical, civic, mental, or moral. These are laws which man knows, but he disregards; he takes chances; he thinks he can dodge results in some way. But nature says, "He who breaks, pays." There are no dead-letter laws on the divine statute-books of life. When a man permits a torchlight procession to parade through a powder magazine, it is not courteous for him to refer to the subsequent explosion as "one of the mysterious workings of Providence."

Nine tenths of the world's sorrow, misfortune, and unhappiness is preventable. The daily newspapers are the great chroniclers of the dominance of the unnecessary. Paragraph after paragraph, column after column, and page after page of the dark story—accidents, disasters, crime, scandal, human weakness, and sin—might be checked off with the word "preventable." In each instance, were our information full enough, our analysis keen enough, we could trace each back to its cause, to the weakness or the wrong from which it emanated. Sometimes it is carelessness, inattention, neglect of duty, avarice, anger, jealousy, dissipation, betrayal of trust, selfishness, hypocrisy, revenge, dishonesty—any of a hundred phases of the preventable.

That which *can* be prevented *should* be prevented. It all rests with the individual. The "preventable" exists in three degrees: first, that which is due to the individual solely and directly; second, that which he suffers through the wrong-doing of those around him, other individuals; third, those instances wherein he is the unnecessary victim of the wrongs of society, the innocent legatee of the folly of humanity—and society is but the massing of thousands of individuals with the heritage of manners, customs, and laws they have received from the past.

We sometimes feel heart-sick and weary in facing failure, when the fortune that seemed almost in our fingers slips away because of the envy, malice, or treachery of someone else. We bow under the weight of a sorrow that makes all life grow dark, and the star of hope fade from our vision; or we meet some unnecessary misfortune with a dumb, helpless despair. "It is all wrong," we say, "it is cruel, it is unjust. Why is it permitted?" And in the very intensity of our feeling, we half-unconsciously repeat the words over and over again, in monotonous iteration, as if in some way the very repetition might bring relief, might somehow soothe us. Yet, in most instances, it could be prevented. No suffering is caused in the world by right. Whatever sorrow there is that is preventable comes from inharmony or wrong of some kind.

In the divine economy of the universe most of the evil, pain, and suffering are unnecessary, even when overruled for good, and perhaps, if our knowledge were perfect, it would be seen that none is necessary, that all is preventable. The fault is mine, or yours, or the fault of the world. It is always individual. The world itself is but the cohesive united force of the thoughts, words, and deeds of millions who have lived or who are living, like you and me. By individuals has the great wrong that causes our preventable sorrow been built up; by individuals must it be weakened and transformed to right. And in this, too, it is to a great degree our fault; we care so little about rousing public sentiment and lashing it into activity unless it concerns us individually.

The old Greek fable of Atlas, the African king, who supported the world on his shoulders, has a modern application. The *individual* is the Atlas upon whom the fate of the world rests to-day. Let each individual do his best—and the result is foreordained; it is but a matter of the unconquerable massing of the units. Let each individual bear his part as faithfully as though all the responsibility rested on him, yet as calmly, as gently, and as unworried as though all the responsibility rested on others.

Most accidents are preventable—as at Balaclava, "someone has blundered." One of the great disasters of the nineteenth century was the Johnstown flood, where the bursting of a dam caused the loss of more than six thousand lives. The flood was not a mere accident, it was a crime. A leaking dam, for more than a year known to be unsafe, known to be unable to withstand any increased pressure, stood at the head of the valley. Below it lay a chain of villages containing over forty-five thousand persons in the direct line of the flood. When the heavy rains came the weakened dam gave way. Had there been *one* individual, one member of the South Fork Fishing Club brave enough to have done merely his duty, *one member* with the courage to so move his fellows, and to stir up public action to make the barrier safe, over six thousand murders could have been prevented.

When a tired engineer, sleepy from overwork, can no longer cheat nature of her needed rest, and, drowsing for a moment in his box, fails to see the red signal light of danger, or to heed the exploding of the warning torpedo, the wreck that follows is not chargeable to the Almighty. It is but an awful memorial of a railway company's struggle to save two dollars. One ounce of prevention is worth six pounds of coroner's inquest. It is a crime to balance the safety and sacredness of human life in the scales with the petty saving that comes from transforming a man into a mechanism and forgetting he has either a soul or a body. True, just and wise labour laws are part of society's weapon for fighting the preventable.

When a terrible fire makes a city desolate and a nation mourn, the investigation that follows usually shows that a little human foresight could have prevented it, or, at least, lessened the horror of it all. If chemicals or dynamite are stored in any building in excess of what wise legislation declares is safe, someone has been cruelly careless. Perhaps it is some inspector who has been disloyal to his trust, by permitting bribes to chloroform his sense of duty. If the lack of fire-escapes adds its quota to the list of deaths, or if the avarice of the owner has made his building a fire-trap, public feeling becomes intense, the newspapers are justly loud in their protests, and in demands that the guilty ones be punished. "If the laws already on the statute-books do not cover the situation," we hear from day to day, "new laws will be framed to make a repetition of the tragedy impossible"; we are promised all kinds of reforms; the air seems filled with a spirit of regeneration; the mercury of public indignation rises to the point where "fever-heat" seems a mild, inadequate term.

Then, as the horror begins to fade in the perspective of the past, men go quietly back to their own personal cares and duties, and the mighty wave of righteous protest that threatened so much dies in gentle lapping on the shore. What has been all men's concern seems soon to concern no one. The tremendous energy of the authorities seems like the gesture of a drunken man, that starts from his shoulder with a force that would almost fell an ox, but when it reaches the hand it has expended itself, and the hand drops listlessly in the air with hardly power enough to disturb the serenity of a butterfly. There is always a little progress, a slight advance, and it is only the constant accumulation of these steps that is giving to the world greater dominion over the preventable.

Constant vigilance is the price of the conquest of the preventable. We have no right to admit any wrong or evil in the world as necessary until we have exhausted every precaution that human wisdom can suggest to prevent it. When a man with a pistol in his right hand, clumsily covered with a suspicious-looking handkerchief, moved along in a line of people, and presenting his left hand to President McKinley, pressed his weapon to the breast of the Chief Executive of the American people, some one of the secret service men, paid by the nation to guard their ruler, should have watched so zealously that the tragedy would have been impossible. Two Presidents had already been sacrificed, but twenty years of immunity had brought a dreamy sense of security that lessened the vigilance. We should emulate the example of the insurance companies who decline certain risks that are "extra hazardous."

Poverty has no necessary place in life. It is a disease that results from the weakness, sin, and selfishness of humanity. Nature is boundless in her generosity; the world produces sufficient to give food, clothing, and comfort to every individual. Poverty is preventable. Poverty may result from the shiftlessness, idleness, intemperance, improvidence, lack of purpose, or evil-doing of the individual himself.

If the causes do not exist in the individual, they may be found in the second class, in the wrong-doing of those around him, in the oppression of labor by capital, in the grinding process by which corporations seek to crush the individual. The individual may be the victim of any of a thousand phases of the wrong of others. The poverty caused by the third class, the weakness and injustice of human laws and human institutions, is also preventable; but to reach the cause requires time and united heroic effort of all individuals.

In the battle against poverty, those writers who seek to inflame the poor against the rich, to foment discontent between labor and capital, do grievous wrong to both. What the world needs is to have the two brought closer together in the bonds of human brotherhood. The poor should learn more of the cares, responsibilities, unrecorded charities, and absorbing worries of the rich; the rich should learn more intimately the sorrows, privations, struggles, and despair of poverty.

The world is learning the great truth, that the best way to prevent crime is to study the sociological conditions in which it flourishes, to seek to give each man a better chance of living his real life by removing, if possible, the elements that make wrong easy, and to him, almost necessary, and by inspiring him to fight life's battle bravely with all the help others can give him. Science is cooperating with religion in striving to conquer the evil at the root instead of the evil manifest as crime in the fruit of the branches. It is so much wiser to prevent than to cure; to keep someone from being burned is so much better than inventing new poultices for unnecessary hurts.

It is ever the little things that make up the sum of human misery. All the wild animals of the world combined do but trifling damage when compared with the ravages of insect pests. The crimes of humanity, the sins that make us start back affrighted, do not cause as much sorrow and unhappiness in life as the multitude of little sins, of omission and commission, that the individual, and millions like him, must meet every day. They are not the evil deeds that the law can reach or punish, they are but the infinity of petty wrongs for which man can never be tried until he stands with bowed head before the bar of justice of his own conscience.

The bitter words of anger and reproach that rise so easily to our lips and give us a moment's fleeting satisfaction in thus venting our feelings, may change the current of the whole life of someone near to us. The thoughtless speech, revealing our lack of tact and sympathy, cannot be recalled and made nothing by the plea, "I didn't think." To sensitive souls this is no justification; they feel that our hearts should be so filled with the instinct of love that our lips would need no tutor or guardian.

Our unfulfilled duty may bring unhappiness and misery to hundreds. The dressmaker's bill that a rich woman may toss lightly aside, as being an affair of no moment, to be settled at her serene pleasure, may bring sorrow, privation, or even failure to her creditor, and through her to a long chain of others. The result, if seen in all its stern reality, seems out of all proportion to the cause. There are places in the Alps where great masses of snow are so lightly poised that even the report of a gun might start a vibration that would dislodge an avalanche, and send it on its death-mission into the valley.

The individual who would live his life to the best that is within him must make each moment one of influence for good. He must set before him as one of his ideals, to be progressively realized in each day of his living: "If I cannot accomplish great deeds in the world, I will do all the good I can by the faithful performance of the duties that come to my hand and being ever ready for all opportunities. And I will consecrate myself to the conquest of the preventable."

Let the individual say each day, as he rises new-created to face a new life: "To-day no one in the world shall suffer because I live. I will be kind, considerate, careful in thought and speech and act. I will seek to discover the element that weakens me as a power in the world, and that keeps me from living up to the fulness of my possibility. That weakness I will master to-day. I will conquer it, at any cost."

When any failure or sorrow comes to the individual, he should be glad if he can prove to himself that it was his fault—for then he has the remedy in his own hands. Lying, intrigue, jealousy are never remedies that can *prevent* an evil. They postpone it, merely to augment it. They are merely deferring payment of a debt which has to be met later—with compound interest. It is like trying to put out a fire by pouring kerosene on the flames.

Jealousy in the beginning is but a thought—in the end it may mean the gallows. Selfishness often assumes seemingly harmless guises, yet it is the foundation of the world's unhappiness. Disloyalty may seem to be a rare quality, but society is saturated with it. Judas acquired his reputation because of his proficiency in it. Sympathy which should be the atmosphere of every individual life is as rare as human charity. The world is suffering from an over-supply of unnecessary evils, created by man. They should be made luxuries, then man could dispense with them.

The world needs societies formed of members pledged to the individual conquest of preventable pain and sorrow. The individual has no right that runs counter to the right of anyone else. There are no solo parts in the eternal music of life. Each must pour out his life in duo with every other. Every moment must be one of choice, of good or of evil. Which will the individual choose? His life will be his answer. Let him dedicate his life to making the world around him brighter, sweeter, and better, and by his conquest of preventable pain and sorrow he will day by day get fuller revelation of the glory of the possibilities of individual living, and come nearer and nearer to the realization of his ideals.

The Companionship of Tolerance

Intolerance is part of the unnecessary friction of life. It is prejudice on the war-path. Intolerance acknowledges only one side of any question—its own. It is the assumption of a monopoly in thinking, the attitude of the man who believes he has the sole command of wisdom and truth in some phase of life.

Tolerance is a calm, generous respect for the opinions of others, even of one's enemies. It recognises the right of every man to think his own thoughts, to live his own life, to be himself in all things, so long as he does not run counter to the rights of others. It means giving to others the same freedom that we ourselves crave. Tolerance is silent justice, blended with sympathy. If he who is tolerant desires to show to others the truth as he sees it, he seeks with gentleness and deference to point out the way in which he has found peace and certainty and rest; he tries to raise them to the recognition of higher ideals, as he has found them inspiring; he endeavours in a spirit of love and comradeship with humanity to lead others rather than to drive them, to persuade and convince, rather than to overawe and eclipse.

Tolerance does not use the battering-ram of argument, or the club of sarcasm, or the rapier of ridicule, in discussing the weakness or wrongs of individuals. It may lash or scourge the evil of an age, but it is kind and tender with the individual; it may flay the sin, but not the sinner. Tolerance makes the individual regard truth as higher than personal opinion; it teaches him to live with the windows of his life open towards the east to catch the first rays of the sunlight of truth, no matter from whom it comes, and to realize that the faith which he so harshly condemns may have the truth he desires if he would only look into it and test it before he repudiates it so cavalierly.

This world of ours is growing better, more tolerant and liberal. The days when a difference in political opinions was solved and cured by the axe and the block; when a mans' courage to stand by his religion meant facing the horrors of the Inquisition or the cruelty of the stake; when daring to think their own thoughts on questions of science brought noble men to a pallet of straw and a dungeon cell—these days have, happily, passed away. Intolerance and its twin brother, Ignorance, weaken and die when the pure white light of wisdom is thrown upon them. Knowledge is the death-knell of intolerance—not mere book-learning, nor education in schools or colleges, nor accumulation of mere statistics, nor shreds of information, but the large, sympathetic study of the lives, manners, customs, aims, thoughts, struggles, progress, motives and ideals of other ages, other nations, other individuals.

Tolerance unites men in closer bonds of human brotherhood, brings them together in unity and sympathy in essentials, and gives them greater liberality and freedom in non-essentials. Napoleon, when First Consul, said, "Let there be no more Jacobins, nor Moderates, nor Royalists: let all be Frenchmen." Sectionalism and sectarianism always mean concentration on the body of a part at the expense of the soul of the whole. The religious world to-day needs more Christ and less sects in its gospel. When Christ lived on earth Christianity was a unit; when He died sects began.

There are in America to-day, hundreds of small towns, scattered over the face of the land, that are over-supplied with churches. In many of these towns, just emerging from the short dresses of villagehood, there are half a dozen or more weak churches, struggling to keep their organization alive. Between these churches there is often only a slight difference in creed, the tissue-paper wall of some technicality of belief. Half-starved, dragging out of mere existence, trying to fight a large mortgage with a small congregation and a small contribution box, there is little spiritual fervor. By combination, by cooperation, by tolerance, by the mutual surrender of non-essentials and a strong, vital concentration and unity on the great fundamental realities of Christianity, their spiritual health and possibilities could be marvellously increased. Three or four sturdy, live, growing churches would then take the place of a dozen strugglers. Why have a dozen weak bridges across a stream, if greater good can come from three or four stronger ones, or even a single strongest bridge? The world needs a great religious trust which will unite the churches into a single body of faith, to precede and prepare the way for the greater religious trust predicted in Holy Writ—the millennium.

We can ever be loyal to our own belief, faithful to our own cause, without condemning those who give their fidelity in accord with their own conscience or desires. The great reformers of the world, men who are honestly and earnestly seeking to solve the great social problems, to provide means for meeting human sin and wrong, agreeing perfectly in their estimate of the gravity and awfulness of the situation, often propose diametrically opposite methods. They are regarding the subject from different points of view, and it would be intolerance for us, who are looking on, to condemn the men on either side merely because we cannot accept their verdict as our own.

On the great national questions brought before statesmen for their decision, men equally able, equally sincere, just and unselfish, differ in their remedies. One, as a surgeon, suggests cutting away the offending matter, the use of the knife—this typifies the sword or war. Another, as a doctor, urges medicine that will absorb and cure—this is the prescription of the diplomat. The third suggests waiting for developments, leaving the case with time and nature—this is the conservative. But all three classes agree as to the evil and the need of meeting it.

The conflict of authorities on every great question to be settled by human judgment should make us tolerant of the opinion of others, though we may be as confident of the rightness of the judgment we have formed as if it were foreordained from the day of the creation. But if we receive any new light that makes us see clearer, let us change at once, without that foolish consistency of some natures that continue to use last year's almanac as a guide to this year's eclipses. Tolerance is ever progressive.

Intolerance believes it is born with the peculiar talent for managing the affairs of others, without any knowledge of the details, better than the men themselves, who are giving their life's thought to the vital questions. Intolerance is the voice of the Pharisee still crying through the ages and proclaiming his infallibility.

Let us not seek to fit the whole world with shoes from our individual last. If we think that all music ceased to be written when Wagner laid down the pen, let us not condemn those who find enjoyment in light opera. Perhaps they may sometime rise to our heights of artistic appreciation, and learn the proper parts to applaud. If their lighter music satisfies their souls, is our Wagner doing more for us? It is not fair to take from a child its rag doll in order to raise it to the appreciation of the Venus de Milo. The rag doll is its Venus; it may require a long series of increasingly better dolls to lead it to realise the beauties of the marble woman of Melos.

Intolerance makes its great mistakes in measuring the needs of others from its own standpoint. Intolerance ignores the personal equation in life. What would be an excellent book for a man of forty might be worse than useless for a boy of thirteen. The line of activity in life that we would choose as our highest dream of bliss, as our Paradise, might, if forced on another, be to him worse than the after-death fate of the wicked, according to the old-fashioned theologians. What would be a very acceptable breakfast for a sparrow would be a very poor meal for an elephant.

When we sit in solemn judgment on the acts and characters of those around us and condemn them with the easy nonchalance of our ignorance, yet with the assumption of omniscience, we reveal our intolerance. Tolerance ever leads us to recognize and respect the differences in the natures of those who are near to us, to make allowance for differences in training, in opportunities, in ideals, in motives, in tastes, in opinions, in temperaments and in feelings. Intolerance seeks to live other people's lives *for* them; sympathy helps us to live their lives *with* them. We must accept humanity with all its weakness, sin, and folly, and seek to make the best of it, just as humanity must accept us. We learn this lesson as we grow older, and, with the increase of our knowledge of the world, we see how much happier life would have been for us and for others if we had been more tolerant, more charitable, more generous.

No one in the world is absolutely perfect; if he were he would probably be translated from earth to heaven, as was Elijah of old, without waiting for the sprouting of wings or the passport of death. It is a hard lesson for youth to learn, but we must realise, as the old college professor said to his class of students, bowed with the consciousness of their wisdom: "No one of us is infallible; no, not even the youngest." Let us accept the little failings of those around us as we accept facts in nature, and make the best of them, as we accept the hard shells of nuts, the skin of fruits, the shadow that always accompanies light. These are not absolute faults, they are often but individual peculiarities. Intolerance sees the mote in its neighbor's eye as larger than the beam in its own.

Instead of concentrating our thought on the one weak spot in a character, let us seek to find some good quality that off-sets it, just as a credit may more than cancel a debt on a ledger account. Let us not constantly speak of roses having thorns, let us be thankful that the thorns have roses. In Nature there are both thorns and prickles; thorns are organic, they have their root deep in the fibre and the being of the twig; prickles are superficial, they are lightly held in the cuticle or covering of the twig. There are thorns in character that reveal an internal inharmony, that can be controlled only from within; there are also prickles, which are merely peculiarities of temperament, that the eye of tolerance may overlook and the finger of charity can gently remove.

The tenderness of tolerance will illuminate and glorify the world—as moonlight makes all things beautiful—if we only permit it. Measuring a man by his weakness alone is unjust. This little frailty may be but a small mortgage on a large estate, and it is narrow and petty to judge by the mortgage on a character. Let us consider the "equity," the excess of the real value over the claim against it.

Unless we sympathetically seek to discover the motive behind the act, to see the circumstances that inspired a course of living, the target at which a man is aiming, our snap condemnations are but arrogant and egotistic expressions of our intolerance. All things must be studied relatively instead of absolutely. The hour hand on a clock does just as valuable work as the minute hand, even though it is shorter and seems to do only one-twelfth as much.

Intolerance in the home circle shows itself in overdiscipline, in an atmosphere of severity heavy with prohibitions. The home becomes a place strewn with "Please keep off the grass" signs. It means the suppression of individuality, the breaking of the wills of children, instead of their development and direction. It is the foolish attempt to mould them from the outside, as a potter does clay; the higher conception is the wise training that helps the child to help himself in his own growth. Parents often forget their own youth; they do not sympathize with their children in their need of pleasure, of dress, of companionship. There should be a few absolutely firm rules on essentials, the basic principles of living, with the largest possible leeway for the varying manifestations of individuality in unimportant phases. Confidence, sympathy, love, and trust would generate a spirit of tolerance and sweetness that would work marvels. Intolerance converts live, natural children into prigs of counterfeit virtue and irritatingly good automatons of obedience.

Tolerance is a state of mutual concessions. In the family life there should be this constant reciprocity of independence, this mutual forbearance. It is the instinctive recognition of the sacredness of individuality, the right of each to live his own life as best he can. When we set ourselves up as dictators to tyranize over the thoughts, words, and acts of others, we are sacrificing the kingly power of influence, with which we may help others for the petty triumphs of tyranny which repels and loses them.

Perhaps one reason why the sons of great and good men so often go astray is, that the earnestness, strength, and virtue of the father exacting strict obedience to the letter of the law, kills the appreciation of the spirit of it, breeding an intolerance that forces submission under which the fire of protest and rebellion is smouldering, ready to burst into flame at the first breath of freedom. Between brother and sister, husband and wife, parent and child, master and servant, the spirit of tolerance of "making allowances," transforms a house of gloom and harshness into a home of sweetness and love.

In the sacred relation of parent to child there always comes a time when the boy becomes a man, when she whom the father still regards but as a little girl faces the great problems of life as an individual. The coming of years of discretion brings a day when the parents must surrender their powers of trusteeship, when the individual enters upon his heritage of freedom and responsibility. Parents have still the right and privilege of counsel, and of helpful, loving insight, their children should respect. But in meeting a great question, when the son or daughter stands before a problem that means happiness or misery for a lifetime, it must be for him or for her to decide. Coercion, bribery, undue influence, threats of disinheritance and the other familiar weapons are cruel, selfish, arrogant, and unjust. A child is a human being, free to make his own life, not a slave. There is a clearly marked dead-line that it is intolerance to cross.

Let us realize that tolerance is ever broadening; it develops sympathy, weakens worry, and inspires calmness. It is but charity and optimism; it is Christianity as a living, eternal fact, not a mere theory. Let us be tolerant of the weakness of others, sternly intolerant of our own. Let us seek to forgive and forget the faults of others, losing sight, to a degree, of what they are in the thought of what they may become. Let us fill their souls with the inspiring revelation of their possibilities in the majestic evolution march of humanity. Let us see, for ourselves and for them, in the acorn of their present the towering oak of their future.

We should realize the right of every human soul to work out its own destiny, with our aid, our sympathy, our inspiration if we are thus privileged to help him to live his life; but it is intolerance to try to live it for him. He sits alone on the throne of his individuality; he must reign alone, and at the close of his rule must give his own account to the God of the ages of the deeds of his kingship. Life is a dignified privilege, a glorious prerogative of every man, and it is arrogant intolerance that touches the sacred ark with the hand of unkind condemnation.

The Things That Come Too Late

Time seems a grim old humorist, with a fondness for afterthoughts. The things that come too late are part of his sarcasm. Each generation is engaged in correcting the errors of its predecessors, and in supplying new blunders for its own posterity to set right. Each generation bequeaths to its successor its wisdom and its folly, its wealth of knowledge and its debts of error and failure. The things that come too late thus mean only the delayed payments on old debts. They mean that the world is growing wiser, and better, truer, nobler, and more just. It is emerging from the dark shadows of error into the sunshine of truth and justice. They prove that Time is weaving a beauteous fabric from the warp and woof of humanity, made up of shreds and tangles of error and truth.

The things that come too late are the fuller wisdom, the deferred honors, the truer conception of the work of pioneers, the brave, sturdy fighters who battled alone for truth and were misunderstood and unrecognized. It means the world's finer attitude toward life. If looked at superficially, the things that come too late make us feel helpless, hopeless, pessimistic; if seen with the eye of deeper wisdom, they reveal to us the grand evolution march of humanity toward higher things. It is Nature's proclamation that, in the end, Right *must* triumph, Truth *must* conquer, and Justice *must* reign. For us, as individuals, it is a warning and an inspiration,—a warning against withholding love, charity, kindness, sympathy, justice, and helpfulness, till it is too late; an inspiration for us to live ever at our best, ever up to the maximum of effort, not worrying about results, but serenely confident that they *must* come.

It takes over thirty years for the light of some of the stars to reach the earth, some a hundred, some a thousand years. Those stars do not become visible till their light reaches and reacts on human vision. It takes an almost equal time for the light of some of the world's great geniuses to meet real, seeing eyes. Then we see these men as the brilliant stars in the world's gallery of immortal great ones. This is why contemporary reputation rarely indicates lasting fame. We are constantly mistaking fireflies of cleverness for stars of genius. But Time brings all things right. The fame, though, brings no joy, or encouragement, or inspiration to him who has passed beyond this world's lights and shadows; it has the sadness of the honours that come too late, a touch of the farcical mingled with its pathos. Tardy recognition is better than none at all—it is better, though late, than never; but it is so much truer and kinder and more valuable if never late. We are so inclined to send our condemnation and our snapshot criticisms by express, and our careful, honest commendation by slow freight.

In October, 1635, Roger Williams, because of his inspiring pleas for individual liberty, was ordered by the General Court of Massachusetts to leave the colony forever. He went to Rhode Island, where he lived for nearly fifty years. But the official conscience grew a little restless, and in April, 1899, Massachusetts actually made atonement for its rash act. The original papers, yellow, faded, and crumbling, were taken from their pigeon-hole tomb, and "by an ordinary motion made, seconded, and adopted," the order of banishment was solemnly "annulled and repealed, and made of no effect whatever." The ban under which Roger Williams had lain for over 260 years was lifted. And there is no reason now, according to law, why Roger Williams cannot enter the state of Massachusetts and reside therein. The action was to the credit and honour of the state; it was right in its spirit, and Roger, being in the spirit for more than two centuries, may have smiled gently and understood. But the reparation was really—over-delayed.

The mistakes, the sin and folly of one age may be partially atoned for by a succeeding age, but the individual stands alone. For what we do and for what we leave undone we alone are responsible. If we permit the golden hours that might be consecrated to higher things to trickle like sand through our fingers, no one can ever restore them to us.

Human affection is fed by signs and tokens of that affection. Merely having kindly feelings is not enough; they should be made manifest in action. The parched earth is not refreshed by the mere fact of water in the clouds; it is only when the blessing of rain actually descends that it awakens to new life. We are so ready to say, "He knows how much I think of him," and to assume that as a fitting substitute for expression. We may know that the sun is shining somewhere, and still shiver for lack of its glow and warmth. Love should be constantly made evident in little acts of thoughtfulness, words of sweetness and appreciation, smiles and handclasps of esteem. It should be shown to be a loving reality instead of a memory by patience, forbearance, courtesy, and kindness.

This theory of presumed confidence in the persistence of affection is one of the sad phases of married life. We should have roses of love, ever blooming, ever breathing perfume, instead of dried roses pressed in the family Bible, merely for reference, as a memorial of what was, instead of guarantee of what is. Matrimony too often shuts the door of life and leaves sentiment, consideration, and chivalry on the outside. The feeling may possibly be still alive, but it does not reveal itself rightly; the rhymed poetry of loving has changed to blank verse, and later into dull prose. As the boy said of his father: "He's a Christian, but he's not working much at it now." Love without manifestation does not feed the heart any more than a locked bread-box feeds the body; it does not illuminate and brighten the round of daily duties any more than an unlit lamp lightens a room. There is often such a craving in the heart of a husband or a wife for expression in words of human love and tenderness, that they are welcomed no matter from what source they may come. If there were more courtships continued after marriage, the work of the divorce courts would be greatly lessened. This realization is often one of the things that come too late.

There are more people in this world hungering for kindness, sympathy, comradeship, and love, than are hungering for bread. We often refrain from giving a hearty word of encouragement, praise, or congratulation to someone, even where we recognize that our feelings are known, for fear of making him conceited or over-confident. Let us tear down these dykes of reserve, these walls of petty repression, and let in the flood of our feelings. There have been few monuments reared to the memory of those who have failed in life because of over-praise. There is more chiseled flattery on tombstones than was ever heard in life by the dead those stones now guard. Man does not ask for flattery, he does not long for fulsome praise, he wants the honest, ringing sound of recognition of what he has done, fair appreciation of what he is doing, and sympathy with what he is striving to do.

Why is it that death makes us suddenly conscious of a hundred virtues in a man who seemed commonplace and faulty in life? Then we speak as though an angel had been living in our town for years and we had suddenly discovered him. If he could only have heard these words while living, if he could have discounted the eulogies at, say, even sixty per cent, they would have been an inspiration to him when weary, worn, and worried by the problems of living. But now the ears are stilled to all earthly music, and even if they could hear our praise the words would be but useless messengers of love that came too late.

It is right to speak well of the dead, to remember their strength and to forget their weakness, and to render to their memory the expression of honour, justice, love, and sorrow that fill our hearts. But it is the living, ever the living that need it most. The dead have passed beyond the helpfulness; our wildest cries of agony and regret bring no answering echo from the silences of the unknown. Those who are facing the battle of life, still seeking bravely to do and to be—they need our help, our companionship, our love, all that is best in us. Better is the smallest flower placed in our warm, living hands than mountains of roses banked round our coffin.

If we have failed in our expressions to the dead, the deep sense of our sorrow and the instinctive rush of feeling proclaim the vacuum of duty we now seek too late to fill. But there is one atonement that is not too late. It is in making all humanity legatees of the kindness and human love that we regret has been unexpended, it is in bringing brightness, courage, and cheer into the lives of those around us. Thus our regret will be shown to be genuine, not a mere temporary gush of emotionalism.

It is during the formative period, the time when a man is seeking to get a foot-hold, that help counts for most, when even the slightest aid is great. A few books lent to Andrew Carnegie when he was beginning his career were to him an inspiration; he has nobly repaid the loan, made posterity his debtor a million-fold by his beneficence in sprinkling libraries over the whole country. Help the saplings, the young growing trees of vigor; the mighty oaks have no need of your aid.

The heartening words should come when needed, not when they seem only hypocritic protestations, or dexterous preparations for future favors. Columbus, surrounded by his mutinous crew, threatening to kill him, alone amid the crowd, had no one to stand by him. But he neared land, and riches opened before them; then they fell at his feet, proclaimed him almost a god, and said he truly was inspired from Heaven. Success transfigured him; a long line of pebbly beach and a few trees made him divine. A little patience along the way, a little closer companionship, a little brotherly love in his hours of watching, waiting, and hoping, would have been great balm to his soul.

It is in childhood that pleasures count most, when the slightest investment of kindness brings largest returns. Let us give the children sunlight, love, companionship, sympathy with their little troubles and worries that seem to them so great, genuine interest in their growing hopes, their vague, unproportioned dreams and yearnings. Let us put ourselves into their places, view the world through their eyes, so that we may gently correct the errors of their perspective by our greater wisdom. Such trifles will make them genuinely happy, happier by far than things a thousand times greater that come too late.

Procrastination is the father of a countless family of things that come too late. Procrastination means making an appointment with opportunity to "call again to-morrow." It kills self-control, saps mental energy, makes man a creature of circumstances instead of their creator. There is one brand of procrastination that is a virtue. It is never doing to-day a wrong that can be put off till to-morrow, never performing an act to-day that may make to-morrow ashamed.

There are little estrangements in life, little misunderstandings that are passed by in silence between friends, each too closely armored with pride, and enamoured with self to break. There is a time when a few straightforward words would set it all right, the clouds would break and the sunshine of love burst forth again. But each nurses a weak, petty sense of dignity, the rift grows wider, they drift apart, and each goes his lonely way, hungering for the other. They may waken to realization too late to piece the broken strands of affection into a new life.

The wisdom that comes too late in a thousand phases of life usually has an irritating, depressing effect on the individual. He should charge a large part of it to the account of experience. If no wisdom came too late there would be no experience. It means, after all, only that we are wiser to-day than we were yesterday, that we see all things in truer relation, that our pathway of life has been illuminated.

The world is prone to judge by results. It is glad to be a stockholder in our success and prosperity, but it too often avoids the assessments of sympathy and understanding. The man who pulls against the stream may have but a staunch two or three to help him. When the tide turns and his craft swiftens its course and he is carried along without effort, he finds boats hurrying to him from all directions as if he had suddenly woke up and found himself in a regatta. The help then comes too late; he does not need it. He himself must then guard against the temptation of cynicism and coldness and selfishness. Then he should realise and determine that what he terms "the way of the world" shall not be his "way." That he will not be too late with his stimulus to others who have struggled bravely as he has done, but who, being less strong may drop the oars in despair for the lack of the stimulus of even a friendly word of heartening in a crisis.

The old song of dreary philosophy says: "The mill will never grind again with the water that is past." Why should the mill expect to use the same water over and over? That water may now be merrily turning mill-wheels farther down the valley, continuing without ceasing its good work. It is folly to think so much of the water that is past. Think more of the great stream that is ever flowing on. Use that as best you can, and when it has passed you will be glad that it came, and be satisfied with its service.

Time is a mighty stream that comes each day with unending flow. To think of this water of past time with such regret that it shuts our eyes to the mighty river of the present is sheer folly. Let us make the best we can of to-day in the best preparation for tomorrow; then even the things that come too late will be new revelations of wisdom to use in the present now before us, and in the future we are forming.

The Way of the Reformer

The reformers of the world are its men of mighty purpose. They are men with the courage of individual conviction, men who dare run counter to the criticism of inferiors, men who voluntarily bear crosses for what they accept as right, even with out the guarantee of a crown. They are men who gladly go down into the depths of silence, darkness, and oblivion, but only to emerge finally like divers, with pearls in their hands.

He who labors untiringly toward the attainment of some noble aim, with eyes fixed on the star of some mighty purpose, as the Magi followed the star in the East, is a reformer. He who is loyal to the inspiration of some great religious thought, and with strong hand leads weak, trembling steps of faith into the glory of certainty, is a reformer. He who follows the thin thread of some revelation of Nature in any of the sciences, follows it in the spirit of truth through a maze of doubt, hope, experiment, and questioning, till the tiny guiding thread grows stronger and firmer to his touch, leading him to some wondrous illumination of Nature's law, is a reformer.

He who goes up alone into the mountains of truth, and, glowing with the radiance of some mighty revelation, returns to force the hurrying world to listen to his story, is a reformer. Whoever seeks to work out for himself his destiny, the life-work that all his nature tells him should be his, bravely, calmly, and with due consideration of the rights of others and his duties to them, is a reformer.

These men who renounce the commonplace and conventional for higher things are reformers because they are striving to bring about new conditions; they are consecrating their lives to ideals. They are the brave aggressive vanguard of progress. They are men who can stand a siege, who can take long forced marches without a murmur, who set their teeth and bow their heads as they fight their way through the smoke, who smile at the trials and privations that dare to daunt them. They care naught for the handicaps and perils of the fight, for they are ever inspired by the flag of triumph that seems already waving on the citadel of their hopes.

If we are facing some great life ambition, let us see if our heroic plans are good, high, noble, and exalted enough for the price we must pay for their attainment. Let us seriously and honestly look into our needs, our abilities, our resources, our responsibilities, to assure ourselves that it is no mere passing whim that is leading us. Let us hear or consider all counsel, all light that may be thrown on every side; let us hear it as a judge on the bench listens to the evidence, and then makes his own decision. The choice of a life-work is too sacred a responsibility to the individual to be lightly decided for him by others less thoroughly informed than himself. When we have weighed in the balance the mighty question and have made our decision, let us act, let us concentrate our lives upon that which we feel is supreme, and, never forsaking a real duty, never be diverted from the attainment of the highest things, no matter what honest price we have to pay for their realization and conquest.

When Nature decides on any man as a reformer she whispers to him her great message, she places in his hand the staff of courage, she wraps around him the robes of patience and self-reliance, and starts him on his way. Then, in order that he may have strength to live through it all, she mercifully calls him back for a moment, and makes him—an optimist.

The way of the reformer is hard—very hard. The world knows little of it, for it is rare that the reformer reveals the scars of the conflict, the pangs of hope deferred, the mighty waves of despair that wash over a great purpose. Sometimes men of sincere aim and unselfish high ambition, weary and worn with the struggle, have permitted the world to hear an uncontrolled sob of hopelessness or a word of momentary bitterness at the seeming emptiness of all effort. But men of great purpose and noble ideals must know the path of the reformer is loneliness. They must live from within rather than in dependence on sources of help from without. Their mission, their exalted aim, their supreme object in living, which focuses all their energy, must be their source of strength and inspiration. The reformer must ever light the torch of his own inspiration. His own hand must ever guard the sacred flame as he moves steadily forward on his lonely way.

The reformer in morals, in education, in religion, in sociology, in invention, in philosophy, in any line of aspiration, is ever a pioneer. His privilege is to blaze the path for others, to mark at his peril a road that others may follow in safety. He must not expect that the way will be laid and asphalted for him. He must realize that he must face injustice, ingratitude, opposition, misunderstanding, the cruel criticism of contemporaries, and often, hardest of all, the wondering reproach of those who love him best.

He must not expect the tortoise to sympathize with the flight of the eagle. A great purpose is ever an isolation. Should a soldier leading the forlorn hope complain that the army is not abreast of him? The glorious opportunity before him should so inspire him, so absorb him, that he will care nought for the army except to know that if he lead as he should, and do that which the crisis demands, the army *must* follow.

The reformer must realize without a trace of bitterness that the busy world cares little for his struggles, it cares only to joy in his final triumph; it will share his feasts, but not his fasts. Christ was alone in Gethsemane, but—at the sermon in the wilderness, where food was provided, the attendance was four thousand.

The world is honest enough in its attitude. It takes time for the world to realize, to accept, and to assimilate a large truth. Since the dawn of history, the great conservative spirit of every age, that ballast that keeps the world in poise, makes the slow acceptance of great truths an essential for its safety. It wisely requires proof, clear, absolute, undeniable attestation, before if fully accepts. Sometimes the perfect enlightenment takes years, sometimes generations. It is but the safeguard of truth. Time is the supreme test, the final court of appeal that winnows out the chaff of false claims, pretended revelation, empty boast, and idle dreams. Time is the touchstone that finally reveals all true gold. The process is slow, necessarily so, and the fate of the world's geniuses and reformers in the balance of their contemporary criticism should have a sweetness of consolation rather than the bitterness of cynicism. If the greatest leaders of the world have had to wait for recognition, should we, whose best work may be but trifling in comparison with theirs, expect instant sympathy, appreciation, and cooperation, where we are merely growing toward our own attainment?

The world ever says to its leaders, by its attitude if not in words, "If you would lead us to higher realms of thought, to purer ideals of life, and flash before us, like the handwriting on the wall, all the possible glories of development, *you* must pay the price for it, not we." The world has a law as clearly defined as the laws of Kepler: "Contemporary credit for reform works in any line will be in inverse proportion to the square root of their importance." Give us a new fad and we will prostrate ourselves in the dust; give us a new philosophy, a marvelous revelation, a higher conception of life and morality, and we may pass you by, but posterity will pay for it. Send your messages C.O.D. and posterity will settle for them. You ask for bread; posterity will give you a stone, called a monument.

There is nothing in this to discourage the highest efforts of genius. Genius is great because it is decades in advance of its generation. To appreciate genius requires comprehension and the same characteristics. The public can fully appreciate only what is a few steps in advance; it must grow to the appreciation of great thought. The genius or the reformer should accept this as a necessary condition. It is the price he must pay for being in advance of his generation, just as front seats in the orchestra cost more than those in the back row of the third gallery.

The world is impartial in its methods. It says ever, "you may suffer now, but we will give you later fame." Posthumous fame means that the individual may shiver with cold, but his grandchildren will get fur-lined ulsters; the individual plants acorns, his posterity sells the oaks. Posthumous fame or recognition is a cheque made out to the individual, but payable only to his heirs.

There is nothing the world cries out for so constantly as a new idea; there is nothing the world fears so much. The milestones of progress in the history of the ages tell the story. Galileo was cast into prison in his seventieth year, and his works were prohibited. He had committed no crime, but he was in advance of his generation. Harvey's discovery of the circulation of the blood was not accepted by the universities of the world till twenty-five years after its publication. Froebel, the gentle inspired lover of children, suffered the trials and struggles of the reformer, and his system of teaching was abolished in Prussia because it was "calculated to bring up our young people in atheism." So it was with thousands of others.

The world says with a large airy sweep of the hand, "the opposition to progress is all in the past; the great reformer or the great genius is recognized to-day." No, in the past they tried to kill a great truth by opposition; now we gently seek to smother it by making it a fad.

So it is written in the book of human nature: The saviours of the world must ever be martyrs. The death of Christ on the cross for the people He had come to save typifies the temporary crucifixion of public opinion that comes to all who bring to the people the message of some great truth, some clearer revelation of the divine. Truth, right, and justice must triumph. Let us never close the books of a great work and say "it has failed."

No matter how slight seem results, how dark the outlook, the glorious consummation of the past, the revelation of the future, *must* come. And Christ lived thirty years; and He had twelve disciples—one denied Him, one doubted Him, one betrayed Him, and the other nine were very human. And in the supreme crisis of His life "they *all* forsook Him and fled," but to-day—His followers are millions.

Sweet indeed is human sympathy, the warm hand-clasp of confidence and love brings a rich inflow of new strength to him who is struggling, and the knowledge that someone dear to us sees with love and comradeship our future through our eyes is a wondrous draught of new life. If we have this, perhaps the loyalty of two or three, what the world says or thinks about us should count for little. But if this be denied us, then must we bravely walk our weary way alone, toward the sunrise that must come.

The little world around us that does not understand us, does not appreciate our ambition or sympathize with our efforts, that seem to it futile, is not intentionally cruel, callous, bitter, blind or heartless. It is merely that busied with its own pursuits, problems, and pleasures, it does not fully realize, does not see as we do.

The world does not see our ideal as we see it, does not feel the glow of inspiration that makes our blood tingle, our eye brighten, and our soul seem flooded with a wondrous light. It sees naught but the rough block of marble before us and the great mass of chips and fragments of seemingly fruitless effort at our feet, but it does not see the angel of achievement slowly emerging from its stone prison, from nothingness into being, under the tireless strokes of our chisel. It hears no faint rustle of wings that seem already real to us, nor the glory of the music of triumph already ringing in our ears.

There come dark, dreary days in all great work, when effort seems useless, when hope almost appears a delusion, and confidence the mirage of folly. Sometimes for days your sails flap idly against the mast, with not a breath of wind to move you on your way, and with a paralyzing sense of helplessness you just have to sit and wait and wait. Sometimes your craft of hope is carried back by a tide that seems to undo in moments your work of months. But it may not be really so; you may be put into a new channel that brings you nearer your haven than you dared to hope. This is the hour that tests us, that determines whether we are masters or slaves of conditions. As in the battle of Marengo, it is the fight that is made when all seems lost that really counts and wrests victory from the hand of seeming defeat.

If you are seeking to accomplish any great serious purpose that your mind and your heart tell you is right, you must have the spirit of the reformer. You must have the courage to face trial, sorrow, and disappointment, to meet them squarely and to move forward unscathed and undaunted. In the sublimity of your perfect faith in the outcome, you can make them as powerless to harm you as a dewdrop falling on the Pyramids.

Truth, with time as its ally, always wins in the end. The knowledge of the inappreciation, the coldness, and the indifference of the world should never make you pessimistic. They should inspire you with that large, broad optimism that sees that all the opposition of the world can never keep back the triumph of truth, that your work is so great that the petty jealousies, misrepresentations, and hardships caused by those around you dwindle into nothingness. What cares the messenger of the king for his trials and sufferings if he know that he has delivered his message? Large movements, great plans, always take time for development. If you want great things, pay the price like a man.

Anyone can plant radishes; it takes courage to plant acorns and to wait for the oaks. Learn to look not merely *at* the clouds, but through them to the sun shining behind them. When things look darkest, grasp your weapon firmer and fight harder. There is always more progress than you can perceive, and it is really only the outcome of the battle that counts.

And when it is all over and the victory is yours, and the smoke clears away and the smell of the powder is dissipated, and you bury the friendships that died because they could not stand the strain, and you nurse back the wounded and faint-hearted who loyally stood by you, even when doubting, then the hard years of fighting will seem but a dream. You will stand brave, heartened, strengthened by the struggle, re-created to a new, better, and stronger life by a noble battle, nobly waged in a noble cause. And the price will then seem to you—nothing.

THE MAJESTY OF CALMNESS

William George Jordan

The Majesty of Calmness, a collection of essays by William George Jordan, was often given as a gift by President Heber J. Grant. First published in 1900, it was reprinted in 1970 as a small booklet by Deseret Book Company. The title essay emphasizes the importance of inner peace, as admonished by the Lord: "Let your hearts be comforted concerning Zion; for all flesh is in mine hands; *be still and know that I am God.*" (D&C 101:16; italics added.)

Similarly, President Brigham Young taught, "This is the counsel I have for the Latter-day Saints today. Stop, do not be in a hurry. I do not know that I could find a man in our community but what wishes wealth, would like to have everything in his possession that would conduce to his comfort and convenience. Do you know how to get it? 'Well,' replies one, 'if I do not, I wish I did; but I do not seem to be exactly fortunate—fortune is somewhat against me.' I will tell you the reason of this—you are in too much of a hurry; you do not go to meeting enough, you do not pray enough, you do not read the Scriptures enough, you do not meditate enough, you are all the time on the wing, and in such a hurry that you do not know what to do first. This is not the way to get rich. I merely use the term 'rich' to lead the mind along, until we obtain eternal riches in the celestial kingdom of God." (*Discourses of Brigham Young* [Salt Lake City: Deseret Book Co., 1954], 310.)

THE MAJESTY OF CALMNESS

Calmness is the rarest quality in human life. It is the poise of a great nature, in harmony with itself and its ideals. It is the moral atmosphere of a life self-centered, self-reliant, and self-controlled. Calmness is singleness of purpose, absolute confidence, and conscious power,—ready to be focused in an instant to meet any crisis.

The Sphinx is not a true type of calmness—petrifaction is not calmness, it is death, the silencing of all the energies; while no one lives his life more fully, more intensely and more consciously than the man who is calm.

The Fatalist is not calm. He is the coward slave of his environment, hopelessly surrendering to his present condition, recklessly indifferent to his future. He accepts his life as a rudderless ship, drifting on the ocean of time. He has no compass, no chart, no known port to which he is sailing. His self-confessed inferiority to all nature is shown in his existence of constant surrender. It is not—calmness.

The man who is calm has his course in life clearly marked on his chart. His hand is ever on the helm. Storm, fog, night, tempest, danger, hidden reefs,—he is prepared and ready for them. He is made calm and serene by the realization that in these crises of his voyage he needs a clear mind and a cool head; that he has naught to do but to do each day the best he can by the light he has; that he will never flinch nor falter for a moment; that, though he may have to tack and leave his course for a time, he will never drift, he will get back into the true channel, he will keep ever headed toward his harbor. *When* he will reach it, *how* he will reach it, matters not to him. He rests in calmness, knowing he has done his best. If his best seems to be overthrown or overruled, then he must still bow his head,—in calmness. To no man is permitted to know the future of his life, the finality. God commits to man only new beginnings, new wisdom, and new days to use the best of his knowledge.

Calmness comes from within. It is the peace and restfulness of the depths of our nature. The fury of storm and of wind agitate only the surface of the sea; they can penetrate only two or three hundred feet,—below that is the calm, unruffled deep. To be ready for the great crises of life we must learn serenity in our daily living. Calmness is the crown of self-control.

When the worries and cares of the day fret you, and begin to wear upon you, and you chafe under the friction,—be calm. Stop, rest for a moment, and let calmness and peace assert themselves. If you let these irritating outside influences get the better of you, you are confessing your inferiority to them by permitting them to dominate you. Study the disturbing elements, each by itself, bring all the will power of your nature to bear upon them, and you will find that they will, one by one, melt into nothingness, like vapors fading before the sun. The glow of calmness that will then pervade your mind, the tingling sensation of an inflow of new strength, may be to you the beginning of the revelation of the supreme calmness that is possible for you. Then, in some great hour of your life, when you stand face to face with some awful trial, when the structure of your ambition and lifework crumbles in a moment, you will be brave. You can then fold your arms calmly, look out undismayed and undaunted upon the ashes of your hope, upon the wreck of what you have faithfully built, and with brave heart and unfaltering voice you may say, "So let it be,—I will build again."

When the tongue of malice and slander, the persecution of inferiority, tempt you for just a moment to retaliate, when for an instant you forget yourself so far as to hunger for revenge,—be calm. When the gray heron is pursued by its enemy, the eagle, it does not run to escape; it remains calm, takes a dignified stand, and waits quietly, facing the enemy unmoved. With the terrific force with which the eagle makes its attack, the boasted king of birds is often impaled and run through on the quiet, lance-like bill of the heron. The means that man takes to kill another's character becomes suicide of his own.

No man in the world ever attempted to wrong another without being injured in return,—someway, somehow, sometime. The only weapon of offense that Nature seems to recognize is the boomerang. Nature keeps her books admirably; she puts down every item, she closes all accounts finally, but she does not always balance them at the end of the month. To the man who is calm, revenge is so far beneath him that he cannot reach it,—even by stooping. When injured, he does not retaliate; he wraps around him the royal robes of Calmness, and he goes quietly on his way.

When the hand of Death touches the one we hold dearest, paralyzes our energy, and eclipses the sun of our life, the calmness that has been accumulating in long years becomes in a moment our refuge, our reserve strength.

The most subtle of all temptations is the *seeming* success of the wicked. It requires moral courage to see, without flinching, material prosperity coming to men who are dishonest; to see politicians rise into prominence, power and wealth by trickery and corruption; to see virtue in rags and vice in velvets; to see ignorance at a premium, and knowledge at a discount. To the man who is really calm these puzzles of life do not appeal. He is living his life as best he can; he is not worrying about the problems of justice, whose solution must be left to Omniscience to solve.

When man has developed the spirit of calmness until it becomes so absolutely part of him that his very presence radiates it, he has made great progress in life. Calmness cannot be acquired of itself and by itself; it must come as the culmination of a series of virtues. What the world needs and what individuals need is a higher standard of living, a great realization of the privilege and dignity of life, a higher and nobler conception of individuality.

With this great sense of calmness permeating an individual, man becomes able to retire more into himself, away from the noise, the confusion and strife of the world, which come to his ears only as faint, far-off rumblings, or as the tumult of the life of a city heard only as a buzzing hum by the man in a balloon.

The man who is calm does not selfishly isolate himself from the world, for he is intensely interested in all that concerns the welfare of humanity. His calmness is but a Holy of Holies into which he can retire *from* the world to get strength to live *in* the world. He realizes that the full glory of individuality, the crowning of his self-control is,—the majesty of calmness.

Hurry, the Scourge of America

The first sermon in the world was preached at the Creation. It was a Divine protest against Hurry. It was a Divine object lesson of perfect law, perfect plan, perfect order, perfect method. Six days of work carefully planned, scheduled and completed were followed by,—rest. Whether we accept the story as literal or as figurative, as the account of successive days or of ages comprising millions of years, matters little if we but learn the lesson.

Nature is very un-American. Nature never hurries. Every phase of her working shows plan, calmness, reliability, and the absence of hurry. Hurry always implies lack of definite method, confusion, impatience of slow growth. The Tower of Babel, the world's first skyscraper, was a failure because of hurry. The workers mistook their arrogant ambition for inspiration. They had too many builders,—and no architect. They thought to make up the lack of a head by a superfluity of hands. This is a characteristic of Hurry. It seeks ever to make energy a substitute for a clearly defined plan,—the result is as hopeless as trying to transform a hobbyhorse into a real steed by brisk riding.

Hurry is a counterfeit of haste. Haste has an ideal, a distinct aim to be realized by the quickest, direct methods. Haste has a single compass upon which it relies for direction and in harmony with which its course is determined. Hurry says, "I must move faster. I will get three compasses; I will have them different; I will be guided by all of them. One of them will probably be right." Hurry never realizes that slow, careful foundation work is the quickest in the end.

Hurry has ruined more Americans than has any other word in the vocabulary of life. It is the scourge of America, and is both a cause and a result of our high-pressure civilization. Hurry adroitly assumes so many masquerades of disguise that its identity is not always recognized.

Hurry always pays the highest price for everything, and usually the goods are not delivered. In the race for wealth, men often sacrifice time, energy, health, home, happiness and honor,—everything that money cannot buy, the very things that money can never bring back. Hurry is a phantom of paradoxes. Businessmen, in their desire to provide for the future happiness of their family, often sacrifice the present happiness of wife and children on the altar of Hurry. They forget that their place in the home should be something greater than being merely "the man who pays the bills"; they expect consideration and thoughtfulness that they are not giving.

We hear too much of a wife's duties to a husband and too little of the other side of the question. "The wife," they tell us, "should meet her husband with a smile and a kiss, should tactfully watch his moods and be ever sweetness and sunshine." Why this continual swinging of the censer of devotion to the man of business? Why should a woman have to look up with timid glance at the face of her husband, to "size up his mood"? Has not her day, too, been one of care, and responsibility, and watchfulness? Has not mother-love been working over perplexing problems and worries of home and of the training of the children that wifely love may make her seek to solve in secret? Is man, then, the weaker sex that he must be pampered and treated as tenderly as a boil trying to keep from contact with the world?

In their hurry to attain some ambition, to gratify the dream of a life, men often throw honor, truth, and generosity to the winds. Politicians dare to stand by and see a city poisoned with foul water until they "see where they come in" on a water-works appropriation. If it be necessary to poison an army,—that too is but an incident in the hurry for wealth.

This is the Age of the Hothouse. The element of natural growth is pushed to one side and the hothouse and the force-pump are substituted. Nature looks on tolerantly as she says: "So far you may go, but no farther, my foolish children."

The educational system of to-day is a monumental institution dedicated to Hurry. The children are forced to go through a series of studies that sweep the circle of all human wisdom. They are given everything that the ambitious ignorance of the age can force into their minds; they are taught everything but the essentials,—how to use their senses and how to think. Their minds become congested by a great mass of undigested facts, and still the cruel, barbarous forcing goes on. You watch it until it seems you cannot stand it a moment longer, and you instinctively put out your hand and say: "Stop! This modern slaughter of the

Innocents must *not* go on!" Education smiles suavely, waves her hand complacently toward her thousands of knowledge-prisons over the country, and says: "Who are you that dares speak a word against our sacred, school system?" Education is in a hurry. Because she fails in fifteen years to do what half the time should accomplish by better methods, she should not be too boastful. Incompetence is not always a reason for pride. And they hurry the children into a hundred textbooks, then into ill-health, then into the colleges, then into a diploma, then into life,—with a dazed mind, untrained and unfitted for the real duties of living.

Hurry is the deathblow to calmness, to dignity, to poise. The old-time courtesy went out when the new-time hurry came in. Hurry is the father of dyspepsia. In the rush of our national life, the bolting of food has become a national vice. The words "Quick Lunches" might properly be placed on thousands of headstones in our cemeteries. Man forgets that he is the only animal that dines; the others merely feed. Why does he abrogate his right to dine and go to the end of the line with the mere feeders? His self-respecting stomach rebels, and expresses its indignation by indigestion. Then man has to go through life with a little bottle of pepsin tablets in his vest pocket. He is but another victim to this craze for speed. Hurry means the breakdown of the nerves. It is the royal road to nervous prostration.

Everything that is great in life is the product of slow growth; the newer, and greater, and higher, and nobler the work, the slower is its growth, the surer is its lasting success. Mushrooms attain their full power in a night; oaks require decades. A fad lives its life in a few weeks; a philosophy lives through generations and centuries. If you are sure you are right, do not let the voice of the world, or of friends, or of family swerve you for a moment from your purpose. Accept slow growth if it must be slow, and know the results *must* come, as you would accept the long, lonely hours of the night,—with absolute assurance that the heavy-leaded moments *must* bring the morning.

Let us as individuals banish the word "Hurry" from our lives. Let us care for nothing so much that we would pay honor and self-respect as the price of hurrying it. Let us cultivate calmness, restfulness, poise, sweetness,—doing our best, bearing all things as bravely as we can; living our life undisturbed by the prosperity of the wicked or the malice of the envious. Let us not be impatient, chafing at delay, fretting over failure, wearying over results, and weakening under opposition. Let us ever turn our face toward the future with confidence and trust, with the calmness of a life in harmony with itself, true to its ideals, and slowly and constantly progressing toward their realization.

Let us see that cowardly word Hurry in all its most degenerating phases; let us see that it ever kills truth, loyalty, thoroughness; and let us determine that, day by day, we will seek more and more to substitute for it the calmness and repose of a true life, nobly lived.

The Power of Personal Influence

The only responsibility that a man cannot evade in this life is the one he thinks of least,—his personal influence. Man's conscious influence, when he is on dress parade, when he is posing to impress those around him,—is woefully small. But his unconscious influence, the silent, subtle radiation of his personality, the effect of his words and acts, the trifles he never considers,—is tremendous. Every moment of life he is changing to a degree the life of the whole world. Every man has an atmosphere which is affecting every other. So silent and unconsciously is this influence working, that man may forget that it exists.

All the forces of Nature,—heat, light, electricity and gravitation,— are silent and invisible. We never *see* them; we only know that they exist by seeing the effects they produce. In all Nature the wonders of the "seen" are dwarfed into insignificance when compared with the majesty and glory of the "unseen." The great sun itself does not supply enough heat and light to sustain animal and vegetable life on the earth. We are dependent for nearly half of our light and heat upon the stars, and the greater part of this supply of life-giving energy come from *invisible* stars, millions of miles from the earth. In a thousand ways Nature constantly seeks to lead men to a keener and deeper realization of the power and the wonder of the invisible.

Into the hands of every individual is given a marvelous power for good or for evil,—the silent, unconscious, unseen influence of his life.

This is simply the constant radiation of what a man really *is,* not what he pretends to be. Every man, by his mere living, is radiating sympathy, or sorrow, or morbidness, or cynicism, or happiness, or hope, or any of a hundred other qualities. Life is a state of constant radiation and absorption; to exist is to radiate; to exist is to be the recipient of radiations.

There are men and women whose presence seems to radiate sunshine, cheer and optimism. With them you feel calmed and rested and restored in a moment to a new and stronger faith in humanity. There are others who focus in an instant all your latent distrust, morbidness and rebellion against life. Without knowing why, you chafe and fret in their presence. You lose your bearings on life and its problems. Your moral compass is disturbed and unsatisfactory. It is made untrue in an instant, as the magnetic needle of a ship is deflected when it passes near great mountains of iron ore.

There are men who float down the stream of life like icebergs,— cold, reserved, unapproachable and self-contained. In their presence you involuntarily draw your wraps closer around you, as you wonder who left the door open. These refrigerated human beings have a most depressing influence on all those who fall under the spell of their radiated chilliness. But there are other natures, warm, helpful, genial, who are like the Gulf Stream, following their own course, flowing undaunted and undismayed in the ocean of colder waters. Their presence brings warmth and life and the glow of sunshine, the joyous, stimulating breath of spring.

There are men who are like malarious swamps,—poisonous, depressing and weakening by their very presence. They make heavy, oppressive and gloomy the atmosphere of their own homes; the sound of the children's play is stilled, the ripples of laughter are frozen by their presence. They go through life as if each day were a new big funeral, and they were always chief mourners. There are other men who seem like the ocean; they are constantly bracing, stimulating, giving new draughts of tonic life and strength by their very presence.

There are men who are insincere in heart, and that insincerity is radiated by their presence. They have a wondrous interest in your welfare,—when they need you. They put on a "property" smile so suddenly, when it serves their purpose, that it seems the smile must be connected with some electric button concealed in their clothes. Their voice has a simulated cordiality that long training may have made almost natural. But they never play their part absolutely true, the mask *will* slip down sometimes; their cleverness cannot teach their eyes the look of sterling honesty; they may deceive some people, but they cannot deceive all. There is a subtle power of revelation which makes us say: "Well, I cannot explain how it is, but I know that man is not honest."

Man cannot escape for one moment from this radiation of his character, this constant weakening or strengthening of others. He cannot evade the responsibility by saying it is an unconscious influence. He can *select* the qualities that he will permit to be radiated. He can cultivate sweetness, calmness, trust, generosity, truth, justice, loyalty, nobility,—make them vitally active in his character,—and by these qualities he will constantly affect the world.

Discouragement often comes to honest souls trying to live the best they can, in the thought that they are doing so little good in the world. Trifles unnoted by us may be links in the chain of some great purpose. In 1797, William Godwin wrote The Inquirer, a collection of revolutionary essays on morals and politics. This book influenced Thomas Malthus to write his Essay on Population, published in 1798. Malthus' book suggested to Charles Darwin a point of view upon which he devoted many years of his life, resulting, in 1859, in the publication of The Origin of Species,—the most influential book of the nineteenth century, a book that has revolutionized all science. These were but three links of influence extending over sixty years. It might be possible to trace this genealogy of influence back from Godwin, through generation and generation, to the word or act of some shepherd in early Britain, watching his flock upon the hills, living his quiet life, and dying with the thought that he had done nothing to help the world.

Men and women have duties to others,—and duties to themselves. In justice to ourselves we should refuse to live in an atmosphere that keeps us from living our best. If the fault be in us, we should master it. If it be the personal influence of others that, like a noxious vapor, kills our best impulses, we should remove from that influence,—if we can *possibly* move without forsaking duties. If it be wrong to move, then we should take strong doses of moral quinine to counteract the malaria of influence. It is not what those around us *do* for us that counts,—it is what they *are* to us. We carry our houseplants from one window to another to give them the proper heat, light, air and moisture. Should we not be at least as careful of ourselves?

To make our influence felt, we must live our faith, we must practice what we believe. A magnet does not attract iron, as iron. It must first convert the iron into another magnet before it can attract it. It is useless for a parent to try to teach gentleness to her children when she herself is cross and irritable. The child who is told to be truthful and who hears a parent lie cleverly to escape some little social unpleasantness is not going to cling very zealously to truth. The parent's words say "don't lie," the influence of the parent's life says "do lie."

No man can ever isolate himself to evade this constant power of influence, as no single corpuscle can rebel and escape from the general course of the blood. No individual is so insignificant as to be without influence. The changes in our varying moods are all recorded in the delicate barometers of the lives of others. We should ever let our influence filter through human love and sympathy. We should not be merely an influence,—we should be an inspiration. By our very presence we should be a tower of strength to the hungering human souls around us.

The Dignity of Self-Reliance

Self-confidence, without self-reliance, is as useless as a cooking recipe,—without food. Self-confidence sees the possibilities of the individual; self-reliance realizes them. Self-confidence sees the angel in the unhewn block of marble; self-reliance carves it out for himself.

The man who is self-reliant says ever: "No one can realize my possibilities for me, but me; no one can make me good or evil but myself." He works out his own salvation,—financially, socially, mentally, physically, and morally. Life is an individual problem that man must solve for himself. Nature accepts no vicarious sacrifice, no vicarious service. Nature never recognizes a proxy vote. She has nothing to do with middlemen,—she deals only with the individual. Nature is constantly seeking to show man that he is his own best friend, or his own worst enemy. Nature gives man the option on which he will be to himself.

All the athletic exercises in the world are of no value to the individual unless he compels those bars and dumb-bells to yield to him, in strength and muscle, the power for which he himself pays in time and effort. He can never develop his muscles by sending his valet to a gymnasium.

The medicine-chests of the world are powerless, in all the united efforts, to help the individual until he reaches out and takes for himself what is needed for his individual weakness.

All the religions of the world are but speculations in morals, mere theories of salvation, until the individual realizes that he must save himself by relying on the law of truth, as he sees it, and living his life in harmony with it, as fully as he can. But religion is not a Pullman car, with soft-cushioned seats, where he has but to pay for his ticket,—and someone else does all the rest. In religion, as in all other great things, he is ever thrown back on his self-reliance. He should accept all helps, but,—he must live his own life. He should not feel that he is a mere passenger; he is the engineer, and the train is his life. We must rely on ourselves, live our own lives, or we merely drift through existence,—losing all that is best, all that is greatest, all that is divine.

All that others can do for us is to give us opportunity. We must be prepared for the opportunity when it comes, and go after it and find it when it does not come, or that opportunity is to us,—nothing. Life is but a succession of opportunities. They are for good or evil,—as we make them.

Many of the alchemists of old felt that they lacked but one element; if they could obtain that one, they believed they could transmute the baser metals into pure gold. It is so in character. There are individuals with rare mental gifts and delicate spiritual discernment who fail utterly in life because they lack the one element,—self-reliance. This would unite all their energies and focus them into strength and power.

The man who is not self-reliant is weak, hesitating and doubting in all he does. He fears to take a decisive step because he dreads failure, because he is waiting for someone to advise him or because he dares not act in accordance with his own best judgment. In his cowardice and his conceit he sees all his non-success due to others. He is "not appreciated," "not recognized," he is "kept down." He feels that in some subtle way "society is conspiring against him." He grows almost vain as he thinks that no one has had such poverty, such sorrow, such affliction, such failure as have come to him.

The man who is self-reliant seeks to discover and conquer the weakness within him that keeps him from the attainment of what he holds dearest; he seeks within himself the power to battle against all outside influences. He realizes that all the greatest men in history, in every phase of human effort, have been those who have had to fight against the odds of sickness, suffering, sorrow. To him, defeat is no more than passing through a tunnel is to a traveller,—he knows he must emerge again into the sunlight.

The nation that is strongest is the one that is most self-reliant, the one that contains within its boundaries all that its people need. If, with its ports all blockaded, it has not within itself the necessities of life and the elements of its continual progress then,—it is weak, held by the enemy, and it is but a question of time till it must surrender. Its independence is in proportion to its self-reliance, to its power to sustain itself from within. What is true of nations is true of individuals. The history of nations is but the biography of individuals magnified, intensified, multiplied, and projected on the screen of the past. History is the biography of a nation; biography is the history of an individual. So it must be that the individual who is strongest in any trial, sorrow or need is he who can live from his inherent strength, who needs no scaffolding of commonplace sympathy to uphold him. He must ever be self-reliant.

The wealth and prosperity of ancient Rome, relying on her slaves to do the real work of the nation, proved the nation's downfall. The constant dependence on the captives of war to do the thousand details of life for them killed self-reliance in the nation and in the individual. Then, through weakened self-reliance and the increased opportunity for idle, luxurious ease that came with it, Rome, a nation of fighters, became,—a nation of men more effeminate than women. As we depend on others to do those things we should do for ourselves, our self-reliance weakens and our powers, and our control of them, become continuously less.

Man to be great must be self-reliant. Though he may not be so in all things, he must be self-reliant in the one in which he would be great. This self-reliance is not the self-sufficiency of conceit. It is daring to stand alone. Be an oak, not a vine. Be ready to give support, but do not crave it; do not be dependent on it. To develop your true self-reliance, you must see from the very beginning that life is a battle you must fight for yourself,—you must be your own soldier. You cannot buy a substitute, you cannot win a reprieve, you can never be placed on the retired list. The retired list of life is,—death. The world is busy with its own cares, sorrows and joys, and pays little heed to you. There is but one great password to success,—self-reliance.

If you would learn to converse, put yourself into positions where you *must* speak. If you would conquer your morbidness, mingle with the bright people around you, no matter how difficult it may be. If you desire the power that someone else possesses, do not envy his strength and dissipate your energy by weakly wishing his force were yours. Emulate the process by which it became his, depend on your self-reliance, pay the price for it, and equal power may be yours. The individual must look upon himself as an investment of untold possibilities if rightly developed,—a mine whose resources can never be known but by going down into it and bringing out what is hidden.

Man can develop his self-reliance by seeking constantly to surpass himself. We try too much to surpass others. If we seek ever to surpass ourselves, we are moving on a uniform line of progress that gives a harmonious unifying to our growth in all its parts. Daniel Morrell, at one time President of the Cambria Rail Works that employed 7,000 men and made a rail famed throughout the world, was asked the secret of the great success of the works. "We have no secret," he said, "but this,—we always try to beat our last batch of rails." Competition is good, but it has its danger side. There is a tendency to sacrifice real worth to mere appearance, to have seeming rather than reality. But the true competition is the competition of the individual with himself,—his present seeking to excel his past. This means real growth from within. Self-reliance develops it, and it develops self-reliance. Let the individual feel thus as to his own progress and possibilities, and he can almost create his life as he will. Let him never fall down in despair at dangers and sorrows at a distance; they may be harmless, like Bunyan's stone lions, when he nears them.

The man who is self-reliant does not live in the shadow of someone else's greatness; he thinks for himself, depends on himself, and acts for himself. In throwing the individual thus back upon himself it is not shutting his eyes to the stimulus and light and new life that come with the warm pressure of the hand, the kindly word and the sincere expressions of true friendship. But true friendship is rare; its great value is in a crisis,—like a lifeboat. Many a boasted friend has proved a leaking, worthless "lifeboat" when the storm of adversity might make him useful. In these great crises of life, man is strong only as he is strong from within, and the more he depends on himself the stronger will he become, and the more able will he be to help others in the hour of their need. His very life will be a constant help and a strength to others, as he becomes to them a living lesson of the dignity of self-reliance.

Failure as a Success

It oftimes requires heroic courage to face fruitless effort, to take up the broken strands of a life-work, to look bravely toward the future, and proceed undaunted on our way. But what, to our eyes, may seem hopeless failure is often but the dawning of a greater success. It may contain in its débris the foundation material of a mighty purpose, or the revelation of new and higher possibilities.

Some years ago, it was proposed to send logs from Canada to New York, by a new method. The ingenious plan of Mr. Joggins was to bind great logs together by cables and iron girders and to tow the cargo as a raft. When the novel craft neared New York and success seemed assured, a terrible storm arose. In the fury of the tempest, the iron bands snapped like icicles and the angry waters scattered the logs far and wide. The chief of the Hydrographic Department at Washington heard of the failure of the experiment, and at once sent word to shipmasters the world over, urging them to watch carefully for these logs which he described;

and to note the precise location of each in latitude and longitude and the time the observation was made. Hundreds of captains sailing over the waters of the earth noted the logs, in the Atlantic Ocean, in the Mediterranean, in the South Seas—for into all waters did these venturesome ones travel. Hundreds of reports were made, covering a period of weeks and months. These observations were then carefully collated, systematized and tabulated, and discoveries were made as to the course of ocean currents that otherwise would have been impossible. The loss of the Joggins raft was not a real failure, for it led to one of the great discoveries in modern marine geography and navigation.

In our superior knowledge we are disposed to speak in a patronizing tone of the follies of the alchemists of old. But their failure to transmute the baser metals into gold resulted in the birth of chemistry. They did not succeed in what they attempted, but they brought into vogue the natural processes of sublimation, filtration, distillation, and crystallization; they invented the alembic, the retort, the sand-bath, the water-bath and other valuable instruments. To them is due the discovery of antimony, sulphuric ether and phosphorus, the cupellation of gold and silver, the determining of the properties of saltpetre and its use in gunpowder, and the discovery of the distillation of essential oils. This was the success of failure, a wondrous process of Nature for the highest growth,—a mighty lesson of comfort, strength, and encouragement if man would only realize and accept it.

Many of our failures sweep us to greater heights of success than we ever hoped for in our wildest dreams. Life is a successive unfolding of success from failure. In discovering America Columbus failed absolutely. His ingenious reasoning and experiment led him to believe that by sailing westward he would reach India. Every redman in America carries in his name "Indian" the perpetuation of the memory of the failure of Columbus. The Genoese navigator did not reach India; the cargo of "souvenirs" he took back to Spain to show to Ferdinand and Isabella as proofs of his success, really attested his failure. But the discovery of America was a greater success than was any finding of a "back-door" to India.

When David Livingstone had supplemented his theological

education by a medical course, he was ready to enter the missionary field. For over three years he had studied tirelessly, with all energies concentrated on one aim,—to spread the gospel in China. The hour came when he was ready to start out with noble enthusiasm for his chosen work, to consecrate himself and his life to his unselfish ambition. Then word came from China that the "opium war" would make it folly to attempt to enter the country. Disappointment and failure did not long daunt him; he offered himself as missionary to Africa,—and he was accepted. His glorious failure to reach China opened a whole continent to light and truth. His study proved an ideal preparation for his labors as physician, explorer, teacher and evangel in the wilds of Africa.

Business reverses and the failure of his partner threw upon the broad shoulders and the still broader honor and honesty of Sir Walter Scott a burden of responsibility that forced him to write. The failure spurred him to almost superhuman effort. The masterpieces of Scotch historic fiction that have thrilled, entertained and uplifted millions of his fellow-men are a glorious monument on the field of a seeming failure.

When Millet, the painter of the "Angelus," worked on his almost divine canvas in which the very air seems pulsing with the regenerating essence of spiritual reverence, he was painting against time, he was antidoting sorrow, he was racing against death. His brush strokes, put on in the early morning hours before going to his menial duties as a railway porter, in the dusk like that perpetuated on his canvas,—meant strength, food and medicine for the dying wife he adored. The art failure that cast him into the depths of poverty unified with marvelous intensity all the finer elements of his nature. This rare spiritual unity, this purging of all the dross of triviality as he passed through the furnace of poverty, trial, and sorrow gave eloquence to his brush and enabled him to paint as never before,—as no prosperity would have made possible.

Failure is often the turning-point, the pivot of circumstance that swings us to higher levels. It may not be financial success, it may not be fame; it may be new draughts of spiritual, moral or mental inspiration that will change us for all the later years of our life. Life is not really what comes to us, but what we get from it.

Whether man has had wealth or poverty, failure or success, counts for little when it is past. There is but one question for him to answer, to face boldly and honestly as an individual alone with his conscience and his destiny:

"How will I let that poverty or wealth affect me? If that trial or deprivation has left me better, truer, nobler then,—poverty has been riches, failure has been a success. If wealth has come to me and has made me vain, arrogant, contemptuous, uncharitable, cynical, closing from me all the tenderness of life, all the channels of higher development, of possible good to my fellow-man, making me the mere custodian of a money-bag, then,—wealth has lied to me, it has been failure, not success; it has not been riches, it has been dark, treacherous poverty that stole from me even Myself." All things become for us then what we take from them.

Failure is one of God's educators. It is experience leading man to higher things; it is the revelation of a way, a path hitherto unknown to us. The best men in the world, those who have made the greatest real successes look back with serene happiness on their failures. The turning of the face of Time shows all things in a wondrously illuminated and satisfying perspective.

Many a man is thankful to-day that some petty success for which he once struggled melted into thin air as his hand sought to clutch it. Failure is often the rock-bottom foundation of real success. If man, in a few instances of his life can say, "Those failures were the best things in the world that could have happened to me," should he not face new failures with undaunted courage and trust that the miraculous ministry of Nature may transform these new stumbling-blocks into new stepping-stones?

Our highest hopes are often destroyed to prepare us for better things. The failure of the caterpillar is the birth of the butterfly; the passing of the bud is the becoming of the rose; the death or destruction of the seed is the prelude to its resurrection as wheat. It is at night in the darkest hours, those preceding dawn, that plants grow best, that they most increase in size. May this not be one of Nature's gentle showings to man of the times when he grows best, of the darkness of failure that is evolving into the sunlight of success? Let us fear only the failure of not living the right as we see it, leaving the results to the guardianship of the Infinite.

If we think of any supreme moment of our lives, any great success, anyone who is dear to us, and then consider how we reached that moment, that success, that friend, we will be surprised and strengthened by the revelation. As we trace each one back, step by step, through the genealogy of circumstances, we will see how logical has been the course of our joy and success, from sorrow and failure, and that what gives us most happiness to-day is inextricably connected with what once caused us sorrow. Many of the rivers of our greatest prosperity and growth have had their source and their trickling increase into volume among the dark, gloomy recesses of our failure.

There is no honest and true work, carried along with constant and sincere purpose, that ever really fails. If it sometime seem to be wasted effort, it will prove to us a new lesson of "how" to walk; the secret of our failures will prove to us the inspiration of possible successes. Man, living with the highest aims as best he can, in continuous harmony with them, is a success, no matter what statistics of failure a near-sighted and half-blind world of critics and commentators may lay at his door.

High ideals, noble efforts will make seeming failures but trifles, they need not dishearten us; should prove sources of new strength. The rocky way may prove safer than the slippery path of smoothness. Birds cannot fly best with the wind, but against it; ships do not progress in calm when the sails flap idly against the unstrained masts.

The alchemy of Nature, superior to that of the Paracelsians, constantly transmutes the baser metals of failure into the later pure gold of higher success, if the mind of the worker is kept true, constant and untiring in the service, and he have that sublime courage that defies fate to its worst while he does his best.

Doing Our Best at All Times

Life is a wondrously complex problem for the individual until, some day, in a moment of illumination, he awakens to the great realization that he can make it simple,—never quite simple, but always simpler. There are a thousand mysteries of right and wrong that have baffled the wise men of the ages. There are depths in the great fundamental questions of the human race that no plummet of philosophy has ever sounded. There are wild cries of honest hunger for truth that seek to pierce the silence beyond the grave, but to them ever echo back,—only a repetition of their unanswered cries.

To us all, comes, at times, the great note of questioning despair that darkens our horizon and paralyzes our effort: "If there really be a God, if eternal justice really rules the world," we say, "why should life be as it is? Why do some men starve while others feast? Why does virtue often languish in the shadow while vice triumphs in the sunshine? Why does failure so often dog the footsteps of honest effort, while the success that comes from trickery and dishonor is greeted with the world's applause? How is it that the loving father of one family is taken by death, while the worthless incumbrance of another is spared? Why is there so much unnecessary pain, sorrowing and suffering in the world—why, indeed, should there be any?"

Neither philosophy nor religion can give any final satisfactory answer that is capable of logical demonstration, of absolute proof. There is ever, even after the best explanations, a residuum of the unexplained. We must then fall back in the eternal arms of faith and be wise enough to say, "I will not be disconcerted by these problems of life; I will not permit them to plunge me into doubt, and to cloud my life with vagueness and uncertainty. Man arrogates much to himself when he demands from the Infinite the full solution of all His mysteries. I will found my life on the impregnable rock of a simple fundamental truth:—'This glorious creation with its millions of wondrous phenomena pulsing ever in harmony with eternal law must have a Creator; that Creator must be omniscient and omnipotent. But that Creator Himself cannot, in justice, demand of any creature more than the best that that individual can give.' I will do each day, in every moment, the best I can by the light I have; I will ever seek more light, more perfect illumination of truth, and live as best I can in harmony with the truth as I see it. If failure comes I will meet it bravely; if my pathway then lies in the shadow of trial, sorrow and suffering, I shall have the restful peace and the calm strength of one who has done his best, who can look back upon the past with no pang of regret, and who has heroic courage in facing the results, whatever they be, knowing that he could not make them different."

Upon this life-plan, this foundation, man may erect any superstructure of religion or philosophy that he conscientiously can erect; he should add to his equipment for living every shred of strength and inspiration, moral, mental or spiritual that is in his power to secure. This simple working faith is opposed to no creed, is a substitute for none; it is but a primary belief, a citadel, a refuge where the individual can retire for strength when the battle of life grows hard.

A mere theory of life, that remains but a theory, is about as useful to a man, as a gilt-edged menu is to a starving sailor on a raft in mid-ocean. It is irritating but not stimulating. No rule for higher living will help a man in the slightest until he reaches out and appropriates it for himself, until he makes it practical in his daily life, until that seed of theory in his mind blossoms into a thousand flowers of thought and word and act.

If a man honestly seeks to live his best at all times, that determination is visible in every moment of his living; no trifle in his life can be too insignificant to reflect his principle of living. The sun illuminates and beautifies a fallen leaf by the roadside as impartially as a towering mountain peak in the Alps. Every drop of water in the ocean is an epitome of the chemistry of the whole ocean; every drop is subject to precisely the same laws as dominate the united infinity of billions of drops that make that miracle of Nature men call the Sea. No matter how humble the calling of the individual, how uninteresting and dull the round of his duties, he should do his best. He should dignify what he is doing by the mind he puts into it; he should vitalize what little he has of power or energy or ability or opportunity, in order to prepare himself to be equal to higher privileges when they come. This will never lead man to that weak content that is satisfied with whatever falls to his lot. It will rather fill his mind with that divine discontent that cheerfully accepts the best,—merely as a temporary substitute for something better.

The man who is seeking ever to do his best is the man who is keen, active, wide-awake, and aggressive. He is ever watchful of himself in trifles; his standard is not "What will the world say?" but "Is it worthy of me?"

Edwin Booth, one of the greatest actors on the American stage, would never permit himself to assume an ungraceful attitude, even in his hours of privacy. In this simple thing, he lived his best. On the stage every move was one of unconscious grace. Those of his company who were conscious of their motions were the awkward ones who were seeking in public to undo or to conceal the carelessness of the gestures and motions of their private life. The man who is slipshod and thoughtless in his daily speech, whose vocabulary is a collection of anæmic commonplaces, whose repetitions of phrases and extravagance of interjections act but as feeble disguises to his lack of ideas, will never be brilliant on an occasion when he longs to outshine the stars. Living at one's best is constant preparation for instant use. It can never make one overprecise, self-conscious, affected, or priggish. Education, in its highest sense, is *conscious* training of mind or body to act *unconsciously.* It is conscious formation of mental habits, not mere acquisition of information.

One of the many ways in which the individual unwisely eclipses himself is in his worship of the fetish of luck. He feels that all others are lucky, and that whatever he attempts, fails. He does not realize the untiring energy, the unremitting concentration, the heroic courage, the sublime patience that is the secret of some men's success. Their "luck" was that they had prepared themselves to be equal to their opportunity when it came and were awake to recognize it and receive it. His own opportunity came and departed unnoted; it would not waken him from his dreams of some untold wealth that would fall into his lap. So he grows discouraged and envies those whom he should emulate; he bandages his arm, chloroforms his energies and performs his duties in a perfunctory way; or he passes through life, just ever "sampling" lines of activity.

The honest, faithful struggler should always realize that failure is but an episode in a true man's life,—never the whole story. It is never easy to meet and no philosophy can make it so, but the steadfast courage to master conditions, instead of complaining of them, will help him on his way; it will ever enable him to get the best out of what he has. He never knows the long series of vanquished failures that give solidity to someone else's success; he does not realize the price that some rich man, the innocent football of political malcontents and demagogues, has heroically paid for wealth and position.

The man who has a pessimist's doubt of all things; who demands a certified guarantee of his future; who fears his work will not be recognized or appreciated, or that after all, it is really not worth while, will never live his best. He is dulling his capacity for real progress by his hypnotic course of excuses for inactivity, instead of using a strong tonic of reasons for action.

One of the most weakening elements in the individual make-up is the surrender to the oncoming of years. Man's self-confidence dims and dies in the fear of age. "This new thought," he says of some suggestion tending to higher development, "is good; it is what we need. I am glad to have it for my children; I would have been happy to have had some help when I was at school, but it is too late for me. I am a man advanced in years."

This is but blind closing of life to wondrous possibilities. The knell of lost opportunity is never tolled in this life. It is never too late to recognize truth and to live by it. It requires only greater effort, closer attention, deeper consecration; but the impossible does not exist for the man who is self-confident and is willing to pay the price in time and struggle for his success or development. Later in life, the assessments are heavier in progress, as in life insurance, but that matters not to that mighty self-confidence that *will* not grow old while knowledge can keep it young.

Socrates, when his hair whitened with the snow of age, learned to play on instruments of music. Cato, at fourscore, began his study of Greek, and the same age saw Plutarch beginning, with the enthusiasm of a boy, his first lessons in Latin. The Character of Man, Theophrastus' greatest work, was begun on his ninetieth birthday. Chaucer's Canterbury Tales was the work of the poet's declining years. Ronsard, the father of French poetry, whose sonnets even translation cannot destroy, did not develop his poetic faculty until nearly fifty. Benjamin

Franklin at this age had just taken his really first steps of importance in philosophic pursuits. Arnauld, the theologian and sage, translated Josephus in his eightieth year. Winekelmann, one of the most famous writers on classic antiquities, was the son of a shoemaker, and lived in obscurity and ignorance until the prime of life. Hobbes, the English philosopher, published his version of the Odyssey in his eighty-seventh year, and his Iliad one year later. Chevreul, the great French scientist, whose untiring labors in the realm of color have so enriched the world, was busy, keen and active when Death called him, at the age of 103.

These men did not fear age; these few names from the great muster-roll of the famous ones who defied the years, should be voices of hope and heartening to every individual whose courage and confidence is weak. The path of truth, higher living, truer development in every phase of life, is never shut from the individual—until he closes it himself. Let man feel this, believe it and make this faith a real and living factor in his life and there are no limits to his progress. He has but to live his best at all times, and rest calm and untroubled no matter what results come to his efforts. The constant looking backward to what might have been, instead of forward to what may be, is a great weakener of self-confidence. This worry for the old past, this wasted energy, for that which no power in the world can restore, ever lessens the individual's faith in himself and weakens his efforts to develop himself for the future to the perfection of his possibilities.

Nature, in her beautiful love and tenderness, says to man, weakened and worn and weary with the struggle, "Do in the best way you can the trifle that is under your hand at this moment; do it in the best spirit of preparation for the future your thought suggests; bring all the light of knowledge from all the past to aid you. Do this and you have done your best. The past is forever closed to you. No worry, no struggle, no suffering, no agony of despair can alter it. It is as much beyond your power as if it were a million years of eternity behind you. Turn all that past, with its sad hours, weakness and sin, its wasted opportunities, as light, in confidence and hope, upon the future. Turn it all in fuller truth and light so as to make each trifle of this present a new past it will be joy to look back to; each trifle a grander, nobler, and more perfect preparation for the future.

The present and the future you can make from it is yours; the past has gone back, with all its messages, all its history, all its records, to the God who loaned you the golden moments to use in obedience to His law.

The Royal Road to Happiness

"During my whole life I have not had twenty-four hours of happiness." So said Prince Bismarck, one of the greatest statesmen of the nineteenth century. Eighty-three years of wealth, fame, honors, power, influence, prosperity and triumph,—years when he held an empire in his fingers,—but not one day of happiness!

Happiness is the greatest paradox in Nature. It can grow in any soil, live under any conditions. It defies environment. It comes from within; it is the revelation of the depths of the inner life as light and heat proclaim the sun from which they radiate. Happiness consists not of having, but of being; not of possessing, but of enjoying. It is the warm glow of a heart at peace with itself. A martyr at the stake may have happiness that a king on his throne might envy. Man is the creator of his own happiness; it is the aroma of a life lived in harmony with high ideals. For what a man *has*, he may be dependent on others; what he *is*, rests with him alone. What he *ob*tains in life is but acquisition; what he *at*tains is growth. Happiness is the soul's joy in the possession of the intangible. Absolute, perfect, continuous happiness in life is impossible for the human. It would mean the consummation of attainments, the individual consciousness of a perfectly fulfilled destiny. Happiness is paradoxical because it may coexist with trial, sorrow and poverty. It is the gladness of the heart,—rising superior to all conditions.

Happiness has a number of under studies,—gratification, satisfaction, content, and pleasure,—clever imitators that simulate its appearance rather than emulate its method. Gratification is a harmony between our desires and our possessions. It is ever incomplete, it is the thankful acceptance of part. It is a mental pleasure in the quality of what one receives, a dissatisfaction as to the quantity. It may be an element in happiness, but, in itself,—it is not happiness.

Satisfaction is perfect identity of our desires and our possessions. It exists only so long as this perfect union and unity can be preserved. But every realized ideal gives birth to new ideals, every step in advance reveals large domains of the unattained; every feeding stimulates new appetites,—then the desires and possessions are no longer identical, no longer equal; new cravings call forth new activities, the equipoise is destroyed, and dissatisfaction reënters. Man might possess everything tangible in the world and yet not be happy, for happiness is the satisfying of the soul, not of the mind or the body. Dissatisfaction, in its highest sense, is the keynote of all advance, the evidence of new aspirations, the guarantee of the progressive revelation of new possibilities.

Content is a greatly overrated virtue. It is a kind of diluted despair; it is the feeling with which we continue to accept substitutes, without striving for the realities. Content makes the trained individual swallow vinegar and try to smack his lips as if it were wine. Content enables one to warm his hands at the fire of a past joy that exists only in memory. Content is a mental and moral chloroform that deadens the activities of the individual to rise to higher planes of life and growth. Man should never be contented with anything less than the best efforts of his nature can possibly secure for him. Content makes the world more comfortable for the individual, but it is the death-knell of progress. Man should be content with each step of progress merely as a station, discontented with it as a destination; contented with it as a step; discontented with it as a finality. There are times when a man should be content with what he *has,* but never with what he *is.*

But content is not happiness; neither is pleasure. Pleasure is temporary, happiness is continuous; pleasure is a note, happiness is a symphony; pleasure may exist when conscience utters protests; happiness,—never. Pleasure may have its dregs and its lees; but none can be found in the cup of happiness.

Man is the only animal that can be really happy. To the rest of the creation belong only weak imitations of the understudies. Happiness represents a peaceful attunement of a life with a standard of living. It can never be made by the individual, by himself, for himself. It is one of the incidental by-products of an unselfish life. No man can make his own happiness the one object of his life and attain it, any more than he can jump on the far end of his shadow. If you would hit the bull's-eye of happiness on the target of life, aim above it. Place other things higher than your own happiness and it will surely come to you. You can buy pleasure, you can acquire content, you can become satisfied,—but Nature never put real happiness on the bargain counter. It is the undetachable accompaniment of true living. It is calm and peaceful; it never lives in an atmosphere of worry or of hopeless struggle.

The basis of happiness is the love of something outside self. Search every instance of happiness in the world and you will find, when all the incidental features are eliminated, that there is always the constant, unchangeable element of love,—love of parent for child; love of man and woman for each other; love of humanity in some form, or a great lifework into which the individual throws all his energies.

Happiness is the voice of optimism, of faith, of simple, steadfast love. No cynic or pessimist can be really happy. A cynic is a man who is morally near-sighted,—and brags about it. He sees the evil in his own heart, and thinks he sees the world. He lets a mote in his eye eclipse the sun. An incurable cynic is an individual who should long for death,—for life cannot bring him happiness, and death might. The keynote of Bismarck's lack of happiness was his profound distrust of human nature.

There is a royal road to happiness; it lies in Consecration, Concentration, Conquest and Conscience.

Consecration is dedicating the individual life to the service of others, to some noble mission, to realizing some unselfish ideal. Life is not something to be lived *through;* it is something to be lived *up to.* It is a privilege, not a penal servitude of so many decades on earth. Consecration places the object of life above the mere acquisition of money as a finality. The man who is unselfish, kind, loving, tender, helpful, ready to lighten the burden of those around him, to hearten the struggling ones, to forget himself sometimes in remembering others,— is on the right road to happiness. Consecration is ever active, bold and aggressive, fearing naught but possible disloyalty to high ideals.

Concentration makes the individual life simpler and deeper. It cuts away the shams and pretenses of modern living and limits life to its truest essentials. Worry, fear, useless regret,—all the great wastes that sap mental, moral or physical energy must be sacrificed, or the individual needlessly destroys half the possibilities of living. A great purpose in life, something that unifies the strands and threads of each day's thinking, something that takes the sting from the petty trials, sorrows, sufferings and blunders of life, is a great aid to Concentration. Soldiers in battle may forget their wounds, or even be unconscious of them, in the inspiration of battling for what they believe is right. Concentration dignifies an humble life; it makes a great life,—sublime. In morals it is a short cut to simplicity. It leads to right for right's sake, without thought of policy or of reward. It brings calm and rest to the individual,—a serenity that is but the sunlight of happiness.

Conquest is the overcoming of an evil habit, the rising superior to opposition and attack, the spiritual exaltation that comes from resisting the invasion of the groveling material side of life. Sometimes when you are worn and weak with the struggle; when it seems that justice is a dream, that honesty and loyalty and truth count for nothing, that the devil is the only good paymaster; when hope grows dim and flickers, then is the time when you must tower in the great sublime faith that Right must prevail, then must you throttle these imps of doubt and despair; you must master yourself to master the world around you. This is Conquest; this is what counts. Even a log can float with the current, it takes a man to fight sturdily against an opposing tide that would sweep his craft out of its course. When the jealousies, the petty intrigues and the meannesses and the misunderstandings in life assail you,—rise above them. Be like a lighthouse that illumines and beautifies the snarling, swashing waves of the storm that threaten it, that seek to undermine it and seek to wash over it. This is Conquest. When the chance to win fame, wealth, success or the attainment of your heart's desire, by sacrifice of honor or principle, comes to you and it does not affect you long enough even to seem a temptation, you have been the victor. That too is Conquest. And Conquest is part of the royal road to happiness.

Conscience, as the mentor, the guide and compass of every act, leads ever to Happiness. When the individual can stay alone with his conscience and get its approval, without using force or specious logic, then he begins to know what real Happiness is. But the individual must be careful that he is not appealing to a conscience perverted or deadened by the wrongdoing and subsequent deafness of its owner. The man who is honestly seeking to live his life in Consecration, Concentration and Conquest, living from day to day as best he can, by the light he has, may rely explicitly on his Conscience. He can shut his ears to "what the world says" and find in the approval of his own conscience the highest earthly tribune,—the voice of the Infinite communing with the Individual.

Unhappiness is the hunger to get; Happiness is the hunger to give. True happiness must have the tinge of sorrow outlived, the sense of pain softened by the mellowing years, the chastening of loss that in the wondrous mystery of time transmutes our suffering into love and sympathy with others.

If the individual should set out for a single day to give Happiness, to make life happier, brighter and sweeter, not for himself but for others, he would find a wondrous revelation of what Happiness really is. The greatest of the world's heroes could not by any series of acts of heroism do as much real good as any individual living his whole life in seeking, from day to day, to make others happy.

Each day there should be fresh resolution, new strength, and renewed enthusiasm. "Just for To-day" might be the daily motto of thousands of societies throughout the country, composed of members bound together to make the world better through constant simple acts of kindness, constant deeds of sweetness and love. And Happiness would come to them in its highest and best form, not because they would seek to *absorb* it, but,—because they seek to *radiate* it.

THE LIFE OF OUR LORD

Charles Dickens

Charles Dickens, born in 1812, is one of the great English novelists, the author of such classics as *A Christmas Carol* and *Oliver Twist*. He spent his childhood in poverty, and his feelings for the downtrodden are often evident in his writing. Dickens once visited an LDS emigrant ship, noting in *The Uncommercial Traveller,* "I went on board . . . to bear testimony against them if they deserved it. . . . To my great astonishment they did not. . . . I [left], feeling it impossible to deny that . . . some remarkable influence had produced a remarkable result, which better known influences have often missed."

Dickens wrote *The Life of Our Lord* in 1849 "expressly for his children" and not for publication, which explains its inconsistent capitalization, punctuation, and so on. His son, Sir Henry Dickens, would not allow the manuscript to be published during his lifetime, but Sir Henry's will provided that it could be published after his death with the approval of the family. It was first published in 1934 in both England and the United States.

Although *The Life of Our Lord* does not strictly follow the scriptures, it represents the author's sincere effort to teach his children about the life of Christ in a simple, beautiful, and instructive way. In 1999 President Gordon B. Hinckley quoted from it during his Christmas address to the Church, emphasizing its closing words: "Remember—It is christianity to do good always—even to those who do evil to us. It is christianity to love our neighbour as ourself, and to do to all men as we would have them Do to us."

THE LIFE OF OUR LORD

Chapter the First

My dear children, I am very anxious that you should know something about the History of Jesus Christ. For everybody ought to know about Him. No one ever lived, who was so good, so kind, so gentle, and so sorry for all people who did wrong, or were in anyway ill or miserable, as he was. And as he is now in Heaven, where we hope to go, and all to meet each other after we are dead, and there be happy always together. You never can think what a good place Heaven is, without knowing who he was and what he did.

He was born, a long long time ago—nearly Two Thousand years ago—at a place called Bethlehem. His father and mother lived in a city called Nazareth, but they were forced, by business to travel to Bethlehem. His father's name was Joseph, and his mother's name was Mary. And the town being very full of people, also brought there by business, there was no room for Joseph and Mary in the Inn or in any house; so they went into a Stable to lodge, and in this stable Jesus Christ was born. There was no cradle or anything of that kind there, so Mary laid her pretty little boy in what is called the Manger, which is the place the horses eat out of. And there he fell asleep.

While he was asleep, some Shepherds who were watching Sheep in the Fields, saw an Angel from God, all light and beautiful, come moving over the grass towards Them. At first they were afraid and fell down and hid their faces. But it said "There is a child born to-day in the City of Bethlehem near here, who will grow up to be so good that God will love him as his own son; and he will teach men to love one another, and not to quarrel and hurt one another; and his name will be Jesus Christ; and people will put that name in their prayers, because they will know God loves it, and will know that they should love it too." And then the Angel told the Shepherds to go to that Stable, and look at that little child in the Manger. Which they did; and they kneeled down by it in its sleep, and said "God bless this child!"

Now the great place of all that country was Jerusalem—just as London is the great place in England—and at Jerusalem the King lived, whose name was King Herod. Some wise men came one day, from a country a long way off in the East, and said to the King "We have seen a Star in the Sky, which teaches us to know that a child is born in Bethlehem who will live to be a man whom all people will love." When King Herod heard this, he was jealous, for he was a wicked man. But he pretended not to be, and said to the wise men, "Whereabouts is this child?" And the wise men said "We don't know. But we think the Star will shew us; for the Star has been moving on before us, all the way here, and is now standing still in the sky." Then Herod asked them to see if the Star would shew them where the child lived, and ordered them, if they found the child, to come back to him. So they went out, and the Star went on, over their heads a little way before them, until it stopped over the house where the child was. This was very wonderful, but God ordered it to be so.

When the Star stopped, the wise men went in, and saw the child with Mary his Mother. They loved him very much, and gave him some presents. Then they went away. But they did not go back to King Herod; for they thought he was jealous, though he had not said so. So they went away, by night, back into their own country. And an Angel came, and told Joseph and Mary to take the child into a Country called Egypt, or Herod would kill him. So they escaped too, in the night—the father, the mother, and the child—and arrived there, safely.

But when this cruel Herod found that the wise men did not come back to him, and that he could not, therefore, find out where this child, Jesus Christ, lived, he called his soldiers and captains to him, and told them to go and Kill all the children in his dominions that were not more than two years old. The wicked men did so. The mothers of the children ran up and down the streets with them in their arms trying to save them, and hide them in caves and cellars, but it was of no use. The soldiers with their swords killed all the children they could find. This dreadful murder was called the Murder of the Innocents. Because the little children were so innocent.

King Herod hoped that Jesus Christ was one of them. But He was not, as you know, for He had escaped safely into Egypt. And he lived there, with his father and mother, until Bad King Herod died.

Chapter the Second

When King Herod was dead, an angel came to Joseph again, and said he might now go to Jerusalem, and not be afraid for the child's sake. So Joseph and Mary, and her Son Jesus Christ (who are commonly called The Holy Family) travelled towards Jerusalem; but hearing on the way that King Herod's son was the new King, and fearing that he, too, might want to hurt the child, they turned out of the way, and went to live in Nazareth. They lived there, until Jesus Christ was twelve years old.

Then Joseph and Mary went to Jerusalem to attend a Religious Feast which used to be held in those days, in the Temple of Jerusalem, which was a great church or Cathedral; and they took Jesus Christ with them. And when the Feast was over, they travelled away from Jerusalem, back towards their own home in Nazareth, with a great many of their friends and neighbours. For people used, then, to travel a great many together, for fear of robbers; the roads not being so safe and well guarded as they are now, and travelling being much more difficult altogether, than it now is.

They travelled on, for a whole day, and never knew that Jesus Christ was not with them; for the company being so large, they thought he was somewhere among the people, though they did not see Him. But finding that he was not there, and fearing that he was lost, they turned back to Jerusalem in great anxiety to look for him. They found him, sitting in the Temple, talking about the goodness of God, and how we should all pray to him, with some learned men who were called Doctors. They were not what you understand by the word "doctors" now; they did not attend sick people; they were scholars and clever men. And Jesus Christ shewed such knowledge in what he said to them, and in the questions he asked them, that they were all astonished.

He went, with Joseph and Mary, home to Nazareth, when they had found him, and lived there until he was thirty or thirty-five years old.

At that time there was a very good man indeed, named John, who was the son of a woman named Elizabeth—the cousin of Mary. And people being wicked, and violent, and killing each other, and not minding their duty towards God, John (to teach them better) went about the country, preaching to them, and entreating them to be better men and women. And because he loved them more than himself, and didn't mind himself when he was doing them good, he was poorly dressed in the skin of a camel, and ate little but some insects called locusts, which he found as he travelled: and wild honey, which the bees left in the Hollow Trees. You never saw a locust, because they belong to that country near Jerusalem, which is a great way off. So do camels, but I think you have seen a camel? At all events they are brought over here, sometimes; and if you would like to see one, I will shew you one.

There was a River, not very far from Jerusalem, called the River Jordan; and in this water, John baptized those people who would come to him, and promise to be better. A great many people went to him in crowds. Jesus Christ went too. But when John saw him, John said, "Why should I baptize you, who are so much better than I!" Jesus Christ made answer, "Suffer it to be so now." So John baptized him. And when he was baptized, the sky opened, and a beautiful bird like a dove came flying down, and the voice of God, speaking up in Heaven, was heard to say "This is my beloved Son, in whom I am well pleased!"

Jesus Christ then went into a wild and lonely country called the Wilderness, and stayed there forty days and forty nights, praying that he might be of use to men and women, and teach them to be better, so that after their deaths, they might be happy in Heaven.

When he came out of the Wilderness, he began to cure sick people by only laying his hand upon them; for God had given him power to heal the sick, and to give sight to the blind, and to do many wonderful and solemn things of which I shall tell you more bye and bye, and which are called *"The Miracles"* of Christ. I wish you would remember that word, because I shall use it again, and I should like you to know that it means something which is very wonderful and which could not be done without God's leave and assistance.

The first miracle which Jesus Christ did, was at a place called Cana, where he went to a Marriage-Feast with Mary his Mother. There was no wine; and Mary told him so. There were only six stone water-pots filled with water. But Jesus turned this water into wine, by only lifting up his hand; and all who were there, drank of it.

For God had given Jesus Christ the power to do such wonders; and he did them, that people might know he was not a common man, and might believe what he taught them, and also believe that God had sent him. And many people, hearing this, and hearing that he cured the sick, did begin to believe in him; and great crowds followed him in the streets and on the roads, wherever he went.

Chapter the Third

That there might be some good men to go about with Him, teaching the people, Jesus Christ chose Twelve poor men to be his companions. These twelve are called *The apostles* or *Disciples,* and he chose them from among Poor Men, in order that the Poor might know—always after that; in all years to come—that Heaven was made for them as well as for the rich, and that God makes no difference between those who wear good clothes and those who go barefoot and in rags. The most miserable, the most ugly, deformed, wretched creatures that live, will be bright Angels in Heaven if they are good here on earth. Never forget this, when you are grown up. Never be proud or unkind, my dears, to any poor man, woman, or child. If they are bad, think that they would have been better, if they had had kind friends, and good homes, and had been better taught. So, always try to make them better by kind persuading words; and always try to teach them and relieve them if you can. And when people speak ill of the Poor and Miserable, think how Jesus Christ went among them and taught them, and thought them worthy of his care. And always pity them yourselves, and think as well of them as you can.

The names of the Twelve apostles were, Simon Peter, Andrew, James the son of Zebedee, John, Philip, Bartholomew, Thomas, Matthew, James the son of Alphaeus, Labbaeus, Simon, and Judas Iscariot. This man afterwards betrayed Jesus Christ, as you will hear bye and bye.

The first four of these, were poor fishermen, who were sitting in their boats by the seaside, mending their nets, when Christ passed by. He stopped, and went into Simon Peter's boat, and asked him if he had caught many fish. Peter said No; though they had worked all night with their nets, they had caught nothing. Christ said, "let down the net again." They did so; and it was immediately so full of fish, that it required the strength of many men (who came and helped them) to lift it out of the water, and even then it was very hard to do. This was another of the miracles of Jesus Christ.

Jesus then said "Come with me." And they followed him directly. And from that time the Twelve disciples or apostles were always with him.

As great crowds of people followed him, and wished to be taught, he went up into a Mountain and there preached to them, and gave them, from his own lips, the words of that Prayer, beginning "Our father which art in Heaven," that you say every night. It is called The Lord's Prayer, because it was first said by Jesus Christ, and because he commanded his disciples to pray in those words.

When he was come down from the Mountain, there came to him a man with a dreadful disease called the leprosy. It was common in those times, and those who were ill with it, were called lepers. This Leper fell at the feet of Jesus Christ, and said "Lord! If thou wilt, thou canst make me well!" Jesus, always full of compassion, stretched out his hand, and said "I will! Be thou well!" And his disease went away, immediately, and he was cured.

Being followed, wherever he went, by great crowds of people, Jesus went, with his disciples, into a house, to rest. While he was sitting inside, some men brought upon a bed, a man who was very ill of what is called the Palsy, so that he trembled all over from head to foot, and could neither stand, nor move. But the crowd being all about the door and windows, and they not being able to get near Jesus Christ, these men climbed up to the roof of the house, which was a low one; and through the tiling at the top, let down the bed, with the sick man upon it, into the room where Jesus sat. When he saw him, Jesus, full of pity, said "Arise! Take up thy bed, and go to thine own home!" And the man rose up and went away quite well; blessing him, and thanking God.

There was a Centurion too, or officer over the Soldiers, who came to him, and said, "Lord! My servant lies at home in my house, very ill."—Jesus Christ made answer, "I will come and cure him." But the Centurion said "Lord! I am not worthy that Thou shouldst come to my house. Say the word only, and I know he will be cured." Then Jesus

Christ, glad that the Centurion believed in him so truly, said "Be it so!" And the servant became well, from that moment.

But of all the people who came to him, none were so full of grief and distress, as one man who was a Ruler or Magistrate over many people, and he wrung his hands, and cried, and said "Oh Lord, my daughter—my beautiful, good, innocent little girl, is dead. Oh come to her, come to her, and lay Thy blessed hand upon her, and I know she will revive, and come to life again, and make me and her mother happy. Oh Lord we love her so, we love her so! And she is dead!"

Jesus Christ went out with him, and so did his disciples and went to his house, where the friends and neighbours were crying in the room where the poor dead little girl lay, and where there was soft music playing; as there used to be, in those days, when people died. Jesus Christ, looking on her, sorrowfully, said—to comfort her poor parents—"She is not dead. She is asleep." Then he commanded the room to be cleared of the people that were in it, and going to the dead child, took her by the hand, and she rose up, quite well, as if she had only been asleep. Oh what a sight it must have been to see her parents clasp her in their arms, and kiss her, and thank God, and Jesus Christ his son, for such great Mercy!

But he was always merciful and tender. And because he did such Good, and taught people how to love God and how to hope to go to Heaven after death, he was called *Our Saviour.*

Chapter the Fourth

There were in that, country where Our Saviour performed his Miracles, certain people who were called Pharisees. They were very proud, and believed that no people were good but themselves; and they were all afraid of Jesus Christ, because he taught the people better. So were the Jews, in general. Most of the Inhabitants of that country, were Jews.

Our Saviour, walking once in the fields with his disciples on a Sunday (which the Jews called, and still call, the Sabbath) they gathered some ears of the corn that was growing there, to eat. This, the Pharisees said, was wrong; and in the same way, when our Saviour went into one of their churches—they were called Synagogues—and looked compassionately on a poor man who had his hand all withered and wasted away, these Pharisees said "Is it right to cure people on a Sunday?" Our Saviour answered them by saying, "If any of you had a sheep and it fell into a pit, would you not take it out, even though it happened on a Sunday? And how much better is a man than a sheep!" Then he said to the poor man, "Stretch out thine hand!" And it was cured immediately, and was smooth and useful like the other. So Jesus Christ told them "You may always do good, no matter what the day is."

There was a city called Nain into which Our Saviour went soon after this, followed by great numbers of people, and especially by those who had sick relations, or friends, or children. For they brought sick people out into the streets and roads through which he passed, and cried out to him to touch them, and when he did, they became well. Going on, in the midst of this crowd, and near the Gate of the city, He met a funeral. It was the funeral of a young man, who was carried on what is called a Bier, which was open, as the custom was in that country, and is now in many parts of Italy. His poor mother followed the bier, and wept very much, for she had no other child. When Our Saviour saw her, he was touched to the heart to see her so sorry, and said "Weep not!" Then, the bearers of the bier standing still, he walked up to it and touched it with his hand, and said "Young Man! Arise." The dead man, coming to life again at the sound of The Saviour's Voice, rose up and began to speak. And Jesus Christ leaving him with his mother—Ah how happy they both were!—went away.

By this time the crowd was so very great that Jesus Christ went down to the waterside, to go in a boat, to a more retired place. And in the boat, He fell asleep, while his Disciples were sitting on the deck. While he was still sleeping a violent storm arose, so that the waves washed over the boat, and the howling wind so rocked and shook it, that they thought it would sink. In their fright the disciples awoke Our Saviour, and said "Lord! Save us, or we are lost!" He stood up, and raising his arm, said to the rolling Sea and to the whistling wind, "Peace! Be still!" And immediately it was calm and pleasant weather, and the boat went safely on, through the smooth waters.

When they came to the other side of the waters they had to pass a wild and lonely burying-ground that was outside the City to which they were going. All burying-grounds were outside cities in those times. In this place there was a dreadful madman who lived among the tombs, and houled all day and night, so that it made travellers afraid, to hear him. They had tried to chain him, but he broke his chains, he was so strong; and he would throw himself on the sharp stones, and cut himself in the most dreadful manner: crying and houling all the while: When this wretched man saw Jesus Christ a long way off, he cried out "It is the son of God! Oh son of God, do not torment me!" Jesus, coming near him, perceived that he was torn by an Evil Spirit, and cast the madness out of him, and into a herd of swine (or pigs) who were feeding close by, and who directly ran headlong down a steep place leading to the sea and were dashed to pieces.

Now Herod, the son of that cruel King who murdered the Innocents, reigning over the people there, and hearing that Jesus Christ was doing these wonders, and was giving sight to the blind and causing the deaf to hear, and the dumb to speak, and the lame to walk, and that he was followed by multitudes and multitudes of people—Herod, hearing this, said "This man is a companion and friend of John the Baptist." John was the good man, you recollect, who wore a garment made of camel's hair, and ate wild honey. Herod had taken him Prisoner, because he taught and preached to the people; and had him then, locked up, in the prisons of his Palace.

While Herod was in this angry humour with John, his birthday came; and his daughter, Herodias, who was a fine dancer, danced before him, to please him. She pleased him so much that he swore an oath he would give her whatever she would ask him for. "Then," said she, "father, give me the head of John the Baptist in a charger." For she hated John, and was a wicked, cruel woman.

The King was sorry, for though he had John prisoner, he did not wish to kill him; but having sworn that he would give her what she asked for, he sent some soldiers down into the Prison, with directions to cut off the head of John the Baptist, and give it to Herodias. This they did, and took it to her, as she had said, in a charger, which was a kind of dish. When Jesus Christ heard from the apostles of this cruel deed, he left that city, and went with them (after they had privately buried John's body in the night) to another place.

Chapter the Fifth

One of the Pharisees begged Our Saviour to go into his house, and eat with him. And while our Saviour sat eating at the table, there crept into the room a woman of that city who had led a bad and sinful life, and was ashamed that the Son of God should see her; and yet she trusted so much to his goodness, and his compassion for all who, having done wrong were truly sorry for it in their hearts, that, by little and little, she went behind the seat on which he sat, and dropped down at his feet, and wetted them with her sorrowful tears; then she kissed them and dried them on her long hair, and rubbed them with some sweet-smelling ointment she had brought with her in a box. Her name was Mary Magdalene.

When the Pharisee saw that Jesus permitted this woman to touch Him, he said within himself that Jesus did not know how wicked she had been. But Jesus Christ, who knew his thoughts, said to him "Simon"—for that was his name—"if a man had debtors, one of whom owed him five hundred pence, and one of whom owed him only fifty pence, and he forgave them, both, their debts, which of those two debtors do you think would love him most?" Simon answered "I suppose that one whom he forgave most." Jesus told him he was right, and said "As God forgives this woman so much sin, she will love Him, I hope, the more." And he said to her, "God forgives you!" The company who were present wondered that Jesus Christ had power to forgive sins, but God had given it to Him. And the woman thanking Him for all his mercy, went away.

We learn from this, that we must always forgive those who have done us any harm, when they come to us and say they are truly sorry for it. Even if they do not come and say so, we must still forgive them, and never hate them or be unkind to them, if we would hope that God will forgive us.

After this there was a great feast of the Jews, and Jesus Christ went to Jerusalem. There was, near the sheep market in that place, a pool, or pond, called Bethesda, having five gates to it; and at the time of the year when that feast took place great numbers of sick people and cripples went to this pool to bathe in it: believing that an Angel came and stirred the water, and that whoever went in first after the Angel had done so, was cured of any illness he or she had, whatever it might be. Among these poor persons, was one man who had been ill, thirty eight years; and he told Jesus Christ (who took pity on him when he saw him lying on his bed alone, with no one to help him) that he never could be dipped in the pool, because he was so weak and ill that he could not move to get there. Our Saviour said to him, "take up thy bed and go away." And he went away, quite well.

Many Jews saw this; and when they saw it, they hated Jesus Christ the more: knowing that the people, being taught and cured by him, would not believe their Priests, who told the people what was not true, and deceived them. So they said to one another that Jesus Christ should be killed, because he cured people on the Sabbath Day (which was against their strict law) and because he called himself the Son of God. And they tried to raise enemies against him, and to get the crowd in the streets to murder Him.

But the crowd followed Him wherever he went, blessing him, and praying to be taught and cured; for they knew He did nothing but Good. Jesus going with his disciples over a sea, called the Sea of Tiberias and sitting with them on a hill-side, saw great numbers of these poor people waiting below, and said to the apostle Philip, "Where shall we buy bread, that they may eat and be refreshed, after their long journey?" Philip answered, "Lord, two hundred pennyworth of bread would not be enough for so many people, and we have none." "We have only," said another apostle—Andrew, Simon Peter's brother—"five small barley loaves, and two little fish, belonging to a lad who is among us. What are they, among so many!" Jesus Christ said, "Let them all sit down!" They did; there being a great deal of grass in that place. When they were all seated, Jesus took the bread, and looked up to Heaven, and blessed it, and broke it, and handed it in pieces to the apostles, who handed it to the people. And of those five little loaves, and two fish, five thousand men, besides women, and children, ate, and had enough; and when they were all satisfied, there were gathered up twelve baskets full of what was left. This was another of the Miracles of Jesus Christ.

Our Saviour then sent his disciples away in a boat, across the water, and said he would follow them presently, when he had dismissed the people. The people being gone, he remained by himself to pray; so that the night came on, and the disciples were still rowing on the water in their boat, wondering when Christ would come. Late in the night, when the wind was against them and the waves were running high, they saw Him coming walking towards them on the water, as if it were dry land. When they saw this, they were terrified, and cried out, but Jesus said, "It is I. Be not afraid!" Peter taking courage, said, "Lord, if it be thou, tell me to come to thee upon the water." Jesus Christ said, "Come!" Peter then walked towards Him, but seeing the angry waves, and hearing the wind roar, he was frightened and began to sink, and would have done so, but that Jesus took him by the hand, and led him into the boat. Then, in a moment, the wind went down; and the Disciples said to one another, "It is true! He is the Son of God!"

Jesus did many more miracles after this happened and cured the sick in great numbers: making the lame walk, and the dumb speak, and the blind see. And being again surrounded by a great crowd who were faint and hungry, and had been with him for three days eating little, he took from his disciples seven loaves and a few fish, and again divided them among the people who were four thousand in number. They all ate, and had enough; and of what was left, there were gathered up seven baskets full.

He now divided the disciples, and sent them into many towns and villages, teaching the people, and giving them power to cure, in the name of God, all those who were ill. And at this time He began to tell them (for he knew what would happen) that he must one day go back to Jerusalem where he would suffer a great deal, and where he would certainly be put to Death. But he said to them that on the third day after he was dead, he would rise from the grave, and ascend to Heaven, where he would sit at the right hand of God, beseeching God's pardon to sinners.

Chapter the Sixth

Six days after the last Miracle of the loaves and fish, Jesus Christ went up into a high Mountain, with only three of the Disciples—Peter, James, and John. And while he was speaking to them there, suddenly His face began to shine as if it were the Sun, and the robes he wore, which were white, glistened and shone like sparkling silver, and he stood before them like an angel. A bright cloud overshadowed them at the same time; and a voice, speaking from the cloud, was heard to say "This is my beloved Son in whom I am well pleased. Hear ye him!" At which the three disciples fell on their knees and covered their faces: being afraid.

This is called the Transfiguration of our Saviour.

When they were come down from this mountain, and were among the people again, a man knelt at the feet of Jesus Christ, and said, "Lord have mercy on my son, for he is mad and cannot help himself, and sometimes falls into the fire, and sometimes into the water, and covers himself with scars and sores. Some of Thy Disciples have tried to cure him, but could not." Our Saviour cured the child immediately; and turning to his disciples told them they had not been able to cure him themselves, because they did not believe in Him so truly as he had hoped.

The Disciples asked him, "Master, who is greatest in the Kingdom of Heaven?" Jesus called a little child to him, and took him in his arms, and stood him among them, and answered, "a child like this. I say unto you that none but those who are as humble as little children shall enter into Heaven. Whosoever shall receive one such little child in my name receiveth me. But whosoever hurts one of them, it were better for him that he had a millstone tied about his neck, and were drowned in the depths of the sea. The angels are all children." Our Saviour loved the child, and loved all children. Yes, and all the world. No one ever loved all people, so well and so truly as He did.

Peter asked Him, "Lord, How often shall I forgive any one who offends me? Seven times?" Our Saviour answered "Seventy times seven times, and more than that. For how can you hope that God will forgive you, when you do wrong, unless you forgive all other people!"

And he told his disciples this Story—He said, there was once a Servant who owed his master a great deal of money, and could not pay it. At which the Master, being very angry, was going to have this servant sold for a Slave. But the servant kneeling down and begging his Master's pardon with great sorrow, the Master forgave him. Now this same servant had a fellow-servant who owed him a hundred pence, and instead of being kind and forgiving to this poor man, as his Master had been to him, he put him in prison for the debt. His master hearing of it, went to him, and said "oh wicked Servant, I forgave you. Why did you not forgive your fellow servant!" And because he had not done so, his Master turned him away with great misery. "So," said Our Saviour; "how can you expect God to forgive you, if you do not forgive others!" This is the meaning of that part of the Lord's prayer, where we say "forgive us our trespasses"—that word means faults—"as we forgive them that trespass against us."

And he told them another story, and said There was a certain Farmer once, who had a Vineyard, and he went out early in the morning, and agreed with some labourers to work there all day, for a Penny. And bye and bye, when it was later, he went out again and engaged some more labourers on the same terms; and bye and bye went out again; and so on, several times, until the afternoon. When the day was over, and they all came to be paid, those who had worked since morning complained that those who had not begun to work until late in the day had the same money as themselves, and they said it was not fair. But the Master, said, "Friend, I agreed with you for a Penny; and is it less money to you, because I give the same money to another man?"

Our Saviour meant to teach them by this, that people who have done good all their lives long, will go to Heaven after they are dead. But that people who have been wicked, because of their being miserable, or not having parents and friends to take care of them when young, and who are truly sorry for it, however late in their lives, and pray God to forgive them, will be forgiven and will go to Heaven too. He taught His disciples in these stories, because he knew the people liked to hear them, and would remember what He said better, if he said it in that way. They are called Parables—THE PARABLES OF OUR SAVIOUR; and I wish you to remember that word, as I shall soon have some more of these Parables to tell you about.

The people listened to all that our Saviour said, but were not agreed among themselves about Him. The Pharisees and Jews had spoken to some of them against Him, and some of them were inclined to do Him harm and even to murder Him. But they were afraid, as yet, to do Him any harm, because of His goodness, and His looking so divine and grand—although he was very simply dressed; almost like the poor people—that they could hardly bear to meet his eyes.

One morning, He was sitting in a place called the Mount of Olives, teaching the people who were all clustered round Him, listening and learning attentively, when a great noise was heard, and a crowd of Pharisees, and some other people like them, called Scribes, came running in, with great cries and shouts, dragging among them a woman who had done wrong, and they all cried out together, "Master! Look at this woman. The law says she shall be pelted with stones until she is dead. But what say you? what say you?"

Jesus looked upon the noisy crowd attentively, and knew that they had come to make Him say the law was wrong and cruel; and that if He said so, they would make it a charge against Him and would kill him. They were ashamed and afraid as He looked into their faces, but they still cried out, "Come! What say you Master? what say you?"

Jesus stooped down, and wrote with his finger in the sand on the ground, "He that is without sin among you, let him throw the first stone at her." As they read this, looking over one another's shoulders, and as He repeated the words to them, they went away, one by one, ashamed, until not a man of all the noisy crowd was left there; and Jesus Christ, and the woman, hiding her face in her hands, alone remained.

Then said Jesus Christ, "Woman, where are thine accusers? Hath no man condemned Thee?" She answered, trembling, "No, Lord!" Then said our Saviour, "Neither do *I* condemn Thee. Go! and sin no more!"

Chapter the Seventh

As Our Saviour sat teaching the people and answering their questions, a certain lawyer stood up, and said "Master what shall I do, that I may live again in happiness after I am dead?" Jesus said to him "*The first of all the commandments is, the Lord our God is one Lord: and Thou shalt love the Lord Thy God with all Thy heart, and with all Thy Soul, and with all thy mind, and with all thy Strength. And the second is like unto it. Thou shalt love thy neighbour as thyself. There is none other commandment greater than these.*"

Then the Lawyer said "But who *is* my neighbour? Tell me that I may know." Jesus answered in this Parable:

"There was once a traveller," he said, "journeying from Jerusalem to Jericho, who fell among Thieves; and they robbed him of his clothes, and wounded him, and went away, leaving him half dead upon the road. A Priest, happening to pass that way, while the poor man lay there, saw him, but took no notice, and passed by, on the other side. Another man, a Levite, came that way, and also saw him; but he only looked at him for a moment, and then passed by, also. But a certain Samaritan who came travelling along that road, no sooner saw him than he had compassion on him, and dressed his wounds with oil and wine, and set him on the beast he rode himself, and took him to an Inn, and next morning took out of his pocket Two pence and gave them to the Landlord, saying 'take care of him and whatever you may spend beyond this, in doing so, I will repay you when I come here again.'—Now which of these three men," said our Saviour to the Lawyer, "do you think should be called the neighbour of him who fell among the Thieves?" The Lawyer said, "The man who shewed compassion on him." "True," replied our Saviour. "Go Thou and do likewise! Be compassionate to all men. For all men are your neighbours and brothers."

And he told them this Parable, of which the meaning is, that we are never to be proud, or think ourselves very good, before God, but are always to be humble. He said, "when you are invited to a Feast or Wedding, do not sit down in the best place, lest some more honored man should come, and claim that seat. But sit down in the lowest place, and a better will be offered you if you deserve it. For whosoever exalteth himself shall be abased, and whosoever humbleth himself shall be exalted."

He also told them this Parable.—"There was a certain man who prepared a great supper, and invited many people, and sent his Servant round to them when supper was ready to tell them they were waited for. Upon this, they made excuses. One said he had bought a piece of ground and must go to look at it. Another that he had bought five yoke of Oxen, and must go to try them. Another, that he was newly married, and could not come. When the Master of the house heard this, he was angry, and told the servant to go into the streets, and into the high roads, and among the hedges, and invite the poor, the lame, the maimed, and the blind to supper instead."

The meaning of Our Saviour in telling them this Parable, was, that those who are too busy with their own profits and pleasures, to think of God and of doing good, will not find such favor with him as the sick and miserable.

It happened that our Saviour, being in the city of Jericho, saw, looking down upon him over the heads of the crowd, from a tree into which he had climbed for that purpose, a man named Zaccheus, who was regarded as a common kind of man, and a Sinner, but to whom Jesus Christ called out, as He passed along, that He would come and eat with him in his house that day. Those proud men, the Pharisees and Scribes, hearing this, muttered among themselves, and said "he eats with Sinners." In answer to them, Jesus related this Parable, which is usually called THE PARABLE OF THE PRODIGAL SON.

"There was once a Man," he told them, "who had two sons: and the younger of them said one day, 'Father, give me my share of your riches now, and let me do with it what I please?' The father granting his request, he travelled away with his money into a distant country, and soon spent it in riotous living.

"When he had spent all, there came a time, through all that country, of great public distress and famine, when there was no bread, and when the corn, and the grass, and all the things that grow in the ground were all dried up and blighted. The Prodigal Son fell into such distress and hunger, that he hired himself out as a servant to feed swine in the fields. And he would have been glad to eat, even the poor coarse husks that the swine were fed with, but his Master gave him none. In this distress, he said to himself 'How many of my father's servants have bread enough, and to spare, while I perish with hunger! I will arise and go to my father, and will say unto him, Father! I have sinned against Heaven, and before thee, and am no more worthy to be called Thy Son!'

"And so he travelled back again, in great pain and sorrow and difficulty, to his father's house. When he was yet a great way off, his father saw him, and knew him in the midst of all his rags and misery, and ran towards him, and wept, and fell upon his neck, and kissed him. And he told his servants to clothe this poor repentant Son in the best robes, and to make a great feast to celebrate his return. Which was done; and they began to be merry.

"But the eldest Son, who had been in the field and knew nothing of his brother's return, coming to the house and hearing the music and Dancing, called to one of the Servants, and asked him what it meant. To this the Servant made answer that his brother had come home, and that his father was joyful because of his return. At this, the elder brother was angry and would not go into the house; so the father, hearing of it, came out to persuade him.

"'Father,' said the elder brother, 'you do not treat me justly, to shew so much joy for my younger brother's return. For these many years I have remained with you constantly, and have been true to you, yet you have never made a feast for me. But when my younger brother returns, who has been prodigal, and riotous, and spent his money in many bad ways, you are full of delight, and the whole house makes merry!'—'Son,' returned the father, 'you have always been with me, and all I have is yours. But we thought your brother dead, and he is alive. He was lost, and he is found; and it is natural and right that we should be merry for his unexpected return to his old home.'"

By this, our Saviour meant to teach, that those who have done wrong and forgotten God, are always welcome to him and will always receive his mercy, if they will only return to Him in sorrow for the sin of which they have been guilty.

Now the Pharisees received these lessons from our Saviour, scornfully; for they were rich, and covetous, and thought themselves superior to all mankind. As a warning to them, Christ related this Parable:—OF DIVES AND LAZARUS.

"There was a certain rich man who was clothed in purple and fine linen, and fared sumptuously every day. And there was a certain beggar, named Lazarus, who was laid at his gate, full of sores, and desiring to be fed with the crumbs which fell from the rich man's table. Moreover, the dogs came and licked his sores.

"And it came to pass that the Beggar died, and was carried by the angels into Abraham's bosom—Abraham had been a very good man who lived many years before that time, and was then in Heaven. The rich man also died, and was buried. And in Hell, he lifted up his eyes, being in torments, and saw Abraham afar off, and Lazarus. And he cried and said, 'Father Abraham have mercy on me, and send Lazarus that he may dip the tip of his finger in water and cool my tongue, for I am tormented in this flame. But Abraham said, 'Son, remember that in thy life time thou receivedst good things, and likewise Lazarus evil things. But now, he is comforted, and thou art tormented!'"

And among other Parables, Christ said to these same Pharisees, because of their pride, That two men once went up into the Temple, to pray; of whom, one was a Pharisee, and one a Publican. The Pharisee said, "God I thank Thee, that I am not unjust as other men are, or bad as this Publican is!" The Publican, standing afar off, would not lift up his eyes to Heaven, but struck his breast, and only said, "God be merciful to me, a Sinner!" And God,—our Saviour told them—would be merciful to that man rather than the other, and would be better pleased with his prayer, because he made it with a humble and a lowly heart.

The Pharisees were so angry at being taught these things, that they employed some spies to ask Our Saviour questions, and try to entrap Him into saying something which was against the Law. The Emperor of that country, who was called Caesar, having commanded tribute-money to be regularly paid to him by the people, and being cruel against any one who disputed his right to it, these spies thought they might, perhaps, induce our Saviour to say it was an unjust payment, and so to bring himself under the Emperor's displeasure. Therefore, pretending to be very humble, they came to Him and said, "Master you teach the word of God rightly, and do not respect persons on account of their wealth or high station. Tell us, is it lawful that we should pay tribute to Caesar?"

Christ, who knew their thoughts, replied, "Why do you ask? Shew me a penny." They did so. "Whose image, and whose name, is this upon it?" he asked them. They said "Caesar's." "Then," said He, "Render unto Caesar, the things that are Caesar's."

So they left him; very much enraged and disappointed that they could not entrap Him. But our Saviour knew their hearts and thoughts, as well as He knew that other men were conspiring against him, and that he would soon be put to Death.

As he was teaching them thus, he sat near the Public Treasury, where people as they passed along the street, were accustomed to drop money into a box for the poor; and many rich persons, passing while Jesus sat there, had put in a great deal of money. At last there came a poor Widow who dropped in two mites, each half a farthing in value, and then went quietly away. Jesus, seeing her do this as he rose to leave the place, called his disciples about him, and said to them that that poor widow had been more truly charitable than all the rest who had given money that day; for the others were rich and would never miss what they had given, but she was very poor, and had given those two mites which might have bought her bread to eat.

Let us never forget what the poor widow did, when we think we are charitable.

Chapter the Eighth

There was a certain man named Lazarus of Bethany, who was taken very ill; and as he was the Brother of that Mary who had anointed Christ with ointment and wiped his feet with her hair, she and her sister Martha sent to him in great trouble, saying, Lord, Lazarus whom you love is sick, and like to die.

Jesus did not go to them for two days after receiving this message; but when that time was past, he said to his Disciples, "Lazarus is dead. Let us go to Bethany." When they arrived there (it was a place very near to Jerusalem) they found, as Jesus had foretold, that Lazarus was dead, and had been dead and buried, four days.

When Martha heard that Jesus was coming, she rose up from among the people who had come to condole with her on her poor brother's death, and ran to meet him: leaving her sister Mary weeping, in the house. When Martha saw Him she burst into tears, and said "Oh Lord if Thou hadst been here, my brother would not have died."— "Thy brother shall rise again," returned Our Saviour. "I know he will, and I believe he will, Lord, at the Resurrection on the Last Day," said Martha.

Jesus said to her, "I am the Resurrection and the Life. Dost Thou believe this?" She answered "Yes Lord"; and running back to her sister Mary, told her that Christ was come. Mary hearing this, ran out, followed by all those who had been grieving with her in the house, and coming to the place where he was, fell down at his feet upon the ground and wept; and so did all the rest. Jesus was so full of compassion for their sorrow, that He wept too, as he said, "where have you laid him?"— They said, "Lord, come and see!"

He was buried in a cave; and there was a great stone laid upon it. When they all came to the Grave, Jesus ordered the stone to be rolled away, which was done. Then, after casting up his eyes, and thanking God, he said, in a loud and solemn voice, "Lazarus, come forth!" and the dead man, Lazarus, restored to life, came out among the people, and went home with his sisters. At this sight, so awful and affecting, many of the people there, believed that Christ was indeed the Son of God, come to instruct and save mankind. But others ran to tell the Pharisees; and from that day the Pharisees resolved among themselves—to prevent more people from believing in him, that Jesus should be killed. And they agreed among themselves—meeting in the Temple for that purpose—that if he came into Jerusalem before the Feast of the Passover, which was then approaching, he should be seized.

It was six days before the Passover, when Jesus raised Lazarus from the dead; and, at night, when they all sat at supper together, with Lazarus among them, Mary rose up, and took a pound of ointment (which was very precious and costly, and was called ointment of Spikenard) and anointed the feet of Jesus Christ with it, and, once again, wiped them on her hair; and the whole house was filled with the pleasant smell of the ointment. Judas Iscariot, one of the Disciples, pretended to be angry at this, and said that the ointment might have been sold for Three Hundred Pence, and the money given to the poor. But he only said so, in reality, because he carried the Purse, and was (unknown to the rest, at that time) a Thief, and wished to get all the money he could. He now began to plot for betraying Christ into the hands of the chief Priests.

The Feast of the Passover now drawing very near, Jesus Christ, with his disciples, moved forward towards Jerusalem. When they were come near to that city, He pointed to a village and told two of his disciples to go there, and they would find an ass, with a colt, tied to a tree, which they were to bring to Him. Finding these animals exactly as Jesus had described, they brought them away, and Jesus, riding on the ass, entered Jerusalem. An immense crowd of people collected round him as He went along, and throwing their robes on the ground, and cutting down green branches from the trees, and spreading them in His path, they shouted, and cried "Hosanna to the Son of David!" (David had been a great King there.) "He comes in the name of the Lord! This is Jesus, the Prophet of Nazareth!" And when Jesus went into the Temple, and cast out the tables of the money-changers who wrongfully sat there, together with people who sold Doves; saying "My father's house is a house of prayer, but ye have made it a den of Thieves!"—and when the people and children cried in the Temple "This is Jesus the Prophet of Nazareth," and would not be silenced—and when the blind and lame came flocking there in crowds, and were healed by his hand—the chief Priests, and Scribes, and Pharisees were filled with fear and hatred of Him. But Jesus continued to heal the sick, and to do good, and went and lodged at Bethany; a place that was very near the City of Jerusalem, but not within the walls.

One night, at that place, he rose from Supper at which he was seated with his Disciples, and taking a cloth and a basin of water, washed their feet. Simon Peter, one of the Disciples, would have prevented Him from washing his feet; but our Saviour told Him that He did this, in order that they, remembering it, might be always kind and gentle to one another, and might know no pride or ill-will among themselves.

Then, he became sad, and grieved, and looking round on the Disciples said, "There is one here, who will betray me." They cried out, one after another, "Is it I, Lord!"—"Is it I!" But he only answered, "It is one of the Twelve that dippeth with me in the dish." One of the disciples, whom Jesus loved, happening to be leaning on His breast at that moment listening to his words, Simon Peter beckoned to him that he should ask the name of this false man. Jesus answered, "It is he to whom I shall give a sop when I have dipped it in the dish." And when he had dipped it, He gave it to Judas Iscariot, saying "What thou doest, do quickly." Which the other disciples did not understand, but which Judas knew to mean that Christ had read his bad thoughts.

So Judas, taking the sop, went out immediately. It was night, and he went straight to the chief Priests and said "what will you give me, if I deliver him to you?" They agreed to give him thirty pieces of Silver; and for this, he undertook soon to betray into their hands, his Lord and Master Jesus Christ.

Chapter the Ninth

The feast of the Passover being now almost come, Jesus said to two of his disciples, Peter and John, "Go into the city of Jerusalem, and you will meet a man carrying a pitcher of water. Follow him home, and say to him, 'the Master says where is the guest-chamber, where he can eat the Passover with his Disciples.' And he will shew you a large upper room, furnished. There, make ready the supper."

The two disciples found that it happened as Jesus had said; and having met the man with the pitcher of water, and having followed him home, and having been shewn the room, they prepared the supper, and Jesus and the other ten apostles came at the usual time, and they all sat down to partake of it together.

It is always called The Last Supper, because this was the last time that Our Saviour ate and drank with his Disciples.

And he took bread from the table, and blessed it, and broke it, and gave it to them; and he took the cup of Wine, and blessed it, and drank, and gave it to them, saying "Do this in remembrance of Me!" And when they had finished supper, and had sung a hymn, they went out into the Mount of Olives.

There, Jesus told them that he would be seized that night, and that they would all leave him alone and would think only of their own safety. Peter said, earnestly, he never would, for one. "Before the cock crows," returned Our Saviour, "you will deny me thrice." But Peter answered "No Lord. Though I should die with Thee, I will never deny Thee." And all the other Disciples said the same.

Jesus then led the way over a brook, called Cedron, into a garden that was called Gethsemane; and walked with three of the disciples into a retired part of the garden. Then he left them as he had left the others, together; saying "Wait here, and watch!"—and went away and prayed by Himself, while they, being weary, fell asleep.

And Christ suffered great sorrow and distress of mind, in his prayers in that garden, because of the wickedness of the men of Jerusalem who were going to kill Him; and He shed tears before God, and was in deep and strong affliction.

When His prayers were finished, and He was comforted, He returned to the Disciples, and said "Rise! Let us be going! He is close at hand, who will betray me!"

Now, Judas knew that garden well, for Our Saviour had often walked there, with his Disciples; and, almost at the moment when Our Saviour said these words, he came there, accompanied by a strong guard of men and officers, which had been sent by the chief Priests and Pharisees. It being dark, they carried lanterns and torches. They were armed with swords and staves too; for they did not know but that the people would rise and defend Jesus Christ; and this had made them afraid to seize Him boldly in the day, when he sat teaching the people.

As the leader of this guard had never seen Jesus Christ and did not know him from the apostles, Judas had said to them, "The man whom I kiss, will be he." As he advanced to give this wicked kiss, Jesus said to the soldiers "Whom do you seek?"—"Jesus of Nazareth," they answered. "Then," said Our Saviour, "I am He. Let my disciples here, go freely. I am He." Which Judas confirmed, by saying "Hail Master!" and kissing Him. Whereupon Jesus said, "Judas, Thou betrayest me with a kiss!"

The guard then ran forward to seize Him. No one offered to protect Him, except Peter, who, having a sword, drew it, and cut off the right ear of the High Priest's Servant, who was one of them, and whose name was Malchus. But Jesus made him sheath his sword, and gave himself up. Then, all the disciples forsook Him, and fled; and there remained not one—not one—to bear Him company.

Chapter the Tenth

After a short time, Peter and another Disciple took heart, and secretly followed the guard to the house of Caiaphas the High Priest, whither Jesus was taken, and where the Scribes and others were assembled to question Him. Peter stood at the door, but the other disciple, who was known to the High Priest, went in, and presently returning, asked the woman, who kept the door, to admit Peter too. She, looking at him said, "Are you not one of the Disciples?" He said "I am not." So she let him in; and he stood before a fire that was there, warming himself, among the servants and officers who were crowded round it. For it was very cold.

Some of these men asked him the same question as the woman had done, and said "Are you not one of the disciples?" He again denied it, and said, "I am not." One of them, who was related to that man whose ear Peter had cut off with his sword, said "Did I not see you in the garden with him?" Peter again denied it with an oath, and said "I do not know the man." Immediately the cock crew, and Jesus turning round, looked stedfastly at Peter. Then Peter remembered what He had said—that before the cock crew, he would deny Him thrice—and went out, and wept bitterly.

Among other questions that were put to Jesus, the High Priest asked Him what He had taught the people. To which He answered that He had taught them in the open day, and in the open streets, and that the Priests should ask the people what they had learned of Him. One of the officers struck Jesus with his hand for this reply; and two false witnesses coming in, said they had heard Him say that He could destroy the Temple of God and build it again in three days. Jesus answered little;

but the Scribes and Priests agreed that He was guilty of blasphemy, and should be put to death; and they spat upon, and beat him.

When Judas Iscariot saw that His Master was indeed condemned, he was so full of horror for what he had done, that he took the Thirty Pieces of Silver back to the chief Priests, and said "I have betrayed innocent blood! I cannot keep it!" With those words, he threw the money down upon the floor, and rushing away, wild with despair, hanged himself. The rope, being weak, broke with the weight of his body, and it fell down on the ground, after Death, all bruised and burst,—a dreadful sight to see! The chief Priests, not knowing what else to do with the Thirty Pieces of Silver, bought a burying-place for strangers with it, the proper name of which was The Potters' Field. But the people called it The Field of Blood ever afterwards.

Jesus was taken from the High Priests' to the Judgment Hall where Pontius Pilate, the Governor, sat, to administer Justice. Pilate (who was not a Jew) said to Him "Your own Nation, the Jews, and your own Priests have delivered you to me. What have you done?" Finding that He had done no harm, Pilate went out and told the Jews so; but they said "He has been teaching the People what is not true and what is wrong; and he began to do so, long ago, in Galilee." As Herod had the right to punish people who offended against the law in Galilee, Pilate said, "I find no wrong in him. Let him be taken before Herod!"

They carried Him accordingly before Herod, where he sat surrounded by his stern soldiers and men in armour. And these laughed at Jesus, and dressed him, in mockery, in a fine robe, and sent him back to Pilate. And Pilate called the Priests and People together again, and said "I find no wrong in this man; neither does Herod. He has done nothing to deserve death." But they cried out, "He has, he has! Yes, yes! Let him be killed!"

Pilate was troubled in his mind to hear them so clamorous against Jesus Christ. His wife, too, had dreamed all night about it, and sent to him upon the Judgment Seat saying "Have nothing to do with that just man!" As it was the custom at the feast of the Passover to give some prisoner his liberty, Pilate endeavoured to persuade the people to ask for the release of Jesus. But they said (being very ignorant and passionate, and being told to do so, by the Priests) "No no, we will not have him released. Release Barabbas, and let this man be crucified!"

Barabbas was a wicked criminal, in jail for his crimes, and in danger of being put to death.

Pilate, finding the people so determined against Jesus, delivered him to the soldiers to be scourged—that is, beaten. They plaited a crown of thorns, and put it on his head, and dressed Him in a purple robe, and spat upon him, and struck him with their hands, and said "Hail, King of the Jews!"—remembering that the crowd had called him the Son of David when he entered into Jerusalem. And they ill-used him in many cruel ways but Jesus bore it patiently, and only said "Father! Forgive them! They know not what they do!"

Once more, Pilate brought Him out before the people, dressed in the purple robe and crown of thorns, and said Behold the man!" They cried out, savagely, "Crucify him! Crucify him!" So did the chief Priests and officers. "Take him and crucify him yourselves," said Pilate. "I find no fault in him." But they cried out, "He called himself the Son of God; and that, by the Jewish Law is Death! And he called himself King of the Jews; and that is against the Roman Law, for we have no King but Caesar, who is the Roman Emperor. If you let him go, you are not Caesar's friend. Crucify him! Crucify him!"

When Pilate saw that he could not prevail with them, however hard he tried, he called for water, and washing his hands before the crowd, said, "I am innocent of the blood of this just person." Then he delivered Him to them to be crucified; and they, shouting and gathering round Him, and treating him (who still prayed for them to God) with cruelty and insult, took Him away.

Chapter the Eleventh

That you may know what the People meant when they said "Crucify him!" I must tell you that in those times, which were very cruel times indeed (let us thank God and Jesus Christ that they are past!) it was the custom to kill people who were sentenced to Death, by nailing them alive on a great wooden Cross, planted upright in the ground, and leaving them there, exposed to the Sun and Wind, and day and night, until they died of pain and thirst. It was the custom too, to make them walk to the place of execution, carrying the cross-piece of wood to which their hands were to be afterwards nailed; that their shame and suffering might be the greater.

Bearing his Cross, upon his shoulder, like the commonest and most wicked criminal, our blessed Saviour, Jesus Christ, surrounded by the persecuting crowd, went out of Jerusalem to a place called in the Hebrew language, Golgotha; that is, the place of a scull. And being come to a hill called Mount Calvary, they hammered cruel nails through his hands and feet and nailed him on the Cross, between two other crosses on each of which, a common thief was nailed in agony. Over His head, they fastened this writing "Jesus of Nazareth, the King of the Jews"—in three languages; in Hebrew, in Greek, and in Latin.

Meantime, a guard of four soldiers, sitting on the ground, divided His clothes (which they had taken off) into four parcels for themselves, and cast lots for His coat, and sat there, gambling and talking, while He suffered. They offered him vinegar to drink, mixed with gall; and wine, mixed with myrrh; but he took none. And the wicked people who passed that way, mocked him, and said "If Thou be the Son of God, come down from the Cross." The Chief Priests also mocked Him, and said "He came to save Sinners. Let him save himself!" One of the thieves too, railed at him, in his torture, and said, "If Thou be Christ, save thyself, and us." But the other Thief, who was penitent, said "Lord! Remember me when Thou comest into Thy Kingdom!" And Jesus answered, "To-day, thou shalt be with me in Paradise."

None were there, to take pity on Him, but one disciple and four women. God blessed those women for their true and tender hearts! They were, the mother of Jesus, his mother's sister, Mary, the wife of Cleophas, and Mary Magdalene who had twice dried his feet upon her hair. The disciple was he whom Jesus loved—John, who had leaned upon his breast and asked Him which was the Betrayer. When Jesus saw them standing at the foot of the Cross, He said to His mother that John would be her son, to comfort her when He was dead; and from that hour John was as a son to her, and loved her.

At about the sixth hour, a deep and terrible darkness came over all the land, and lasted until the ninth hour, when Jesus cried out, with a loud voice, "My God, My God, why hast Thou forsaken me!" The soldiers, hearing him, dipped a sponge in some vinegar, that was standing there, and fastening it to a long reed, put it up to His Mouth. When He had received it, He said "It is finished!"—And crying "Father! Into thy hands I commend my Spirit!"—died.

Then, there was a dreadful earthquake; and the Great wall of the Temple, cracked; and the rocks were rent asunder. The guards, terrified at these sights, said to each other, "Surely this was the Son of God!"—and the People who had been watching the cross from a distance (among whom were many women) smote upon their breasts, and went, fearfully and sadly, home.

The next day, being the Sabbath, the Jews were anxious that the Bodies should be taken down at once, and made that request to Pilate. Therefore some soldiers came, and broke the legs of the two criminals to kill them but coming to Jesus, and finding Him already dead, they only pierced his side with a spear. From the wound, there came out, blood and water.

There was a good man named Joseph of Arimathea—a Jewish City—who believed in Christ, and going to Pilate privately (for fear of the Jews) begged that he might have the body. Pilate consenting, he and one Nicodemus, rolled it in linen and spices—it was the custom of the Jews to prepare bodies for burial in that way—and buried it in a new tomb or sepulchre, which had been cut out of a rock in a garden near to the place of Crucifixion, and where no one had ever yet been buried. They then rolled a great stone to the mouth of the sepulcher, and left Mary Magdalene, and the other Mary, sitting there, watching it.

The Chief Priests and Pharisees remembering that Jesus Christ had said to his disciples that He would rise from the grave on the third day after His death, went to Pilate and prayed that the Sepulchre might be well taken care of until that day, lest the disciples should steal the Body, and afterwards say to the people that Christ was risen from the dead. Pilate agreeing to this, a guard of soldiers was set over it constantly, and the stone was sealed up besides. And so it remained, watched and sealed, until the third day; which was the first day of the week.

When that morning began to dawn, Mary Magdalene and the other Mary, and some other women, came to the Sepulchre, with some more spices which they had prepared. As they were saying to each other, "How shall we roll away the stone?" the earth trembled and shook, and an angel, descending from Heaven, rolled it back, and then sat resting on it. His countenance was like lightning, and his garments were white as snow; and at sight of him, the men of the guard fainted away with fear, as if they were dead.

Mary Magdalene saw the stone rolled away, and waiting to see no more, ran to Peter and John who were coming towards the place, and said "They have taken away the Lord and we know not where they have laid him!" They immediately ran to the Tomb, but John, being the faster of the two, outran the other, and got there first. He stooped down, and looked in, and saw the linen clothes in which the body had been wrapped, lying there; but he did not go in. When Peter came up, he went in, and saw the linen clothes lying in one place, and a napkin that had been bound about the head, in another. John also went in, then, and saw the same things. Then they went home, to tell the rest.

But Mary Magdalene remained outside the sepulchre, weeping. After a little time, she stooped down, and looked in, and saw Two angels, clothed in white, sitting where the body of Christ had lain. These said to her, "Woman, why weepest Thou?" She answered, "Because they have taken away my Lord, and I know not where they have laid him." As she gave this answer, she turned round, and saw Jesus standing behind her, but did not Then know Him. "Woman," said He, "Why weepest Thou? what seekest thou?" She, supposing Him to be the gardener, replied, "Sir! If thou hast borne my Lord hence, tell me where Thou hast laid him, and I will take him away." Jesus pronounced her name, "Mary." Then she knew him, and, starting, exclaimed "Master!"—"Touch me not," said Christ; "for I am not yet ascended to my father; but go to my disciples, and say unto them, I ascend unto my Father, and your Father; and to my God, and to your God!"

Accordingly, Mary Magdalene went and told the Disciples that she had seen Christ, and what He had said to her; and with them she found the other women whom she had left at the Sepulchre when she had gone to call those two disciples Peter and John. These women told her and the rest, that they had seen at the Tomb, two men in shining garments, at sight of whom they had been afraid, and had bent down, but who had told them that the Lord was risen; and also that as they came to tell this, they had seen Christ, on the way, and had held him by the feet, and worshipped Him. But these accounts seemed to the apostles at that time, as idle tales, and they did not believe them.

The soldiers of the guard too, when they recovered from their fainting-fit, and went to the Chief Priests to tell them what they had seen, were silenced with large sums of money, and were told by them to say that the Disciples had stolen the Body away while they were asleep.

But it happened that on that same day, Simon and Cleopas— Simon one of the twelve Apostles, and Cleopas one of the followers of Christ—were walking to a village called Emmaus, at some little distance from Jerusalem, and were talking, by the way, upon the death and resurrection of Christ, when they were joined by a stranger, who explained the Scriptures to them, and told them a great deal about God, so that they wondered at his knowledge. As the night was fast coming on when they reached the village, they asked this stranger to stay with them, which he consented to do. When they all three sat down to supper, he took some bread, and blessed it, and broke it as Christ had done at the Last Supper. Looking on him in wonder they found that his face was changed before them, and that it was Christ himself; and as they looked on him, he disappeared.

They instantly rose up, and returned to Jerusalem, and finding the disciples sitting together, told them what they had seen. While they were speaking, Jesus suddenly stood in the midst of all the company, and said "Peace be unto ye!" Seeing that they were greatly frightened, he shewed them his hands and feet, and invited them to touch Him; and, to encourage them and give them time to recover themselves, he ate a piece of broiled fish and a piece of honeycomb before them all.

But Thomas, one of the Twelve Apostles, was not there, at that time; and when the rest said to him afterwards, "we have seen the Lord!" he answered "Except I shall see in his hands the print of the nails, and thrust my hand into his side, I will not believe!" At that moment, though the doors were all shut, Jesus again appeared, standing among them, and said "Peace be unto you!" Then He said to Thomas, "Reach hither thy finger, and behold my hands; and reach hither thy hand, and thrust it into my side; and be not faithless, but believing." And Thomas answered, and said to him, "My Lord and my God!" Then said Jesus, "Thomas, because thou hast seen me, thou hast believed. Blessed are they that have not seen me, and yet have believed."

After that time, Jesus Christ was seen by five hundred of his followers at once, and He remained with others of them forty days, teaching them, and instructing them to go forth into the world, and preach His gospel and religion; not minding what wicked men might do to them. And conducting his disciples at last, out of Jerusalem as far as Bethany, he blessed them, and ascended in a cloud to Heaven, and took His place at the right hand of God. And while they gazed into the bright blue sky where He had vanished, two white-robed angels appeared among them, and told them that as they had seen Christ ascend to Heaven, so He would, one day, come descending from it, to judge the World.

When Christ was seen no more, the Apostles began to teach the People as He had commanded them. And having chosen a new apostle, named Matthias, to replace the wicked Judas, they wandered into all countries, telling the People of Christ's Life and Death—and of His Crucifixion and Resurrection—and of the Lessons he had taught—and baptizing them in Christ's name. And through the power He had given them they healed the sick, and gave sight to the Blind, and speech to the Dumb, and Hearing to the Deaf, as he had done. And Peter being thrown into Prison, was delivered from it, in the dead of night, by an Angel: and once, his words before God caused a man named Ananias, and his wife Sapphira, who had told a lie, to be struck down dead, upon the Earth.

Wherever they went, they were persecuted and cruelly treated; and one man named Saul who had held the clothes of some barbarous persons who pelted one of the Christians named Stephen, to death with stones, was always active in doing them harm. But God turned Saul's heart afterwards; for as he was travelling to Damascus to find out some Christians who were there, and drag them to prison, there shone about him a great light from Heaven; a voice cried, "Saul, Saul, why persecutest thou me!" and he was struck down from his horse, by an invisible hand, in sight of all the guards and soldiers who were riding with him. When they raised him, they found that he was blind; and so he remained for three days, neither eating nor drinking, until one of the Christians (sent to him by an angel for that purpose) restored his sight in the name of Jesus Christ. After which, he became a Christian, and preached, and taught, and believed, with the apostles, and did great service.

They took the name of Christians from Our Saviour Christ, and carried Crosses as their sign, because upon a Cross He had suffered Death. The religions that were then in the World were false and brutal, and encouraged men to violence. Beasts, and even men, were killed in the churches, in the belief that the smell of their blood was pleasant to the Gods—there were supposed to be a great many Gods—and many most cruel and disgusting ceremonies prevailed. Yet, for all this, and though the Christian Religion was such a true, and kind, and good one, the Priests of the old Religions long persuaded the people to do all possible hurt to the Christians; and Christians were hanged, beheaded, burnt, buried alive, and devoured in Theatres by Wild Beasts for the public amusement, during many years. Nothing would silence them, or terrify them though; for they knew that if they did their duty, they would go to Heaven. So thousands upon thousands of Christians sprung up and taught the people and were cruelly killed, and were succeeded by other Christians, until the Religion gradually became the great religion of the World.

Remember—It is christianity TO DO GOOD always—even to those who do evil to us. It is christianity to love our neighbour as ourself, and to do to all men as we would have them Do to us. It is christianity to be gentle, merciful, and forgiving, and to keep those qualities quiet in our own hearts, and never make a boast of them, or of our prayers or of our love of God, but always to shew that we love Him by humbly trying to do right in everything. If we do this, and remember the life and lessons of Our Lord Jesus Christ, and try to act up to them, we may confidently hope that God will forgive us our sins and mistakes, and enable us to live and die in Peace.

INDEX